THE NEW ZEALAND POLITICAL SYSTEM

Books by Stephen Levine

New Zealand Politics: A Reader (editor)
Learning About Sexism in New Zealand (co-editor)
The New Zealand General Election of 1975 (co-author)
*The New Zealand Voter: A Survey of Public Opinion
  and Electoral Behaviour* (co-author)
Politics in New Zealand: A Reader (editor)

The New Zealand Political System

Politics in a Small Society

STEPHEN LEVINE
School of Political Science and Public Administration
Victoria University of Wellington

Sydney
GEORGE ALLEN & UNWIN
Auckland   London   Boston

First published in 1979 by
George Allen & Unwin Australia Pty Ltd
Distributed in New Zealand by
Book Reps (New Zealand) Ltd
46 Lake Road
Northcote
Auckland 9

National Library of Australia
Cataloguing-in-Publication data:

Levine, Stephen I., 1945–
    The New Zealand political system.

    Index
    Bibliography
    ISBN 0 86861 073 9
    ISBN 0 86861 081 x Paperback

1. New Zealand—Politics and government. I. Title.

320.9'931

Library of Congress Catalog Card Number 78-74191

Set in 10 on 11 Times by Academy Press Pty. Ltd., Brisbane
Printed in Australia by Watson Ferguson & Co.

If it would not look too much like showing off, I would tell the reader where New Zealand is; for he is as I was; he thinks he knows. There are but four or five people in the world who possess this knowledge, and these make their living out of it. It will be a surprise to the reader, as it was to me, to learn that the distance from Australia to New Zealand is really twelve or thirteen hundred miles, and that there is no bridge. I learned this from Professor X., of Yale University. He not only knew where New Zealand was, but he was minutely familiar with every detail of its history, politics, religions, and commerce, its fauna, flora, geology, products, and climatic peculiarities. When he was done, I was lost in words and admiration, and said to myself, he knows everything; in the domain of human knowledge he is king.

Mark Twain, *Following the Equator* (1897)

To

Amelia and Samuel Levine,
my mother and father

Contents

Preface

New Zealanders, for the most part, have been quite casual about their politics. Their interest may be aroused by a government measure directly affecting them, or a sensational event transmitted via the press, radio or television. The vicarious experience of politics is more common, for it allows us to feel pleasure or dismay, and share these emotions with other people, usually of a similar inclination, in a purgative and mutually reassuring exercise. If this pattern of political responsiveness resembles Aristotle's theory of drama, it ought not to be surprising, for the evocation and reinterpretation of political myths was central to the classical Greek theatre. In our time, politics has frequently been thrust from the stage, but, perversely, politics itself has become theatrical. The New Zealand Parliament can be a grand stage, and while the actors upon it are normally subject to professional directions, there are moments when spontaneity works its magic, expectations are upset, and a predictable sequence of scenes is transformed. When the unexpected happens, an audience will rediscover its primitive 'startle' reaction, as when balance is suddenly lost. It is only when control has been restored, and the momentary surprise has passed, that tension has eased. The game commences once more.

That we view politics as a game, an entertainment, an extension of theatre and television, may help us to keep the players at a distance. But in contemporary politics, again as in theatre, the innovative craftsmen are those seeking to persuade audiences that their roles too may be fictional, and need to be abandoned. For the distinction between actor and audience is a fluid one; it can be upset, the roles can be exchanged. MPs are involved in politics; so are we all. It may all be a game, enlivened periodically by passion and farce, but it is a serious business too. Of course humour provides perspective, and the ephemera of political foreplay ensures that there will be no shortage of events, or personalities, to amuse the loyal and the disenchanted alike. Frivolity has its limits, however, and irony tends often to be the literary posture of the powerless.

New Zealand political scientists, like their countrymen generally, have tended to adopt a casual attitude towards politics. Interest may be spasmodically aroused; a political event may serve as a form of

9

shock treatment, setting the patient twitching under the guise of therapy. Political scientists, though, are in a dilemma in New Zealand, and may deserve some sympathy for their plight. The political culture demands, and broadcasters and politicians expect, that the political scientist will remain 'objective'. This tends to require political scientists to be seen to be fair to all sides; thus political scientists, and other commentators too, can be easily satirised for their failure to enunciate a single point of view consistently and with vigour. To do so, however, may jeopardise the prospect of continued media exposure. More importantly, taking a political position may be unfairly juxtaposed by politicians and the public with the norm of 'objectivity', so that all that one subsequently says, on any subject, can be dismissed disparagingly, as tainted goods.

Certainly Victoria University Professor John Roberts' willingness to associate himself with Citizens for Rowling in the 1975 campaign is the exception which proves the rule, for as 'Citizens for Rowling' Roberts, some would deny his views the scrutiny and attention they so often deserve. Not that Roberts' case is typical; he did not express the courage of others' convictions, for New Zealand political scientists do not share a calling. There is no conscious unity of purpose, either intellectual or political, and their rivalry exhibits the same pressures for conformity, the same hostility to innovation and enterprise, as may be found in the New Zealand political culture generally.

Nothing would be easier than to declare one's position on political issues as they arise. Of course the intellectual may be more willing to admit the possibility of error, to confess the inadequacy of information when pressured to decide, to recognise the weaknesses in all parties, than others quicker to come to judgement and more arrogant in posture. Perhaps it is true that most political scientists, faced with the query 'which side are you on?', would respond: 'The losing one, usually.' The political influence of the political scientist is limited, for the most part. Their impact upon affairs is unexciting, like a marshmallow tossed into a well.

Yet if politics is too important to be left to the politicians, New Zealand political science is, similarly, more than the sum of its political scientists. One of the tasks of this book is to develop for readers some of the images political scientists have of their profession, for without an understanding by New Zealanders of the political scientist's roles, commitments and intellectual obligations, their full contribution to the New Zealand public, and to New Zealand society, cannot be made.

Beyond this, of course, the foregoing pages seek to introduce readers to the New Zealand political system. A book of this scope has not hitherto been produced, although Leslie Lipson's *The Politics of Equality* and my late colleague Alan D. Robinson's *Notes on New Zealand Politics* are among the influential predecessors. These books, however, lack the scope of this volume, which seeks briefly to encompass the entire political system in its salient, broad features. Moreover, these earlier works, and others even more limited in scope, are from an earlier time, when politics in New Zealand was seen to be more tranquil, and the New Zealand dream more secure of achievement. The present work emerges at a more sober time in New Zealand, when people are leaving the country in significant numbers, and those who remain do so despite doubt and distress. There is significant unemployment for the first time in a generation, and young people leaving New Zealand for overseas stimulation are being joined in their departure by the disillusioned and the unwanted. They leave behind them a political system characterised by bitter division, a Parliament uncertain of its role, a party system some of whose main contenders are unsure of survival. A revived Maori political culture remains uncertain of its adaptability to modern circumstance. The Maori culture, still vulnerable, faces not a strong and confident European transplant but rather a white culture itself uncertain, lacking roots, sense of purpose, direction. Each culture has been conquered, not by the other, but by confusion.

Politics is inescapable, but political activity of itself may not provide answers to personal stress or collective unease. For activity needs to be preceded by contemplation and understanding, and a recognition that, at least potentially, political affairs involve us all, and can be affected in the long run by thoughtful and energetic participation. To these ends this book ought to contribute. It does so by complementing *Politics in New Zealand: A Reader*, a collection of original essays by New Zealand political scientists and political figures. *Politics in New Zealand* organised material traversing the entire political system. Inevitably, a book of readings of limited size will contain gaps and omissions. Moreover, a book of readings is not a single narrative, and the diversity of points of view, while serving some pedagogic and scholarly purposes, will less satisfactorily fulfil others.

While oriented towards the needs of first-year political studies students at university, this book can be useful to anyone seeking to extend or deepen their acquaintance with New Zealand political life. The themes discussed in it have been developed in and arise out of six years of lectures and tutorials to first-year students at Victoria University of Wellington. The book meets the needs of these students for an interpretative, contemporary treatment of significant issues in New Zealand politics, and this commentary ought to provoke discussion, independent thought and further research.

The book is the first New Zealand political science work written specifically to complement a collection of readings. The chapter headings in this book correspond to the organisation of articles in *Politics in New Zealand*. Moreover, this companion volume provides a commentary on the analysis and major conclusions of the contributors to the book of readings. In doing so, it seeks to remedy some of the more significant gaps in New Zealand political science. Certain areas of inquiry have tended to be neglected, while other features of New Zealand politics have not been systematically updated for the contemporary reader. Until very recently, for example, the last full-length study of a New Zealand general election by political scientists examined the 1960 election. The most recent study of a new Zealand by-election analysed a contest held in the South Island in 1962. The most recent text on New Zealand government has been superceded, in major areas, by the pace of political change in New Zealand.

The non-New Zealand reader ought to find this book of considerable value. Of course, knowledge about New Zealand in other countries, including Australia and the United Kingdom, is remarkably sparse, as New Zealanders travelling overseas will be quick to confirm. In the United States, vague notions about New Zealand's geographical position fittingly augment a near-perfect ignorance about any other facets of the country, suggesting that information about New Zealand is as plentiful today in the United States as it was when Mark Twain journeyed here in 1897. This book may sketch in the political background for the overseas reader, and the guide to further reading which has been included could, if consulted, transform overnight an American graduate student into a venerable sage to university colleagues.

In commenting on the essays in *Politics in New Zealand, The New Zealand Political System: Politics in a Small Society* unifies their collective message, which is certainly that the New Zealand political system, despite the laudable achievements of the past, needs to be fundamentally reshaped in many of its central features. The democratic experiment in New Zealand is at a crisis point. The anger New Zealanders displayed towards the immigrant in 1975 may now be directed towards the emigrant who, by departure, is 'letting the side down' now that rough times have commenced in earnest. Perhaps we will see still greater powers drift to the government, to the executive, to the Prime Minister; the civil liberties tradition in New Zealand is very weak indeed. However, this book, like the collection of essays in which it is integrated conceptually, is dedicated to the proposition that New Zealanders need not be tossed, like tumbleweeds, on the winds of political caprice. This book seeks briefly to inquire into the system, describe its features and suggest some of the available political alternatives. Controlled change can only arise out of a comprehensive examination of the political system, its ·strengths and weaknesses, undertaken with the understanding that while error may be inevitable, the risk is preferable to silent complacency.

At the same time, we all risk being overtaken by events, immersed in the sensational, left to produce an annual chronicle of errors, a history of political infamy in which immediate excitements obscure more profound influences. This narrative, like the essays in *Politics in New Zealand*, has sought to identify and concentrate upon some of the more enduring political and social patterns of importance to the New Zealand community.

Comparative political inquiry assumes that the people and politics of other countries may face problems, and fashion solutions, comparable to ours. Comparison with countries like our own may be helpful; in addition, contrast with political systems unlike ours may illuminate the unfamiliar, to reveal a novel approach which, suitably modified, may be useful. Some of the comparisons in this book are to Australian and British experience, while at other times American examples have been provided, reflecting my own background and experience. The practice of making comparisons mirrors my conviction that New Zealand politics can only benefit from a recognition that while New Zealand's situation in the world is unique, its problems and policy dilemmas are far from exclusive. There is scope for much further comparative analysis that has been undertaken in this brief introductory survey. I have sought to provide a factual basis for further work, and have in many places gone further to point out anomalies and present original research findings. The material on husbands' and wives' voting behaviour, parliamentary reform (particularly revision of Standing Orders), procedures for promoting participation in the parties, referenda, by-elections and political recruitment, alternative voting systems, the political implications of abolition of the Maori seats, the consequences of a constitutional framework, the politics of budgetary choice and New Zealanders' political style, are among the topics whose treatment will, I think, present an original point of view.

This book has a critical orientation, yet my satisfaction with many features of New Zealand political and social life is known to those who know me well. By contrast to the United States, for example, New Zealand seems to me to remain decades ahead (despite current problems) in some of its social and medical programmes, aspects of its political structure, firearms control, broadcasting policy and campaign practices, to name but a few. Yet we can do better in New Zealand, and we should, for the values we uphold remain an aspiration, remote and appealing. In relation to them, any book emerges flawed, incomplete, imperfect, and passive in contrast to the world of action. What an author of a work on New Zealand politics can hope to do is to produce a work 'full of surprises, and adventures, and incongruities, and contradictions, and incredibilities', and hope that some readers, at least, will find the blend familiar, and acknowledge, 'But they are all true, they all happened.'

Any list of acknowledgements must necessarily be incomplete.

However, certain influences ought to be noted, though none can be held responsible for their outcome as expressed in these pages. These include: the late Dr Alan D. Robinson; Nigel Roberts; Tony Wood; Keith Jackson; Raj Vasil; the many contributors to *New Zealand Politics: A Reader* and *Politics in New Zealand: A Reader*; the students at Victoria University of Wellington amongst whom my ideas and impressions about New Zealand politics have been developed; New Zealand's MPs, so accessible and so audible; my wife Susan, often acute and prescient; and my children Alia and Spencer, for direct contributions to morale. Many years ago Professor Gilbert Abcarian, of The Florida State University, provided an example of scholarship that was humane, honest, receptive and good-humoured. It is an example which continues to provide inspiration, and one for which I, among his many students, remain grateful. Finally, the heroic efforts of the secretaries of the School of Political Science and Public Administration, particularly Helen Peard, Jenny Berry, Marian Beardsmore and Lynette McMorran merit special recognition as well, for their cheerful and conscientious efforts in preparing the manuscript for publication.

Stephen Levine
Wellington
31 July 1978

1 Political Science: Roles and Objectives

Introduction

The importance of politics in twentieth-century life is not in dispute; the growth in size and functions of the state, the power of political institutions, and the immediacy of political personalities as communicated through the mass media ensure that everyone acquires a political identity as they develop and mature. The necessity to understand clearly the role and power of government, to consider the range of activities undertaken by the agencies of the state, and to penetrate the complexities of partisan political conflict is unarguable.[1] The role of political science, and of political scientists, in this enterprise has never been well understood, however.

First-year students are often attracted to political science because of their interest in 'current events'. Many of these students are apt to be disappointed when they discover that political science seeks to go beyond the turbulent ephemera of political conflict, as reported in the press or by political journalists, to consider and explore more enduring patterns of political behaviour. Attempts by theorists to ponder the normative or ethical implications of political commitments –by government, or by political parties–may seem unduly abstract. A concern with methods and techniques, to ensure that research approaches scientific standards, may seem remote and pretentious.

The considerable confusion among introductory students about what political scientists *do* is consistent with an ambivalence within the discipline itself. Even amongst political scientists, there is uncertainty about professional roles, obligations, and techniques.[2] In the public arena it may be possible for politicians to exploit this confusion. Thus the New Zealand Prime Minister, Robert Muldoon, has described political scientists on at least one occasion as 'low-grade statisticians'. To some extent the New Zealand political culture is antagonistic to political science. A conflict may be suggested between the claims of 'experts' to specialised knowledge about politics, on the one hand, and a political culture which stresses egalitarian principles.

Political science as a discipline has grown considerably in the

15

twentieth century. The membership of the American Political Science Association, for example, has grown from several hundred to over 20,000 persons.[3] The scope of the discipline has been considerably enlarged as well. An examination of the agenda of the meetings of professional organisations–such as the American Political Science Association, or the International Political Studies Association–provides a clear indication of growth and increasing specialisation.[4] There are several major sub-fields within the discipline: international politics; comparative politics; political philosophy; political behaviour; public administration. Within these broad fields, however, there are many different areas of specialisations which often bear little direct relationship to one another. At any of these professional conferences, papers are presented ranging over subject areas which proliferate annually. Thus generalisations about the professional behaviour of political scientists must become increasingly difficult and tentative. Nevertheless, some generalisations are possible, and may be necessary, for public understanding of and support for the activities of political scientists to be promoted. If political scientists fail to communicate successfully with the public, their profession may become one whose practitioners are most secure when they are most silent.

The Debate Over Science

Political scientists, whatever their specialised interests, may engage in several distinct activities: (1) teaching (usually in a tertiary instituction); (2) research; (3) publication; (4) political commentary, through the press, television and radio; (5) participation in elective politics; (6) consultation with government departments or private organisations; (7) participation in the public service.[5] In general, however, most specialised debate within the discipline concentrates on the various objectives, theories, and techniques appropriate to the teaching and research roles of political scientists. Political scientists disagree about *the criteria to be used in evaluating propositions*, involving competing conceptions of what constitutes appropriate methods of inquiry and standards of evidence. In addition, political scientists disagree about *the purposes of political research*, and the criteria used to determine appropriate subjects for examination.

Traditionalism
Political science emerged as a branch of moral philosophy, and has had history and philosophy as its most important cognate disciplines.[6] Traditional political research involved the formulation of an 'ideal' state, and abstract normative inquiry on the appropriate ends and means of government was common. In the United States, political science had as a primary basis the study of constitutions, with a view

towards demonstrating the superiority of the American system as a model for other nations.[7] The traditional study of government has been described as: (1) *descriptive*, concerned merely with the anatomical structure of government; (2) *parochial*, confined largely to the United States and Western Europe; (3) *static*, involving the study of seemingly permanent institutional features; (4) *monographic*, embracing unsystematically the study of a single country or institution.[8] The underlying assumption of traditional political science appeared to be ethical: that the 'right' institutions of government, the 'right' constitution, would lead inevitably to the 'good' society. The methods of research were abstract, philosophical, and deductive. The foci of research were the laws, structure, and institutions of the state, to the exclusion of more dynamic forces of political life. Thus legalism (a concern with formal legal institutions), moral philosophy (the study of political values), history and at most a moderately reformist political ethic dominated the traditional 'arm-chair' approach to the study of politics.

Behaviouralism/Scientific Method
The behaviouralists emerged in the United States in the late 1940s and 1950s, and sought to extend the boundaries of the discipline in several ways: (1) to include non-Western political systems in the study of comparative politics; (2) to shift the focus of the discipline towards the behaviour of groups, parties, and individuals; (3) to utilise scientific methods in the conduct of political research.[9] Behavioural political scientists have sought as well to utilise advanced computing techniques, and much of their success in understanding patterns of political behaviour has depended on the computer-based manipulation of quantitative information. Political scientists were influenced in their quest for scientific status in the United States by the existence of government research funds. The American Political Science Association was ultimately successful in its effort to secure access to these funds for political scientists, when the United States National Science Foundation formally recognised political science as a 'science' for purposes of eligibility for research support.

Behaviouralists believe that political science must involve research oriented towards the discovery of uniformities in political behaviour. Behaviouralists are interested primarily in the formulation of 'theoretical and useful knowledge, to which both the unique and familiar may contribute'.[10] The scientist's views of *theory*, however, is diametrically opposed to that found in colloquial usage. To the average person, declaring that something is 'just a theory' involves a claim that it is an abstract opinion unsupported by evidence. To the scientist, however, a theory is a verified set of interrelated propositions which have been repeatedly found to correspond with experience. Science is therefore defined as 'the substitution of knowledge for opinion';[11] moreover, since theoretical knowledge (rather than policy reform or social change) is the goal, behavioural political scientists believe in 'objectivity', in the separation of the researcher from their subject, and in the exclusion of value judgements (i.e. statements of preference).[12]

Behaviouralists believe that knowledge can be derived from empirical research. Empiricism, in turn, is a doctrine propounding that all propositions need to be tested by observation before they can be accepted as evidence. However, while experience is to be a guide, the nature of that experience–in particular, whether it is to be *involved* or *detached*–is a subject of dispute.

The Post-Behavioural Revolution

Post-behaviouralism differs from behaviouralism in two major respects: (1) post-behaviouralists tend to be oriented towards the promotion of social change rather than the discovery of empirical theory;[13] (2) many post-behavioural political scientists believe the 'objective' model of scientific inquiry–cool, remote, cerebral–to be inappropriate to political research.[14] The post-behaviouralists believe in *a subjective approach,* in which political scientists oriented to the achievement of certain social values seek to achieve them through their own direct experience and involvement with 'the people', rather than through the observation of the experience of other people.[15]

The post-behavioural orientation emerged in the United States during political conflict over the Vietnam War, and disenchantment with the involvement of political scientists in the management and development of a broad range of government policies. Thus in 1969 David Easton, one of the articulate political scientists earlier responsible for fashioning the behavioural approach, declared:

A new revolution is under way in American political science. The last revolution–behaviouralism–has scarcely been completed before it has been overtaken by the increasing social and political crises of our time. The weight of these crises is being felt within our discipline in the form of a new conflict in the throes of which we now find ourselves. This new and latest challenge is directed against a developing behavioural orthodoxy. This challenge I shall call .the post-behavioural revolution. The initial impulse of this revolution is just being felt. Its battle cries are relevance and action.

The essence of the post-behavioural revolution is not hard to idertify. It consists of a deep dissatisfaction with political research and teaching, especially of the kind that is striving to convert the study of politics into a more rigorously scientific discipline modelled on the methodology of the natural sciences. Although the post-behavioural revolution may have all the appearances of another reaction to behaviouralism, it is in fact notably different. Hitherto resistance to the incorporation of scientific method has come in the form of an appeal to the past–to classical political science, such as natural law, or to the more loosely conceived non-methodology of traditional research . . .

The post-behavioural revolution is, however, future-oriented. It does not especially seek to return to some golden age of political research or to conserve or even to destroy a particular method-ological approach. It does not require an adherent to deny the possibility of discovering testable generalisations about human behaviour. It seeks rather to propel political science in new directions.[16]

Thus, post-behaviouralists, while willing to use scientific method where appropriate, are united more by a malaise with the traditional relationship between political science and the state than by any common methodological outlook. Nevertheless, post-behaviouralists seek to change social and political institutions which they regard as oppressive, and are unconcerned with whether such an approach corresponds perfectly with the established scientific model.[17]

Marxist Approach

This category includes political scientists who conduct their research according to Marxist principles of analysis. This category is not meant to describe 'left-wing' academics, or political scientists who prefer socialism as a form of social, political and economic organisa-tion. Rather this category refers to political scientists whose pro-fessional activity corresponds to Marxist formulae. Thus unlike the traditionalists (who regard empirical political theory as unattainable), behaviouralists (who seek to generate theory through research dis-ciplined by scientific method), and post-behaviouralists (for whom theoretical preoccupations are an indulgent luxury in an oppressive world), Marxist political scientists believe that a science of politics has already been established and that its theoretical propositions and principles need only to be applied.[18] These political scientists do not believe that various empirical research projects, if meticulously under-taken, will produce a science of politics. Rather, Marxist political scientists believe that Marx has already uncovered the laws which govern social and political institutions. However, these political scientists believe as well in large-scale revolutionary social and political change; thus their objectives involve the application of scientific propositions and the fulfilment of inevitable social re-organisation.

The major differences amongst the four groups of political scientists, in the broadest sense, are depicted in the following table.

TABLE 1:1—*Alternative Professional Orientations*

Approach	Objectives	Method	Focus
Traditionalist	Policy reform; improvement in political institutions	Deductive; logical; analysis of written material	State
Behaviouralist	Theory-building	Empirical; 'objective'; inductive	Behaviour of groups/people
Post-Behaviouralist	Policy reform; improvement in political social life of 'people'	Empirical; 'subjective'; participatory	Behaviour of groups/people; govt. policies
Marxist	Application of science; revolutionary change	Empirical; logical; application of theory	Social/economic classes; economic foundations of political life

In New Zealand, political science has generally been of the 'traditional' form. Unsystematic, and largely unconcerned with scientific principles, political scientists have sought to describe features of the political system, and to stimulate various institutional reforms. More recently, behavioural, post-behavioural and Marxist influences have introduced greater variety into the discipline. It would appear, however, that most New Zealand political scientists aspire neither for science nor 'revolution'. While seeking to produce research of a more exacting standard, there is little acceptance of the behavioural objective of 'science' nor of the post-behavioural goal of a 'relevant', action-oriented profession. For example, one study of advanced political science students in New Zealand sought to discover how closely they conformed to the various professional orientations in the discipline.[19] Most of the students rejected 'political science' as a descriptive term, preferring 'political studies' as an alternative. As one student observed: 'I feel that the study of politics is not in the class of a science, perhaps it can never be.' While such a response involved a rejection of the goals and professional norms of the behavioural approach, responses to other questions suggested a similar lack of enthusiasm for organised political involvement by political scientists as argued by post-behaviouralists. Thus one student commented: 'I see no reason why individuals should not take stands, but I think that a department of a university should not, as it presumably is trying to project an objective image.' Observations such as these suggest the absence of a 'consensus of rational opinion'[20] within the discipline which is not, however, peculiar to political science in its New Zealand form. Nor may the rejection of behavioural and post-behavioural models for political inquiry be undesirable, for 'the two customary though extreme grounds of disciplinary analysis–"pure" science on the one hand, raw politics on the other–constitute relatively naive or primitive metaphors of analysis'.[21]

The Political Scientist as Detective

It should be clear that what is available to the aspiring student of politics is not one professional role to emulate, but several. Political science now involves competing images of the professional, with alternative roles and obligations. As we are all socialised in different spheres of activity, so political science now offers at least four models of behaviour, with appropriate activities and objectives. In practice, most political scientists move from one model to the other, without much hesitation or reflection. Different research opportunities and situations impinge upon the political scientist's choice of goals and techniques. Political scientists tend therefore to be unapologetically eclectic, moving from one role or 'model' to another as circumstances dictate.

What political scientists seek to do as investigators is not dissimilar in its essentials to the work of other investigators, including the fictional detective. As Winks observes: 'My vocation as a professional historian often leads me to deal with questions of evidence. The historian must collect, interpret, and then explain his evidence by methods which are not greatly different from those techniques employed by the detective, or at least the detective of fiction . . . '[22] The literature of this genre presents different models as well. Moreover, political scientists and fictional detectives share certain significant qualities: as participants in investigation; as investigators of 'crimes' of one sort or another; as individuals, with limited resources, seeking to penetrate to the truth of a situation. As Dunphy observes about the famous fictional detective, Sherlock Holmes:

> Holmes seemed to have an enormous capacity for the scientist's logical reasoning–an intense curiosity, the ability to frame the important question, to observe with thoroughness and painstaking care, and a willingness to test his hunches against the evidence. Above all, he never lets familiarity dull his insatiable curiosity. Being a scientist and being a detective are pretty close to each other, for they demand some of the same kinds of personal qualities–inquisitiveness and persistence to name two–and they both involve a search for the truth which can be alternatively frustrating and exciting. Being a *social* scientist and being a detective are even closer. Both jobs demand the ability to put yourself imaginatively in the place of the other person and sense how he might think, feel

and act. A geologist does not have to know what it feels like to be a stone, but a basic source of evidence for the social scientist, as for the detective, is his own imaginative reconstruction of other people's experience.[23]

By contrast to Holmes' 'behaviouralist' style the fictional French detective, Inspector Maigret, exhibits the post-behaviouralist approach in his 'method' of discovery:

> At the beginning, he didn't know anything, except precise facts, such as are written in the reports. Then he would find himself among people he had never seen, people he had not known the day before, and he would look at them as one looks at photographs in an album . . . Then . . . the people concerned became at the same time vaguer and more human, in particular they became more complicated . . . he was beginning to see them from the inside.[24]

Contrasting Maigret with an austere, scholarly, and unemotional physician, Simenon observes: 'Their ideas about men and their motives were not very far apart. The difference lay in the attitudes with which they faced the problem. Gouin only made use of what Maigret would have called pure reason. Gouin observed them from on high. Maigret placed himself on the same level as they'.[25]

This analysis of methods and objectives can be extended through the genre. 'Traditionalist' detectives would include Agatha Christie's Hercule Poirot, who relies entirely on his 'little grey cells' and leaves empirical investigation to the clumsy police force. The behavioural approach was well exemplified in one of the earliest detectives, Edgar Allen Poe's Auguste Dupin who, like his successor Sherlock Holmes, penetrates to the truth of a situation through his discerning interpretations of observed phenomena. Post-behavioural radicalism and a reliance upon subjective experience are apparent in more recent creations such as Nicolas Freling's Van der Valk and Maj Sjowall's and Per Wahloo's Martin Beck. These investigators recognise the dependence of personal behaviour on social and political factors, and seek moreover to understand their own position in society through identification with (rather than separation from) persons caught up in the processes of investigation. 'Marxist' detectives are more difficult to discover, although Raymond Chandler's noble outsider Philip Marlowe repeatedly deals with corrupt political institutions and discovers crime to be the product of a decadent capitalist and repugnantly materialist American society.

Common Tasks

Whatever their different methods or purposes, political scientists seek to satisfy exacting intellectual standards. The burden of these standards has tended to direct most political scientists towards ever-increasing specialisation, a narrowing of focus not without its own problems. When fully committed to their enterprise, political scientists share both with fictional investigators and with intellectuals in other disciplines the conviction that knowledge must be sought and shared. At the same time, political scientists may value their independence, appreciating as they do that on many (if not most) political questions, what politicians and government officials propose must be regarded as hypotheses, propositions lacking persuasive evidence that the desirable consequences claimed for them will in fact be forthcoming. For this reason, political scientists recognise the truth of the United States Supreme Court Justice Oliver Wendell Holmes' observation that 'every year if not every day we have to wager our salvation upon some prophecy based on imperfect knowledge'. It is the historic task of political science to reduce these imperfections, to diminish our uncertainty, in order to make possible policy-making which is both humane and non-capricious.

References

1. See, for example, P. Strum and M. Shmidman, *On Studying Political Science*, Pacific Palisades, California: Goodyear Publishing Company Inc., 1969.
2. For some contrasting views, see G.J. Graham, Jr. and G.W. Carey, *The Post-Behavioural Era: Perspectives on Political Science*, New York: David McKay Company Inc., 1972; J.C. Charlesworth (ed.), *Contemporary Political Analysis*, New York: The Free Press, 1967.
3. See H.V. Wiseman, *Politics: The Master Science*, London; Routledge and Kegan Paul, 1969, pp. vii, 7.
4. For example, see *PS* (published by The American Political Science Association), vol. X, no. 1, Winter 1977, pp. 63–7.
5. See S. Levine, 'Introduction' in S. Levine (ed.), *New Zealand Politics: A Reader*, Melbourne: Cheshire, 1975, p. 4.
6. H.V. Wiseman, *op. cit.*, also see H.V. Wiseman, *Political Science: An Outline For the Intending Student of Government, Politics and Political Science*, London: Routledge and Kegan Paul, 1967; W.A. Welsh, *Studying Politics*, London: Thomas Nelson and Sons Ltd, 1973.
7. See A. Somit and J. Tanenhaus, *The Development of American Political Science: From Burgess to Behaviouralism*, Boston: Allyn and Bacon, 1967; C.A. Merriam, and H.F. Gosnell, *The American Party System*, New York: MacMillan, 1949; see H.V. Wiseman, *op. cit.*, pp. 15–16.
8. See H. Eckstein, 'A Perspective on Comparative Politics, Past and Present', in H. Eckstein and D.E. Apter (eds), *Comparative Politics: A Reader*, New York: The Free Press, 1963, pp. 3–32.
9. See D.E. Apter, 'Comparative Politics and Political Thought: Past Influences and Future Development' in H. Eckstein and D.E. Apter, *op. cit.*, pp. 725–40.
10. See H. Eulau, *The Behavioural Persuasion in Politics*, New York: Random House, 1963; E. Meehan, *Contemporary Political Thought*, Illinois: Dorsey Press, 1967.

11. See S.A. Barber et al, *Introduction to Problem Solving in Political Science*, Columbus, Ohio: Charles E. Merrill Publishing Company, 1971, p. vi.
12. See A. Brecht, *Political Theory: The Foundations of Twentieth Century Political Thought*, Princeton, New Jersey: Princeton University Press, 1959; A.D. Kaplan, *The Conduct of Inquiry: Methodology for Behavioural Science*, San Francisco: Chandler Publishing Company, 1964.
13. See P. Green and S. Levinson (eds), *Power and Community: Dissenting Essays in Political Science*, New York: Vintage Books, 1969; M. Surkin and A. Wolfe (eds), *An End to Political Science: The Caucus Papers*, New York: Basic Books, 1970; A. Wolfe, *The Seamy Side of Democracy: Repression in America*, New York: David McKay Company Inc., 1973.
14. See H.S. Kariel, *Open Systems: Arenas for Political Action*, Itasca, Illinois: F.E. Peacock Publishers, Inc., 1969; H.S. Kariel, *Saving Appearances: The Re-establishment of Political Science*, North Scituate, Massachusetts: Duxbury Press, 1972.
15. See A.W. Gouldner, *The Coming Crisis of Western Sociology*, New York: Basic Books, 1970; J.D. Colfax and J.L. Roach (eds), *Radical Sociology*, New York: Basic Books, 1971, especially pp. 3–27.
16. D. Easton, 'The New Revolution in Political Science', *American Political Science Review*, vol. LXIII, no. 4, pp. 1051–61, December 1969.
17. By contrast, see R.A. Dahl, 'The Behavioural Approach in Political Science: Epitaph for a Movement to a Successful Protest', *American Political Science* Review, vol. LV, no. 4, December 1961.
18. For example, see G.D. Carson, 'Marxism as Methodology' in *Handbook of Political Science Methods*, Boston: Holbrook Press, Inc., 1971.
19. For details on methodology and sample, see S. Levine, 'The Politics of Political Science' in S. Levine (ed.), *Politics in New Zealand: A Reader*, Sydney: George Allen & Unwin Ltd, 1978.
20. M.E. Kirn and G. Abcarian, 'Professionalism in American Political Science: Exorcising the Ghost in the Disciplinary Machine', 1976, pp. 39–40; manuscript received from the authors.
21. *Ibid.*
22. R.W. Winks (ed.), *The Historian as Detective: Essays on Evidence*, New York: Harper and Row, 1968, p. xiii.
23. D.C. Dunphy, *Investigators: Social Scientists at Work*, Melbourne: Cheshire, 1971, p. 5.
24. G. Simenon, *Maigret and the Old Lady*, Harmondsworth: Penguin Books, 1958, p. 102.
25. G. Simenon, *Maigret's Mistake*, Harmondsworth: Penguin Books, 1958, p. 133.

2 The Institutional Setting

The Constitutional Framework

The New Zealand 'constitution' is a collection of Acts of Parliament, relevant British precedent and accepted conventions which together embody some of the characteristics of a constitutional document. Thus the New Zealand constitutional framework has been haphazardly developed, incomplete, elastic and uncluttered.[1] It has the advantage, however, of being susceptible to brief description.

The 1852 New Zealand Constitution Act of the United Kingdom Parliament created six provinces, and provided for the election of legislature and executive in each.

> It gave the central government certain controls over the provincial governments. It created a central legislature, the General Assembly, consisting of the Governor, an appointed Legislative Council, and an elected House of Representatives; and gave the General Assembly the power, subject to certain limitations, to legislate for the peace, order and good government of New Zealand. It provided for the appointment of legislative councillors and the election of members of the House of Representatives. It gave the Governor power, when a Bill was submitted for the royal assent, to assent to it, or to refuse his assent, or to reserve the Bill for the signification of the royal pleasure, or to amend it and return it to either of the legislative chambers for further consideration.[2]

In 1876, the provinces were abolished, creating a unitary system of government. The Legislative Council gradually lost power and, in the absence of a significant role, was abolished in 1950, leaving New Zealand central government with a unicameral legislature.[3] The Governor-General has gradually lost effective power as well, so that assent to legislation and acceptance of the advice of his ministry has become a formality. Within Parliament's remaining chamber, the House of Representatives (elected triennially), the emergence of a rigidly disciplined two-party system has contributed to the concentration of power within the Cabinet, formed from amongst the Members of Parliament (MPs) belonging to the majority party. Within Cabinet, in turn, power has gravitated to the Prime Minister. Finally, a sizeable, permanent bureaucracy has ensured that the public service will maintain considerable influence in the formation and implementation of policy irrespective of the identity of the governing party.

The Governor-General

The reigning Monarch of the United Kingdom–presently Queen Elizabeth II–is the New Zealand Head of State. In the absence of the Queen, the Governor-General represents the Crown. The Governor-General participates in meetings of the Executive Council (the Cabinet, and the Governor-General); assents to Acts of Parliament; acts upon the advice of 'his' ministry. The Governor-General participates as Head of State in a variety of symbolic or representational functions. Thus the Governor-General may be the patron of many organisations, is to be found at banquets and other formal gatherings, and is expected to represent the Crown on significant occasions.[4] It has been argued that the monarchy provides several advantages: (1) by separating ceremonial and political functions, the physical burdens on the Prime Minister are eased; (2) the Queen or Governor-General can, in extreme circumstances, intervene to protect the rights and liberties of New Zealanders; (3) the institution of monarchy adds dignity to the political system; (4) the monarchy is a source of political stability; (5) the monarchy provides a continuing association with the United Kingdom, and with the Commonwealth.[5]

Commonwealth membership is not, however, dependent on the maintenance of the monarchy. Former British colonies which have become republics have been permitted to remain in the Commonwealth. Many of the other suggested benefits are intangible, immeasurable, and largely metaphysical. The extent to which 'dignity' and 'stability' are provided by the Crown could possibly be measured by the absence of the Crown, but are otherwise unprovable assertions. A recent poll suggests that support for the Crown is declining, and is likely to continue to do so for the forseeable future.[6]

While the Governor-General has very little tangible political power, it is sometimes maintained that the Governor-General nevertheless holds power in two additional senses. First, the Governor-General may be described as possessing *latent* political power. Thus the Governor-General *can* dissolve Parliament, call a general election, or disregard the advice of a Prime Minister and Cabinet; while this has happened recently in Australia (1975) and in Fiji (1976), it has not happened in New Zealand, nor is there any expectation that it will happen in New Zealand.[7] New Zealand lacks the complicated constitutional arrangements of Australia (with a federal system, and bi-cameral legislative framework), and has been without the intense communal conflict of Fiji. While a New Zealand Governor-General may seek at some stage to utilise the unexercised powers of the office, whether this will occur must be entirely speculative.

The second sort of power often attributed to the Governor-General is more easily measured. The Governor-General, like the Queen, may be expected to possess political power arising out of the affections and loyalties of the citizenry. A recent effort has been made to measure support for the monarchy in New Zealand, and this study indicated a rather less unified and unconditional support than might have been expected.[8] A smaller-scale study of support for the Governor-General indicates quite clearly that the Governor-General, unlike the Queen or an American president, has very little hold on the imagination of New Zealand children.[9] In no sense is the Governor-General viewed as an extension of the Queen's 'person'. There would appear to be little latent affection for a Governor-General, and therefore any attempt to intervene in the New Zealand political system could not mobilise latent public support. Thus any intervention by the Governor-General would depend for its success only upon its absolute necessity. In other words, only a genuinely unpopular and entirely unprecedented pattern of activities by a government would provoke the Governor-General into successfully intervening into the New Zealand political system. Moreover, the possibility of a renewed political role for the Governor-General has declined, perhaps ironically, with the appointment of the former National party Prime Minister Sir Keith Holyoake (rather than, as is customary, a 'non-political' figure), for the appointment created controversy in National as well as Opposition quarters and jeopardised long-term support for the maintenance of the monarchy. It could be argued that *any* appointment of a Governor-General, no matter how distinguished, is a poor one if it engenders public controversy. Even an appointment which receives majority support is flawed if the displeasure of a significant minority has been generated. This is particularly so, of course, when the appointment is made by the government without bi-partisan consultation and support, seemingly indispensable qualities that ought to surround the selection of a figure to be 'above politics'. A Governor-General, by becoming politically controversial, vitiates claims that the office enhances stability, promotes unity, and acts as a calming symbol to the community.

Parliament and Cabinet

The New Zealand Parliament has the power to scrutinise government finance and expenditure, and parliamentary authority is required to pass legislation. Election to Parliament occurs every three years, and boundaries are set by the Representation Commission.[10] Parliamentary authority, while considerable, has been eroded during the last few decades in a process which appears to be increasing geometrically. Thus while only Parliament has the power to pass laws, some legislation which has been enacted grants wide powers to various authorities to enact regulations with the force of law.[11] In addition, it is quite clear that parliamentary scrutiny of expenditure, while laborious and detailed in certain instances, nevertheless has only the most marginal effect on the pattern of government taxation and expenditure.[12]

The *government* is the Cabinet, consisting of the Prime Minister and other MPs holding ministerial portfolios. The government caucus consists of members of Cabinet (ministers), and non-members of Cabinet (backbenchers). In addition, the Speaker of the House is chosen from among MPs of the governing party.

Ministers are involved simultaneously in both executive and legislative roles. Responsible for the operations of their department, Ministers participate as well in a Parliament whose origin, historically, has centred around the control of the executive. New Zealand executive-legislative relations have undergone a considerable evolution from the earlier requirements of democratic theory and the origins of parliamentary institutions.[13]

A Constitution for New Zealand: Costs and Benefits

In describing the New Zealand constitutional framework, certain characteristics are especially prominent: (1) the absence of a written constitution; (2) the absence of a bill of rights; (3) the existence of a single legislative chamber; (4) the unity between the executive and legislative branches of government; (5) the creation of a unitary, rather than a federal, system of centralised government; (6) the limited role of the judiciary in the political process; (7) the restricted authority of the Ombudsman, circumscribed to individual complaints against administrative decisions by members of the public service.

There are few formal impediments to the exercise of executive authority in New Zealand. However, written constitutions do not provide guarantees that they will be observed. Some of the more elegant, libertarian documents have been written for South American republics whose governments have shown remarkably little hesitation in disregarding their provisions.[14] While the New Zealand system is a simple one, there is little that is inherently desirable about complexity. That New Zealand would benefit, or that its resources would be used more efficiently, were a second chamber to be restored, or an independent and politically significant judiciary established, or a constitution enacted, has yet to be demonstrated. Persons asserting that New Zealand requires a constitution are often motivated by the political passions of the moment. If a constitution in New Zealand were to have the effect its proponents ascribe to it–namely, to protect the citizen against the enlargement of executive power and to safeguard basic rights which majorities ought not to disregard–then some form of judicial authority would need to be given power to interpret constitutional provisions in case-by-case situations.

One of the effects of such intervention might be to lower the public regard for courts in New Zealand.[15] Certainly American courts are subject to more partisan attack because of their involvement in the making of what are, essentially, extremely complex and controversial policy choices. On the other hand, greater attention would be paid in New Zealand to the appointment of justices, their backgrounds and education, and the processes by which they arrive at a decision, than is presently the case.[16] This might be a desirable thing, but it is a consequence not normally stressed by proponents of a written constitution. More importantly, the existence of a judicial authority to which citizens can regularly seek redress, against decisions appearing to them to contravene constitutional mandates, tends dramatically to alter the nature, scope, and style of political debate. In the United States, decisions which are *political* nearly always become transformed into decisions which are *legal*. As a consequence, political debate in the United States often comes to centre more often around what is *constitutionally permissible* rather than what is *socially desirable*. As a result, political debate frequently involves a form of legal shadow-boxing, in which participants in partisan conflict seek to discredit their adversary's position through complicated constitutional interpretation.

One consequence of a constitution is to delay decision-making; another is to transfer authority to unelected officials (judges) and to those best able to communicate with them (lawyers); a third is to compel society to become unduly litigious, with legalistic debate serving to replace the making of moral/political judgements by citizens and their representatives. In the United States, there have been *no* significant political decisions which have not involved the judicial authority in constitutional interpretation, involving the nullification of legislative statutes, the allocation of public monies, and most of the other features associated with parliamentary activity.[17] Thus the distinction between Parliament and executive may be further blurred by a judicial authority which, in nearly all significant situations, can transcend roles shared by Parliament and Cabinet through the exercise of constitutional interpretation. The increasing complexity of government may require a document containing fundamental protections for citizens delimiting the outer parameters of government action. It should be realised, nevertheless, that a constitution does *not* terminate a process of political change so much as commence a realignment of political relationships pervading the entire political system. For example, a written constitution provides pressure groups, parties and individuals with new opportunities to seek political change, through *legal* channels. If New Zealanders wish a more complex and forceful political system, in which there are more numerous 'access points' for the attainment of political objectives, then a constitution and a revived judicial authority may be appropriate innovations.[18]

Recent Constitutional Controversy

The Superannuation Case

Constitutional controversy was provoked in 1976 when the Prime Minister (Mr Muldoon) invited employers to cease their compulsory deductions for the New Zealand Superannuation Scheme, enacted by Labour, on the grounds that National had pledged in its manifesto to repeal the Labour programme for a distinct programme of its own. Mr Muldoon reasoned that National had received a mandate to abolish the scheme and, given the disciplined party system ensuring its parliamentary control, would do so once Parliament had been convened. Such a political certainty suggested to the Prime Minister that the continued collection of tax revenue for the programme constituted an unnecessary burden on all parties. This invitation to employers to disregard an Act of Parliament provoked a number of law suits attempting to compel the Act's continued enforcement. Redress to the Courts appeared for a time to have been prevented as well, by the Attorney-General's instructions that certain cases would not be permitted to proceed.

Ultimately, however, an injunction was successfully sought against the Prime Minister and other parties requiring them to comply with the Act. Exercising astute political judgement, however, the Chief Justice (Sir Richard Wild) suspended its enforcement since 'it would be an altogether unwarranted step to require the machinery of the Act now to be set in motion again, when the high probabilities are that all would have to be undone again within a few months'.[19] Consistent with American judicial experience, in which assertions of Court powers over legislative and executive authority tend to be introduced in a manner least likely to provoke retaliation, the case represented a rare display of judicial authority in New Zealand on a political issue. Moreover, the Chief Justice's reasoning was surprisingly bold. Basing his decision on the 1688 Bill of Rights, he declared:

It is a graphic illustration of the depth of our legal heritage and the strength of our constitutional law that a statute passed by the English Parliament nearly three centuries ago to extirpate the abuses of the Stuart kings should be available on the other side of the earth to a citizen of this country which was then virtually unknown in Europe and on which no Englishman was to set foot for almost another hundred years. And yet it is not disputed that the Bill of Rights is part of our law. The fact that no modern instance of its application was cited in argument may be due to the fact that it is rarely that a litigant takes up such a cause as the present, or it may be because governments usually follow established constitutional procedures. But it is not a reason for declining to apply the Bill of Rights where it is invoked and a litigant makes out his case.[20]

The Prime Minister's reaction to the decision was restrained, but suggested a displeasure not merely with the judgement but the Court's exercise of authority as well. Nevertheless a decision was taken not to challenge the ruling any further. For its part, the Court later chose to award costs against the Prime Minister, who advised the media of Cabinet's decision to make the payment on his behalf as the case involved the conduct of Government business.

The Summoning of Parliament
The National Government's delay in summoning Parliament after the 1975 election (more than six months elapsed) was not unusual in New Zealand, as is clear from Table 2:1.

However, given the practice of the third Labour Government of virtually all-year parliamentary sessions, the delay led to accusations of government by decree. Criticism was voiced within the House by Labour MP Jonathan Hunt (New Lynn), who introduced an Electoral Amendment Bill (rejected) designed to augment New Zealand's limited constitutional apparatus.[22] The bill would have required Parliament to assemble not later than ninety days following a general election, and was intended as well to prohibit the dissolution of Parliament by the Governor-General without the consent of an absolute majority of MPs.

Mr J.L. Hunt (Labour, New Lynn):

Under our present system, New Zealand members of Parliament are not able to conduct their business properly because they do not know exactly when Parliament will or will not be sitting . . . This Bill will ensure, if it is passed through the House, that New Zealanders will be able to look forward to a more orderly progression of legislation.

National's response to the proposal, however, was far from sympathetic.

Hon. David Thomson (Minister of Justice):

One of the lessons apparent from the Labour Government's administration is that Governments must prepare legislation properly before Parliament is called together to consider legislation. A Government

TABLE 2:1 *Number of Sitting Days and Length of Each Session, 1951–1978*[21]

Session	Date commenced	Date ended	Total days occupied	Days of meeting	Hours sat before midnight H. M.	Hours sat after midnight H. M.	Total number of hours sat H. M.	Daily average H. M.
1951	26 June	13 July	18	12	56 52	0 8	57 0	4 45
1951	25 September	6 December	73	45	260 6	16 55	277 1	6 9
1952	25 June	24 October	122	70	398 40	5 40	404 20	5 46
1953	8 April	27 November	234	77	437 52	15 35	453 27	5 53
* 1954	12 January	13 January	2	2	1 51		1 51	0 56
1954	22 June	1 October	102	60	343 9	3 15	346 24	5 47
1955	22 March	28 "	221	81	470 58	42 38	513 36	6 20
1956	4 April	26 "	207	67	393 35	25 27	419 2	6 15
1957	11 June	25 "	137	80	461 6	5 42	466 43	5 50
1958	21 January	31 January	11	8	36 33		36 33	4 34
1958	10 June	3 October	116	70	434 10	42 54	477 4	6 49
1959	24 "	23 "	122	71	405 5	0 17	405 22	5 43
1960	22 "	28 "	129	74	453 32	36 28	490 00	6 37
1961	20 "	1 December	165	91	581 38	19 33	601 31	6 36
1962	7 "	14 "	192	90	527 26	4 53	532 19	5 55
* 1963	12 February	12 February	1	1	1 19		1 19	1 19
1963	20 June	25 October	128	69	391 31	11 34	403 5	5 50
1964	10 "	4 December	178	90	550 46	32 18	583 4	6 29
1965	27 May	1 November	159	89	558 0	17 33	575 33	6 35
1966	26 "	21 October	149	78	458 59	15 50	474 49	6 5
1967	26 April	24 November	213	99	574 48	28 14	603 02	6 7
1968	26 June	19 December	178	89	533 12	3 24	536 36	6 1
1969	15 May	24 October	163	85	488 57	3 25	492 22	5 48
1970	12 March	3 December	267	110	657 47	69 50	727 37	6 37
1971	25 February	17 December	297	111	667 54	10 19	678 13	6 10
1972	7 June	20 October	135	75	416 25	2 45	419 10	5 35
1973	14 February	23 November	283	111	625 14	3 25	628 39	5 40
1974	4 February	8 November	278	118	697 23	41 46	739 09	6 14
1975	25 March	10 October	200	97	558 26	29 25	587 51	6 05
1976	22 June	14 December	172	96	542 33	51 01	593 34	6 11
* 1977	28 February	28 February	1	1	50		50	50
1977	19 May	16 December	224	118	679 30	39 49	719 19	5 45
1978	10 May	6 October	150	87	471 19	62 00	533 19	6 07

* Special session opened by Her Majesty the Queen.

must consider matters of taxation and expenditure before it brings Parliament together to vote supply–and that is the great reason for bringing Parliament together.[23]

Subsequently, the government introduced its own measure to allow new MPs to participate in select committee work prior to their taking the oath of allegiance to the Crown. This measure, the Legislative Amendment Bill, also allowed business to be carried over from one session of Parliament to another, and provided for select committees to sit between sessions. The intent of the government was to demonstrate that the continuity of Parliamentary business could be promoted without extensive constitutional reform, and without a new Government summoning Parliament within a short time following a general election.

It is, however, one of the curiosities of the Parliamentary schedule that so significant a proportion of its business should need to be transacted after midnight (see table 2:1). This will be detrimental not merely to fatigued MPs but to the interested and determined public, for debate and decision-making will occur without the customary broadcasting by radio. It seems remarkable that legislative bodies in other political systems, including ones whose members have considerable political independence and whose behaviour may therefore prove difficult to control, should be able nevertheless to conclude their duties with so little recourse to post-midnight or all-night sessions. It might have been expected that a Parliament within which there is relatively meagre scope for legislative initiative could do likewise.

Royal Commissions and Commissions of Inquiry

One of the consequences of a Parliament deprived of independent resources and institutional nourishment is that when the need arises for a thorough investigation of a particular issue or problem, Parliament will be unable to supply the necessary expertise to carry out the task. Certainly parliamentary committees are entirely lacking in the staff, resources, time, technical assistance and sheer stature to grapple with the really vital tasks of social investigation and legislative scrutiny. As a result, most of the more important investigatory tasks will be carried out by commissions specially constituted by the government, normally along quasi-judicial lines. Unfortunately, there is little doubt that a judicial proceeding can be an intimidating affair, at least to persons who are not members of the legal profession. For this reason alone, it is unfortunate that New Zealand governments have adopted the habit of appointing persons with a judicial background to chair Royal Commissions and Commissions of Inquiry, irrespective of their purpose or the scope of inquiry contemplated.[24] Certainly there are subjects for which a magistrate or a judge would be admirably suited to conduct or preside over hearings, the outcome of which would lead unambiguously to a judgement and recommendation. However, most inquiries are research exercises, and it is regrettable that New Zealand governments (in the absence of an independent research institute) have been so reluctant to tap university talent in making their appointments to these commissions.

Perhaps the most controversial recent Commission has been the one appointed by Labour (but reporting to National) to inquire into Contraception, Sterilisation and Abortion in New Zealand. In the course of the Commission's investigations, the Auckland Medical Aid Trust came to be regarded almost as a defendant in a court of law. Indeed, the Commission's hearings, involving the taking of testimony, appeared to resemble more closely a judicial proceeding, a courtroom inquiry, than a research activity. Yet the Commission was charged with gathering information, not adjudicating upon guilt or innocence. The former activity requires an altogether different temperament, procedures and rules from the latter. Unfortunately the Commission's judicial orientation persisted in its final report, transforming a collaborative process of discovery into an adversary one.

Commissions of Inquiry are often created by governments to delay the making of difficult, potentially unpopular decisions.[25] Since there is no tradition or compulsion for Parliament to accept the recommendations of these Commissions, this expedient–the appointment of Commissions for politically tactical purposes–can be a tempting one for a government. However, while many Commissions of Inquiry deal with technical matters, requiring intensive investigation and the application of specialised skills, other Commissions–such as the one on Abortion, Sterilisation and Contraception–are appointed to deal with issues reflecting conflicts over values. In such instances the public may be misled by the government's use of the Commission process, for fact-gathering cannot scientifically establish beyond doubt that one set of values is preferable to another.

Commissions of Inquiry, abstractly fashioned on the scientific model of investigation, face the limitations of that method, and must be especially cautious in enunciating recommendations based more on value preferences than acquired expertise. Ultimately, however, the necessity to make choices about values, and take actions based on them, cannot be evaded either by MPs or by affected individuals. The best that can be expected is that appointed Commissions can, in certain circumstances, usefully augment the parliamentary process of inquiry.

Local and Regional Government

While there is a cliche that local government is 'closer to the people', and thus in some way more directly a part of the democratic process than the 'remote' central government, in fact most people find local body politics boring and trivial.[26] Participation in local elections in New Zealand is much lower than in parliamentary elections, and involvement in local government tends to be provoked only when an essential service fails to be delivered.[27] Organised involvement can be stimulated by amalgamation schemes not because of any interest in the possibility of renewed civic government, but out of a mixture of parochial pride and financial anxiety over the possibility of higher rates (i.e. taxation of property).

Yet it would be helpful for political scientists and citizens alike to redirect their attention towards local and regional government in New Zealand. Local bodies perform significant social services, and constitute an important political infrastructure throughout the country. The efficiency with which they discharge their functions has yet to be measured, though it is clear that citizens derive unequal benefits from local body services. In commenting on the substantial government involvement in social and economic affairs, which exists in curious partnership with a political culture inimical to socialism, Brownlie observes:

> The public sector spent an estimated \$4,350 million in 1975–76, approximately 41 percent of New Zealand's GNP. Transfer payments, including social security benefits, pensions, and various subsidies accounted for some \$1,300 million; nearly a third of total public sector expenditure was therefore transferred directly back to private individuals and enterprises. Public sector current expenditure on goods and services is estimated at approximately \$2,100 million, about half of the total, and public investment at approximately \$1,000 million . . . Local authority expenditure accounted for 20 percent of the total. Over half of this was expenditure by hospital boards, which was financed almost entirely by transfers from the central government revenue account. Including these transfers, nearly three-fifths of local authority expenditure was financed by the central government, with rates, local taxes, trading income, and borrowing providing the rest.[28]

The pattern of revenues and expenditures of one major local body is described in Figure 2:1.

Much of the pressure for reform of local government has been centred on the eroding financial base of local bodies, made especially intense by the increasing demand for costly civic services. The Local Government Commission, in existence for nearly thirty years, and disbanded by National in late 1977, operated under powers which varied according to the strength of central government's wish to enforce local government reform.

As Roberts has observed:

Local Government in New Zealand has always been a matter of political controversy. The balance between central and local power is inherently sensitive even where, as in New Zealand, the ultimate authority lies with the centre . . . Government is largely a process by which the resources are collected from the inhabitants of a particular geographical area and expended upon those activities which must be undertaken as a matter of legislative duty, or which are chosen among all the options available as the most politically desirable at a given moment in time.[30]

When resources become inadequate, pressure for structural reform will increase. An emerging regional amalgamation may be modelled on New Zealand's most successful reorganisation of government

FIGURE 2:1
Income and Expenditure, Wellington City Corporation, 1977–78[29]

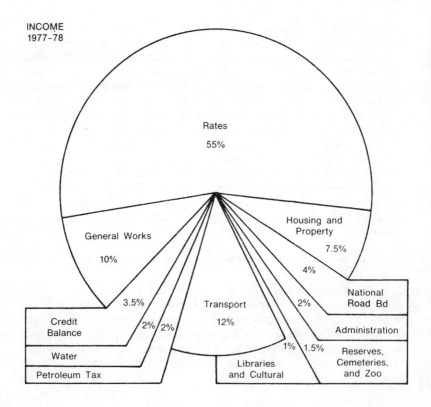

INCOME
1977–78

Rates
55%

General Works
10%

Housing and
Property
7.5%

4%

3.5%

Transport
12%

2%

National
Road Bd

Credit
Balance

2% 2%

Administration

Water

1% 1.5%

Reserves,
Cemeteries,
and Zoo

Petroleum Tax

Libraries
and Cultural

according to the principles of regionalist reform, the Auckland Regional Authority. However, 'regionalism is not . . . a panacea for all political ills nor can it hope to resolve all political conflicts.'[31] This is particularly so if the opportunities for participation in community activities are not to be surrendered through the disappearance of structures untidy to social planners, but beneficial for citizens.

Mr Muldoon has argued that local body problems over finance may be due to inadequate restraints over spending and a tendency for local bodies to undertake activities not normally within their field. However, the problems of local body finance are not peculiar to New Zealand. There may be a need for the promotion of greater revenue-sharing by the central government in partnership with local authorities, or for an enlargement of the tax-base beyond property-owners, lest a

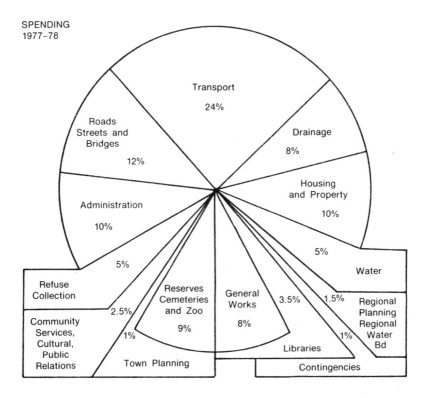

SPENDING 1977–78

ratepayers' revolt emerges, culminating in dramatic and harmful reductions in necessary services.

The Ombudsman

While the office of Ombudsman was initiated in Sweden in 1809, the first non-Scandinavian Ombudsman was the New Zealand one, established by the National Government (over the desultory indifference of Labour and the outright hostility of the Public Service Association) in 1962.[32] This office has served as the model for Ombudsmen established since, in Great Britain, many American states, Canadian provinces and elsewhere throughout the world. In this undramatic yet significant democratic experiment, the office of Ombudsman–a 'perpetual reform institution'–provides a contemporary example of what is more frequently a self-indulgent cliché: New Zealand 'leading the world' through the creativity of its political and social institutions.

The Ombudsman appears to have developed into 'a prestigious, multi-purpose, investigative tool–something like a readily available "mini" Royal Commission'.[33] Sir Guy Powles' Annual Report to Parliament in 1975 underlines the secret of his success as New Zealand's first Ombudsman.

> The office's method of operation, which is wholly investigatory and not adversarial, has lent itself to an objective pursuit of the truth in each case, and in so doing has generated confidence in those persons, be they complainants or departmental officers, whose actions may ultimately be found to be open to criticism.[34]

This approach is in marked contrast to the judicial orientation of Royal Commissions and Commissions of Inquiry, noted earlier. Pursuing a method of investigation based on co-operation and conciliation rather than confrontation, the Ombudsman has been able to ensure compliance with his recommendations despite few formal powers.

The Ombudsman has developed and enlarged the authority of his office over the years, until ultimately the office has emerged as a 'national symbol' acceptable to all parties. Indeed, in controversy over the National Government's appointment of the former Prime Minister, Sir Keith Holyoake, as New Zealand's Governor-General, opponents of the appointment suggested Sir Guy Powles or 'someone like him' as a suitable choice. The office has been neither an irritant to civil servants, nor a panacea for civil libertarians. Rather in small and 'minor' matters, the Ombudsman has been able to initiate a considerable number of reforms whose impact on the lives of individual citizens in their relations with government departments has been significant, and to their benefit. The activities of the Ombudsman during the office's first fourteen years are summarised in Table 2:2.

TABLE 2:2 *Complaints to the Ombudsman, 1962–1975*[35]

Action on Complaint	Year Ended March 1975	1 October 1962 to 31 March 1975
Outside jurisdiction	371	3,285
Declined	9	144
Discontinued	248	1,569
Withdrawn	84	812
Investigated and considered justified	132	1,086
Investigated and considered not justified	282	3,691
Still under investigation	189	189
Total complaints	1,315	10,776

During the 1976–78 period there was a significant growth in the number of investigations undertaken annually, corresponding with the increased jurisdiction and size of the Office. In 1975–6, there were 408 investigations, 134 (33%) of which were sustained; for 1976–7, these figures had risen to 862 investigations, with 349 (40%) considered justified. This proportion, which has been reasonably constant, persisted in 1977–8 as did the continuing rise in workload: 1031 investigations, 381 (36%) sustained.[36]

Surprisingly (given the populist rhetoric surrounding the office), complainants to the Ombudsman appear to be persons already relatively well-placed in the political system to promote their interests and receive satisfactory resolution of their grievances.[37] Moreover, it appears that even those helped by the Ombudsman rarely contact him to express acknowledgement or perfunctory gratitude. To most citizens, the Ombudsman is an access point, an approachable bureaucrat, but little more. He is not able to help citizens opposed to policies carried out by government departments or public servants and his position in the political system–a parliamentary official with limited investigative powers–involves limited, brief interaction with other actors in the system on a one-to-one basis. Complainants do not aggregate their objections, and no organised programme of protest against government policies emerges from this institution.

Indeed, in 1962 the only recorded vote taken on the bill establishing an Ombudsman was an unusual 'free' (or 'conscience') vote taken on the name! More pointedly, while the position appears well established, nevertheless the casual manner of its introduction into New Zealand

and the lack of understanding of its limited role suggests that the strength of the Ombudsman's position in the political system has yet to be tested. In 1975, for example, H.J. Walker (National, Papanui) criticised in sweeping terms Labour's appointment of Sir Guy Powles to conduct an inquiry into the Security Intelligence Service. Mr Walker observed: 'If the proposal is gone on with, the office of Ombudsman will, particularly in the circumstances, be cast into utter contempt and complete disrepute'.[38]

Nevertheless the appointment of successors to Sir Guy Powles, the enlargement of authority to include investigations of complaints involving local bodies, and the establishment of a Privacy Commissioner, suggest that the principle of independent investigative officers of this kind has wide support. Despite some public misunderstanding, however, these innovative positions are responsible to Parliament, and do not comprise a constitutional restraint on Parliamentary or executive authority.

References

1. See W.K. Jackson, *New Zealand: The Politics of Change*, Wellington: A.H. and A.W. Reed, 1972.
2. K.J. Scott, *The New Zealand Constitution*, Oxford: Clarendon Press, 1962, p. 2.
3. W.K. Jackson, *The New Zealand Legislative Council*, Dunedin: John McIndoe, 1972, details quite effectively the evolution and ultimate abolition of this second chamber of the New Zealand Parliament.
4. See, for example, L. Lipson, *The Politics of Equality*, Chicago: University of Chicago Press, 1948, Chapters 7, 13 and 14.
5. See A.D. Robinson, *Notes on New Zealand Politics*, Wellington: School of Political Science and Public Administration, Victoria University of Wellington, 1970. For a more recent look at the place of the Governor-General in the system following the Holyoake appointment, see H. Evans, *Case Against Robert Muldoon and his National Party Government*, Christchurch: Pegasus Press, 1978.
6. See S. Levine and A.D. Robinson, *The New Zealand Voter: An Analysis of A Survey of Public Opinion and Electoral Behaviour*, Wellington: Price Milburn for New Zealand University Press, 1976, pp. 93–5.
7. See D. Butler, 'Politics and the Constitution: Twenty Questions Left by Remembrance Day' in H.R. Penniman (ed.), *Australia at the Polls: The National Elections of 1975*, Washington, D.C.: American Enterprise Institute for Public Policy Research, 1977, pp. 313–36; D. Stevens, 'It Could Happen Here', *The New Zealand Law Journal*, 16 December 1975, pp. 794–7; S. Levine and A.D. Robinson, pp. 89–92, *op. cit.*
8. S. Levine and A.D. Robinson, *op. cit.*, pp. 93–5.
9. W. Gordon, 'Political Socialisation of School Children: A Comparative Study—Urban and Rural', unpublished paper, Victoria University of Wellington, 1977, pp. 1–11.
10. See A.D. McRobie, 'The Politics of Electoral Redistribution', in S. Levine (ed.), *Politics in New Zealand: A Reader*, pp. 255–269.
11. See W.K. Jackson, 'Government Succession in New Zealand' in S. Levine (ed.), *Politics in New Zealand: A Reader*, pp. 1–21.

12. See A.D. McRobie, 'Parliamentary "Control" of Public Expenditure' in S. Levine (ed.), *Politics in New Zealand: A Reader*, pp. 115–130.
13. See R.M. Alley, 'Parliamentary Parties in Office: Government–Backbench Relations', M.J. Minogue, 'Information and Power: Parliamentary Reform and the Right to Know' and M. Waring, 'Power and the New Zealand MP: Selected Myths About Parliamentary Democracy' in S. Levine (ed.), *Politics in New Zealand: A Reader*, pp. 78–114. As the New Zealand system is modelled (increasingly loosely) on the British or 'Westminster' system of government, comparisons with contemporary British political institutions can be quite useful. Perhaps the most successful recent study of the British political system would be R.M. Punnett, *British Government and Politics*, London: Heinemann, 1971.
14. For an interesting analysis of the role of constitutions in securing political democracy, see A. Brecht, 'The New German Constitution', *Social Research*, vol. 16, no. 4, December, 1949.
15. This point of view is expressed by L. Hand, *The Bill of Rights*, New York: Atheneum, 1964.
16. This kind of analysis can be found in N. Christie, 'The Administration of Justice and its Clients' in N.R. Ramsoy, *Norwegian Society*, New York: Humanities Press Inc., 1974; B.N. Cardozo, *The Nature of the Judicial Process*, New Haven, Connecticut: Yale University Press, 1921.
17. An overview of this activity, describing its development, rationale and consequences, can be found in R.H. Jackson, *The Supreme Court in the American System of Government*, New York: Harper and Row, 1955; A.T. Mason and W.M. Beaney, *American Constitutional Law: Introductory Essays and Selected Cases*, Englewood Cliffs, New Jersey: Prentice–Hall, Inc., 1963. R.H. Jackson, *The Struggle for Judicial Supremacy*, New York: Random House, 1941.
18. An excellent discussion of the suitability of a written constitution, Bill of Rights and politically active judicial authority for systems modelled on the British pattern is found in A. Cox's lectures delivered at Oxford University in 1975. See A. Cox, *The Role of the Supreme Court in American Government*, Oxford: Clarendon Press, 1976.
19. S. Levine, 'New Zealand Politics: Annual Review', *Australian Quarterly*, vol. 49, no. 1, March 1977, pp. 101–2.
20. *Ibid.*
21. Annual *Journals of the House of Representatives* (1976; 1978).
22. See W.K. Jackson, 'Government Succession in New Zealand' in S. Levine (ed.), *Politics in New Zealand: A Reader*, pp. 1–21.
23. *New Zealand Parliamentary Debates (N.Z.P.D.)*, vol. 404 pp. 688–93, 16 July 1976. The proposal was debated further on 25 August 1976; pp. 2006–15.
24. See A.C. Simpson, 'Commissions of Inquiry and the Policy Process' in S. Levine (ed.), *Politics in New Zealand: A Reader*, pp. 22–35.
25. *Ibid.*
26. See R.J. Gregory, 'Political Participation in New Zealand: The Democratic Idea in Local Government Reform' in S. Levine (ed.), *Politics in New Zealand: A Reader*, pp. 50–62.
27. See J. Halligan and P. Harris, 'Local Elections and Democracy' in S. Levine (ed.), *Politics in New Zealand: A Reader*, pp. 241–254.
28. New Zealand Monetary and Economic Council, *The Public Sector*, Wellington: Government Printer, 1976, pp. 5–7.
29. *Evening Post*, 5 June 1977.

30. J.L. Roberts, 'Local Government and Reform' in Urban Development Association Inc., *The New Constitution*, August 20–22, 1975, Wellington, pp. 11–12.
31. J.L. Roberts, 'A Greater Wellington Region', unpublished paper, 1976, p. 20.
32. L.B. Hill, *The Model Ombudsman: Institutionalising New Zealand's Democratic Experiment*, Princeton, New Jersey: Princeton University Press, 1976, pp. 67–73.
33. Sir Guy Powles, *Annual Report of the Ombudsman 1975*, Wellington: Government Printer, 1975, pp. 13–15.
34. *Ibid.*
35. *Annual Report of the Ombudsman 1975*, p. 11.
36. See the *Annual Report of the Ombudsman* (Wellington: Government Printer) for 1976, 1977 and 1978.
37. See L.B. Hill, *op. cit.* for an excellent analysis of complainants' backgrounds and the pattern of investigation established by the Ombudsman; especially helpful as models of empirical research are Parts 2 and 3.
38. Hon. H.J. Walker, 'Office of Ombudsman in Disrepute' (Press Release), 3 August 1975.

3 Parliament

The Development of Party Government

The relationship between Parliament and Cabinet has evolved under the influence of the party system of government. Prior to the emergence of the political parties in New Zealand, ministries were unstable coalitions of individuals, and the development of a unified government programme was impeded by the absence of formal and enduring partisan commitments. At the same time, it is possible to exaggerate the degree of instability in government, for the Cabinet lists for the 1854–90 period indicate a high degree of *continuity of personnel* at the highest levels of government.

Prior to John Ballance becoming Premier in 1891, there were 27 different Ministries (during a 37-year period; by contrast, there have been 23 Ministries in the subsequent 87 years). However, of these 27, Harry Atkinson was Prime Minister on no less than five occasions,[1] William Fox held the post four times, while Edward Stafford occupied the position on three separate occasions. While portfolios may have altered quite frequently, the extent of disturbance within the governing elite was not as extensive as is sometimes suggested, and the degree of 'instability' in this non-party system is not comparable to the fractionalised ungovernability of the French Fourth Republic or the parliamentary system of post-war Italy.

TABLE 3:1 *Length of Term of New Zealand Ministries, 1856–1890*[2]

Length of term	Number of ministries
Under two months	9
Two months–1 year	5
One year–two years	6
Two years–three years	2
Over three years	5

Since the emergence of the Liberal party in 1890, however, the balance of power between Parliament and Cabinet has gradually

43

shifted away from the legislative chamber and towards the executive. Party government has ensured a stable base of majority support for an executive's legislative and financial programme, and the influence of the individual MP has been gradually but significantly reduced. It is no longer necessary for a government to manoeuvre to obtain a majority, and ministries in New Zealand since 1890 have been remarkably stable.

TABLE 3:2 *Length of Term of New Zealand Ministries, 1891–1978*[3]

Length of term	Number of ministries
Under two months	2
Two months–1 year	3
One year–two years	3
Two years–three years	2
Over three years	12

On the fall of Atkinson's government in 1891, the Liberals came into office. For the next twenty-one years (1891–1912), it was a continuous ministry of Liberals that held power . . . The year in which the first real change of ministry in the modern period occurred was 1912. Every single member of the Reform Cabinet was new to office . . . This Reform cabinet lasted until 1915, when, as a gesture of wartime unity, a coalition was formed. The coalition ended in 1919, after which cabinets composed purely of Reformers governed the country for a decade. The party composition of the ministry was once more altered in 1928, when the Liberals took office . . . From 1931 to 1935 there was a new cabinet based upon the depression coalition of Reformers and Liberals. In 1935 the Labour ministry was formed, and again the change of office-holders was complete . . . The premier is a party leader, and when the electorate is swayed by a popular personage–a Seddon, a Massey, or a Savage–his ministers and parliamentary followers are likely to share in reflected glory. Because of the party organisation now established in every constituency of the country, the modern prime minister and his colleagues enjoy an expectance of far longer political life than could Vogel, Grey or Atkinson.[4]

This pattern has been extended to the present. The National Party replaced Labour in 1949 and has enjoyed power since, with the exception of two brief interruptions (1957–60; 1972–5). The government of the country has been dominated by a succession of prime ministers: Holland, Holyoake, and Muldoon, under National; Nash and Kirk, under Labour. Less successful leaders unable to capture the imagination of the electorate while in office have been Marshall

(National) and Rowling (Labour).[5] It is interesting, however, that both former leaders have acquired qualities of statesmanship and character not always attributed to them while in office. Thus in retirement, Sir John Marshall has become very much a warmly regarded elder statesman, while Mr Rowling emerged as a forceful leader of his party in 1978 after three years as Opposition leader.

Party Discipline

The unity between legislature and executive is more than a practical outcome of the party system.

> Legally Parliament is a bi-partite body consisting of the House of Representatives and the Governor-General. An Act of Parliament must have been assented to by both parts before it is valid. It is important to remember this legal meaning of Parliament since it is now embodied in the constitutional doctrine that the Government and the House of Representatives are both parts of the legislature and both constitutionally entitled to share in the legislative process. The Government's leadership in the legislative process is not an usurpation of the powers of the legislature; it is rather its traditional constitutional role as a legitimate part of the legislature.[6]

The leadership of the executive has been formally entrenched in the Standing Orders of the House. These ensure executive pre-eminence in every stage of the legislative process. For example, all revenue-raising measures and all bills involving the expenditure of public monies must be introduced by the Crown (i.e. the government). Thus one of the major sources of independent initiative, on the part of government backbench or Opposition MPs, or the Committees of Parliament, is effectively foreclosed by the rules of the House. While party discipline in New Zealand has become even more entrenched in the House in recent years—perhaps, in part, due to its compatibility with pressures for conformity widespread in New Zealand culture—in Westminster it has been steadily crumbling. In Great Britain, the doctrine of collective cabinet responsibility has eroded considerably in the post-war years, at least partially as a consequence of ideological fissures within the Conservative and Labour parties. Thus in 1977, for example, the Labour Prime Minister, Mr Callaghan, was compelled to concede to his Ministerial colleagues the right to *vote*, if they chose—but *not to speak* in debate—against his government's bill to introduce direct elections in Great Britain to the European Parliament.

In New Zealand, backbench power has continued to decline, however, and the improbability of successful rebellion in Parliament continues to be supported by the party basis of electoral politics. Moreover, as Robinson observes:

The mere fact of loyalty to a party produces an impulse to conformity in a member. He cannot let his side down, especially in the midst of intense party struggle in the House. Corresponding to this it is interpreted as treachery to leave one's friends in the lurch. A traitor is not only an opponent; he is also an enemy. Life is much more pleasant and congenial for those who conform.[7]

Indeed the pressures upon potentially dissident MPs may be compelling, and the secrecy of Cabinet and party caucus proceedings almost guarantees that most party divisions will be kept from the press and public. In this respect New Zealand parties approach in practice the philosophy of democratic centralism espoused by socialist and communist parties. Once a decision has been taken, party members in Parliament close ranks absolutely, and departures from agreed-upon policy are viewed with the utmost seriousness.

The model of the process by which 'a bill becomes a law' has been described in graphic detail by Waring.[8] A simpler figure, reproduced below, describes this process irrespective of the identity of the governing party.

FIGURE 3:1 *The Parliamentary Legislative Process*[9]

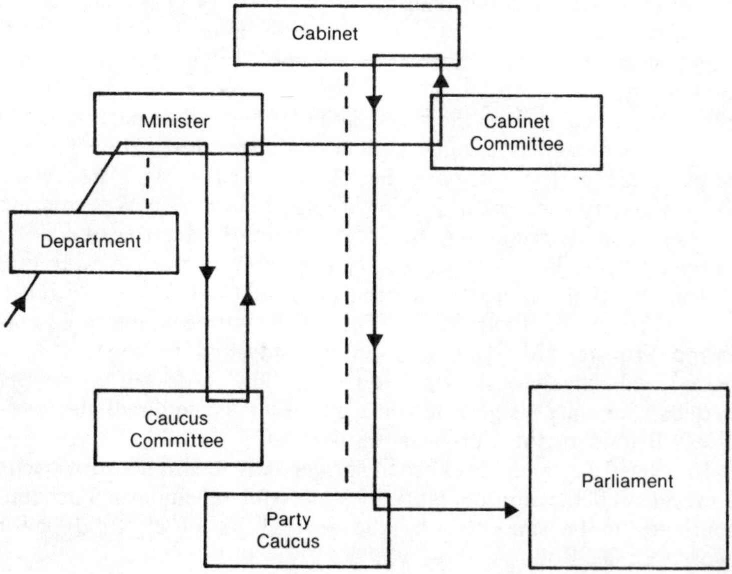

The Committee System

The use of parliamentary committees to study proposed legislation, estimates of expenditure, and petitions is significant though not always crucial. Measures may proceed through the House *without* referral to committees. In particular, parliamentary committees play a very limited role in the development of the government's financial programme, although historically this has been a major prerogative of the legislature. Indeed, Parliament has been conceived as the body required to approve or deny supply to the government. However, this feature of the legislative function has been diminished by the rise of the party system as well as the enormous size and complexity of the financial programme of a modern state.

Select committees include: (1) permanent standing committees of the House; (2) special committees formed on an *ad hoc* basis, usually to coincide with a major piece of legislation likely to attract a considerable number of submissions from individuals and groups.[10] The Parliamentary select committees functioning during 1977 provide an example of the sort of committees commonly established. These included: (1) legislative committees handling public bills: Commerce and Mining; Education; Island Affairs; Labour; Lands and Agriculture; Maori Affairs; Road Safety; Social Services; Statutes Revision; (2) other substantive committees: Defence; Foreign Affairs; Local Bills; Public Expenditure; Selection (Private Bills); Petitions; (3) committees dealing with House matters: Library; House; Privileges. All committees were chaired by Government backbench MPs, with the exception of Library (chaired by the Speaker), Privileges (chaired by the Minister of Justice, Mr Thomson), Lands and Agriculture (chaired by the Minister of Fisheries and Associate Minister of Agriculture, Mr Bolger) and Maori Affairs (also chaired by Mr Bolger). Two committees were chaired by sub-Cabinet MPs: Commerce and Mining, by the Parliamentary Undersecretary to the Minister of Trade and Industry (Mr Allen); Local Bills, by the Parliamentary Undersecretary to the Minister of Internal Affairs, Local Government, Recreation and Sport, Civil Defence and Minister for the Arts (Mr Comber).

In addition, a special select committee was formed in 1977 to consider the National Government's Shop Trading Hours Bill. On the whole, however, the third National Government has been less eager to refer legislation to committee, and this form of deliberation–permitting pressure group participation in the legislative process–has been bypassed on occasion by the government (over Opposition objections). Among the weaknesses of the New Zealand parliamentary system are the absence of formal guarantees to MPs that they may introduce legislation (a first reading, and a printing of the measure, may be denied by Speaker's ruling or a decision by the majority party) and that such legislation may be referred to committees for scrutiny.

The committees of Parliament lack the institutional support and official encouragement necessary for them to make the best possible contribution to the legislative process. Absence of permanent research staff and counsel mean that the capacity to develop an independent, critical perspective is lacking. Of course the political will for such an effort is also inadequate, yet the potential for the committees of Parliament to emerge as centres of initiative and expertise, to augment the government departments and the political parties, is latent. At present, certain committees such as Defence and Foreign Affairs scarcely need to meet at all, while other committees lack the competence to critically examine material provided to them. The committees need to develop an institutional personality, to revitalize their present role as (at best) reactive bodies capable of providing a pressure-group forum. In the short term, it would be useful for parliamentary committees to develop basic procedures and acquire necessary staff, so that (for example) verbatim transcripts of non-sensitive committee testimony might be available as a record of committee work on legislation and estimates.

The formal committee structure of Parliament has been augmented by a committee system which operates more regularly, possesses greater influence and conducts its discussions entirely *in camera*. Committees responsible to each party's caucus have been formed which consider government proposals (and, in the case of the Opposition, possible alternatives). In addition, Cabinet committees composed of Ministers regularly make important, detailed recommendations and decisions embracing the whole of the parliamentary programme. As power has gravitated *from the individual MP to the party*, and *from the legislature to the executive*, so a corresponding shift of power has occurred *from the parliamentary committees to the caucus committees*, and finally *from the caucus committees to those formed from and responsible to Cabinet*.[11]

The Speaker

Parliamentary activities take place according to a variety of rules: Standing Orders, Speakers' Rules, parliamentary custom, party rules and conventions. These are enforced by the Speaker of the House.

The Speaker, the presiding officer of the House, is elected by the House at the beginning of the first session after a general election. While he is expected to be non-partisan, he is nevertheless an MP from the majority party who must campaign for election in a parliamentary electorate. While the Speaker neither votes (except in the case of a tie–an unusual event) nor participates in debates (except to ensure that the procedures of the House are followed), he may nevertheless become the subject of partisan debate. In 1975, Mr Muldoon, then Leader of the Opposition, was ejected from the House by the then Labour Speaker, Sir Stanley Whitehead. The election of a Speaker under National in 1976 (Sir Roy Jack), was vigorously opposed by the Labour Opposition. So sustained was the Labour attack that the Speaker questioned on one occasion how Labour MPs could expect impartial treatment given the tenor and substance of their accusations. During 1976, Jonathan Hunt (Labour, New Lynn) was guilty of a breach of privilege for what Mr Muldoon described as 'a crude attack on the presiding officer of Parliament' after Mr Hunt had characterised the Speaker as 'weak' on a radio programme.[12] In general, however, the Speaker in the New Zealand House of Representatives has been the subject of favourable comment: 'The tradition of the New Zealand Speakership is one of dignity, and fidelity to historic custom . . . In New Zealand the Chair has consistently set a high example'.[13]

An innovation during the 1977 session has involved the surrender of the Chair on several occasions by the Speaker, to an MP from the Labour side of the House, Squadron Leader Drayton. This has been accompanied by the Speaker's suggestions that the post of Speaker be regarded as a bi-partisan one, and the recommendation that a Deputy Speaker be elected from the Opposition side. Clearly the effort to move the New Zealand Speaker more towards the British model, and further from partisan politics, stems from the 1976 controversies. If MPs of the governing party can become socialised to accept a presiding officer of the minority, or Opposition, party, then this experiment in a more mature supervision of parliamentary debate may become institutionalised.

The Legislative Agenda

The legislative agenda is determined by the government, and the programme of the majority party dominates the parliamentary programme. Government bills are introduced into the House through a motion by a Minister that the Bill be introduced. Other types of bills are *private members' bills*, proposed by an Opposition or backbench government MP; *local bills*, which affect a particular locality; *private bills*, which are designed to secure certain benefits or privileges for an individual or group. First reading debates follow the introduction of a bill, and are supposed to concentrate on the purposes of the proposed legislation. The Second Reading debate centres on the principles of the bill, while detailed scrutiny on a clause-by-clause basis occurs during the subsequent debate (when the House forms a Committee of the whole House). The Third Reading debate is a formality, although this debate represents the final opportunity for the Opposition to broadcast its objections and the government to laud the merits of its handiwork. The tedious and repetitious character of these encounters–four debates on a single piece of legislation, with the outcome in little doubt–is not prolonged on every bill, and the Opposition does not force divisions at every opportunity except on more controversial bills (such as Labour's and National's rival super-annuation programmes, each passed only after the most exhaustive and prolonged opposition). The following table summarises in considerable detail some of the formal work undertaken by Parliament during a recent session.

TABLE 3:3 *Schedule of Business*[14]

	(1976–1978) Thirty-Eighth Parliament					
	1976		1977		1978	
1. *Sittings of House–*						
Days of meeting		96		118		87
	h.	m.	h.	m.	h.	m.
Hours of sitting before midnight	542	33	679	30	471	19
Hours of sitting after midnight	51	01	39	49	62	00
	593	34	719	19	533	19
Hours of sitting after 10.30 p.m.	85	32	67	26	76	42
Daily average	6	11	5	45	6	07
2. *Bills—*						
Public—						
Carried over from previous Session	22		14		17	
Introduction by Government during current Session	114*		189**		71***	
Introduced by Private Members during current Session	7		5		13	
		143		208		101

* Statutes Amendment Bill later divided into 57 separate Bills
** Statutes Amendment Bill later divided into 50 spearate Bills; University Acts Amendment Bill later divided into 8 separate Bills; Contraception, Sterilisation and Abortion Bill later divided into 9 separate Bills; Industrial Relations Bill later divided into 4 separate Bills.
*** Statutes Amendment Bill later divided into 50 separate Bills; Contraception, Sterilisation, and Abortion Amendment later divided into 2 separate Bills; Industrial Law Reform Bill later divided into 3 separate Bills; Misuse of Drugs Bill later divided into 4 separate Bills.

TABLE 3:3—*continued*

	1976		1977		1978	
Referred to Select Committees	52		43		26	
(Hearings opened to news media)	39		37		18	
Received the Royal Assent	168		73		137	
Local—						
Carried over from previous Session	—		3		4	
Introduced during recesses	6		4		7	
Introduced during current Session	9		13		7	
		15		20		18
Received the Royal Assent	11		13		11	
Private—						
Carried over from previous Session	—		—		1	
Introduced during current Session	2		2		1	
		2		2		2
Received the Royal Assent	2		1		1	
3. Petitions—						
Presented	35		41		34	
Reported back to House	19		35		17	
Held over	16		15		1	
4. Questions—						
For Oral Answer	1264		1819		1615	
For Written Answer	1156		781		1053	
		2420		2600		2680
Oral transferred to Supplementary Order Papers	445		206		136	
Total on Supplementary Order Papers	2100		2269		2677	
Supplementary Order Papers debated	10		13		10	
		2545		2475		2813
5. Papers Laid Upon Table—						
Papers ordered to be printed	146		162		139	
Papers tabled under S.O. 93(2)	305		283		237	
Papers tabled but not printed	34		37		24	
		485		482		400
6. Notices of Motion—						
Number given	752		525		678	
Number debated	15		38		29	
Days on which debated	8		13		12	

TABLE 3:3—*continued*

	1976		1977		1978	
7. Divisions—						
In the House	111		77		38	
In Committee of Whole House	132		167		22	
		243		244		60
8. Select Committees—						
On public matters	18		18		20	
Other	4		5		3	
		22		23		23
Reports—						
Broadcasting Bill	1		—		—	
Commerce and Mining	2		4		1	
Committee on Bills	—		1		1	
Defence	1		—		—	
Education	1		—		1	
Foreign Affairs	—		1		—	
Human Rights Commission	—		1		—	
Labour	4		4		1	
Lands and Agriculture	11		18		14	
Local Bills	18		22		16	
Maori Affairs	1		2		2	
Petitions	15		17		9	
Private Bills	2		2		2	
Privileges	6		—		1	
Public Expenditure	1		1		1	
Road Safety	3		1		1	
Selection	2		2		1	
Social Services	8		14		3	
Statutes Revision	13		14		8	
Town and Country Planning	—		1		—	
Violent Offending	—		—		1	
		89		105		63

While the content of a government's legislative programme will alter from one session to another, the general pattern of formal parliamentary work is consistent from year to year. The session opens with the Speech from the Throne (made by the Governor-General), setting forth the government's programme. This is followed by the Address-in-Reply debate, on a motion that a reply be given to the Governor-General's address. Later in the session, a similarly wide-ranging debate occurs on the government's budget and on bills (Appropriation; Imprest Supply) required by the government to secure funds for its programme. Other debates may occur over questions, notices of motion, and on 'urgent' public issues.

Petitions may vary considerably, in size, influence and in the response by Parliament to them. For example, on the same day–20 July 1977–two petitions were presented to Parliament. One, the largest in New Zealand history, had 341,159 signatures, and was presented by Dr I. Shearer (National, Hamilton East) on behalf of the signatories. The petition, known as the Maruia Declaration, called for the protection of New Zealand's native forests, and was referred to the Lands and Agriculture Select Committee. The other, presented by Mr A. Malcolm (National, Eden), with 137 signatures, asked that fortune-telling no longer be considered an offence under the Police Offences Act 1952. The petition referred to the law as 'mediaeval and barbaric', and followed the conviction (with a $75 fine) of two persons (tarotmancers by profession) in Auckland for the offence. While some may feel that Parliament is obligated to heed petitions, particularly those which have received considerable community support, the government is under no obligation to do so. Characteristically, Mr Muldoon made his position quite clear when questioned about a petition (promoted by Campaign Half Million) seeking to keep nuclear power (and nuclear ships) out of New Zealand.

> Not even half a million signatures on a petition opposing such visits would bring about a change. Some of the people active in this campaign [against the visits], though naive and confused, are genuinely well-intentioned, but a good deal of the impetus comes from people whose motives cannot be given the benefit of the doubt. Their deliberate aim is to harm this country's national interest. These people . . . seek to raise fear and alarm, to play on honest doubts and ignorance, to induce emotional irrational responses. Their real purpose is to have this country cut its defence links with the United States and Australia in the ANZUS Treaty. The Government is not about to let a tiny disaffected minority dictate our foreign policy.[15]

Parliamentary Conduct

Politicians who are elected to Parliament are often persons of considerable energy and talent, forceful individuals accustomed to influencing others more through strength of personality than intellectual attainments. Yet M.J. Minogue (National, Hamilton West), has cited, approvingly, the analysis of a Welsh MP in the British House of Commons:

> Most [MPs] are characterised as more or less paranoid, and a good deal of what they do is interpreted as a manifestation of Freudian suppression of one kind or another. There have been times when

a psychopathological explanation seems to describe some of the conduct I have witnessed in the New Zealand Parliament.[16]

Elsewhere, describing the operation of the party system in the House, Mr Minogue, a backbench National MP with considerable political experience (as former Mayor of Hamilton and member of the National Roads Board), observed that

the spectacle of debates in Parliament which drag on for endless hours to an inevitable and foregone conclusion have their own particular futility. Awareness of that futility has a destructive impact upon all compelled to participate in it. Some may find escape in paranoid conduct or in some other manifestation of psychopathology. In all situations of futility, the individual ego understandably asserts itself–sometimes in strange and peculiar ways.[17]

On another occasion, following a 23-hour debate over the repeal of Labour's superannuation scheme involving a debilitating all-night sitting of the House, Mr Minogue described this peculiar form of deliberative activity as 'barbaric and uncivilised, an insult to our intelligence'. His backbench National colleague, Ms Waring, observed on television: 'I felt like my brain was dissolving.'[18] Other National MPs–new members of the House–were critical of behaviour in the House during 1976.

Two interpretations suggest themselves, in any attempt to explain the behaviour of adult, reasonably successful individuals within the New Zealand legislature. The behaviour may reflect the pathology of the members, in a setting which permits (or encourages) normally repressed tendencies (including aggressive feelings) to be expressed without fear of social sanctions. Alternatively, the institution itself imposes on its members certain rules and pressures which, to the observer standing apart from the institution, appear bizarre and maladaptive.[19] Such behaviour would have a recognisably Alice-in-Wonderland character about it.

'But I don't want to go among mad people . . . '
'Oh, you can't help that . . . we're all mad here. I'm mad. You're mad.'
'How do you know I'm mad? . . . '
'You must be . . . or you wouldn't have come here.'[20]

Certainly there is nothing unusual about a work environment producing behaviour which, in other settings, would appear most unusual. Moreover, it is customary for new members of legislatures to be advised to be silent, to learn the rules, and to emulate their more experienced colleagues. As a very powerful Speaker of the United States House of Representatives, Sam Rayburn, observed (often): 'To get along, go along.'

However, recent parliamentary sessions have been characterised by repeated disregard for the fundamental courtesies normally prevailing between the leaders of New Zealand's major parties. The withdrawal of these conventions, which discipline and constrain the exercise of power, has been especially serious given New Zealand's dependence on civility and mutual regard (in the absence of formal constitutional safeguards). Without a respect for its own customs and traditions, New Zealand's parliamentary system becomes submerged in momentary passions and ambitions, while the party system ensures that the government can be insulated from legislative sanction.

During National's first year in office, there were numerous 'shocks' to the system; like pebbles, these gathered weight as they accumulated so that by the end of the year, many MPs were willing to agree with the description by Mr Rowling (Labour Opposition leader) of the session as 'the worst since I entered the House'. Mr Rowling's relations with the Prime Minister deteriorated from the commencement of the session, when Mr Muldoon offered him a copy of the Ombudsman's report on the Security Intelligence Service on condition that Mr Rowling give written assurance not to show the report to anyone, including his colleagues and members of his staff. Mr Rowling, who had commissioned the report (which found a continuing need for such a Service) while Prime Minister, described the offer–first revealed on a Wellington radio station–as 'a gratuitous personal insult'.

The 1976 session produced a rash of 'breach of privilege' cases, prompting the Speaker to warn that if further cases kept coming up, MPs might find they were all in the dock with no one to judge them. Not in fifty years had so many charges of breach of privilege arisen in a single session, ranging from an allegation that one MP had uttered a racial slur upon another to claims of lying to Parliament.

Other unusual features of the 1976 session included: the government's moving urgency on its legislation throughout the session; the government's moving urgency on the two major debates of the session, Address-in-Reply and the Budget (the latter for the first time in more than fifty years); the passage of legislation without referral to committees; the closure of debate on the Appropriation Bill dealing with supplementary Estimates of Expenditure. These precedent-setting moves had the effect of diminishing still further the importance of Parliament in the policy-making process.

The 1976 Parliamentary session (which set the tone for Government-Opposition relations during the whole of the Government's term) ended in near-chaos when the Labour Party abandoned the House, after Mr Muldoon's allegation that the former Minister of Agriculture, Colin Moyle, had been picked up by the police for homosexual activities. Mr Moyle, for his part, had charged that the Prime Minister's accountancy firm had been involved in illegal activities. As

on other issues, the Moyle affair (which led to his resignation from
the House) saw a breakdown in the kind of co-operation needed to
restore public confidence and parliamentary harmony.[21]

The Prospect for Parliamentary Reform

During a debate in the United States Senate on reform of the rules,
Senator Douglas observed of his colleague, Senator Clark: 'The
Senator has helped to ring a firebell in the night which I hope will
awaken many people in the country to a realisation of what they dimly
suspected, but which should now stand revealed . . . The tragedy is
that we cannot seem to get together'.[22]

Certainly this failure 'to get together' is one of the disappointments
of the New Zealand House. Legislative reform is not an issue which
has had direct ideological components. Neither party's 1975 manifesto
mentioned reform of the rules or procedures of the House, nor could
a breach of caucus solidarity be suggested by the independent efforts
of new MPs to seek to improve the operations of Parliament. Indeed,
complaints about the conduct of affairs in the House have come from
Labour and National MPs alike. If any coalition appeared to exist
on this issue, it has been more along the lines of length of service
in the House (with newer MPs favouring reform) than any rigid
partisan division.

On one issue in particular, Mr Minogue has repeatedly sounded
'a firebell in the night", with numerous speeches calling for repeal
of the Official Secrets Act and its replacement by a Freedom of
Information Act, containing assumptions of access and openness
diametrically opposed to those underlying the existing legislation.[23] Mr
Minogue has observed that the success of his efforts requires bipartisan
support. Indeed, he has encountered bipartisan opposition from more
long-serving MPs uninterested in institutional reform. Yet an attempt
by Mr Prebble, a first-term Labour MP, to introduce analogous
legislation was attacked by Mr Minogue as 'naive' and indicative of
the efforts of a 'political virgin'. In turn, Mr Prebble's rejoinder
attacked Mr Minogue's sincerity, as Prebble noted Minogue's many
after-dinner speeches in contrast to his opposition to a concrete piece
of legislation. Minogue's objections were sound enough; the bill was
not well drafted, and the success of any Act requires the co-operation
of the public service. Nevertheless, it is remarkable that on this issue,
neither MP was able to suppress partisan rivalry or invective by
engaging in prior consultation and discussion. Given the bipartisan
nature of the issue, it would have been desirable for both MPs to
co-sponsor draft legislation, and to have persuaded as many of their
colleagues as possible to join with them in such an effort. Such
legislation might then have been referred to a committee for research,

hearings and submissions from interested parties. A more useful and less acrimonious exercise might have been undertaken in a co-operative spirit.

Like many institutions, Parliament is most zealous when protecting its own prerogatives. Similarly, the United States Supreme Court, while calling for the greatest tolerance for citizens seeking to restructure the political system, defends the solemnity of its own proceedings with the utmost vigour. There are few areas of public life which the New Zealand Parliament is unwilling to exclude from its coverage. Both parties engage in 'total government', under the assumption that no feature of collective activity can sequester itself from parliamentary sovereignty and popular will. On numerous occasions, the government, in recognition of the burdens of Parliament and the limitations on committee energies and resources, has complemented parliamentary scrutiny by assigning research tasks to Royal Commissions, Commissions of Inquiry, Task Forces, *ad hoc* planning bodies, Caucus committees, Cabinet committees, departmental working groups, and so on. It is interesting that despite the respected dictum that 'no person shall be a judge in their own case,' Parliament has excluded its own procedures, customs and functions from the independent scrutiny so frequently developed for other purposes. Yet it is unrealistic to expect a genuine effort by Parliament oriented towards reform of its proceedings to succeed. Interests are too entrenched; too many MPs benefit from the system, whose ways they have mastered with considerable skill. Only an independent body, with statutory authority, can be expected to provide an assessment of parliamentary structure, functions, procedures and customs which will be both searching and diligent, and which will permit a national debate to emerge on the kind of legislative chamber New Zealanders require at this stage in their political history.

There are benefits to be gained from reform of the rules of the House. However such reforms, while *necessary*, may not be *sufficient* to produce a superior legislative chamber. For example in the United States, perhaps the most iniquitous feature of the Congress has been the *seniority* system. As then Senator Clark observed:

> The Senate establishment, as I see it . . . is almost the antithesis of democracy. It is not selected by any democratic process. It appears to be quite unresponsive to the caucuses of the two parties . . . It is what might be called a self-perpetuating obligarchy . . . The way it operates is something like this: There are a number of States . . . which inevitably and always return . . . members of one party, and under a custom which has grown up over the years of following the rule of seniority in making committee assignments, and in connection with the distribution of other perquisites of Senate

tenure, the result has been that those who have been here longest have . . . exercised virtual control over the distribution of favours.[24]

A seniority system operates in New Zealand as well. There are 'safe' seats in the House, and MPs who occupy these seats can be assured of advancement so long as they do not disturb or threaten basic features of the parliamentary system: caucus solidarity; caucus secrecy; parliamentary rules and procedures. It is paradoxical that some of the more talented MPs, in marginal seats, are unlikely to have the opportunity to make a sustained contribution to the political life of the country because of their relatively insecure tenure. The more politically competitive (and hence genuinely democratic) the seat, the more marginal its status; the more marginal its status, the less likely the MP is to enjoy uninterrupted electoral success, accumulate seniority, and advance in the parliamentary system. In other words, more competitive electorates are 'penalised' for this competitiveness, while less competitive, one-party dominant electorates are 'rewarded' through the perquisites accumulated by their perennial MP.

In the United States Senate, the seniority system, with its pervasive influence, arose as a custom; for a time, reformers used to plead for the abolition of the seniority *rule* in the Congress, only to discover that none existed. Similarly, in New Zealand, it would be possible to alter various rules (Standing Orders) of the House without influencing behaviour very markedly, so long as sanctions were maintained against MPs violating what would then become 'unwritten' rules–i.e. socially and politically sanctioned 'customs'. Nevertheless, the effort needs to be made, for rules do shape behaviour and, over a period of time, customs can be altered.

There has been no shortage of suggested parliamentary reforms; these have included: opening all select committees to the public (the Public Bodies Meetings Act requires all local body and *ad hoc* committees to be open to the public, yet committees of central government continue to be exempt); increasing agreement between the chief whips for the time allocated to a debate, as too much time may be wasted on irrelevant or frivolous activity; ensuring that notices of motion–many of which are demagogic little speeches commencing with the word 'that'–and question time fulfil their historic functions of holding the executive accountable for its actions to Parliament; constitutional safeguards, including a lengthening of the parliamentary term and provisions requiring a regular review of all legislation; modification of procedures for the appointment of permanent department heads and other senior officials; enlargement of the functions of select committees; early summoning of Parliament; reform of breach of privileges procedures; referral to all draft bills to standing committees; improvement in the ability of the General Assembly Library to supply members with information; closer parliamentary scrutiny of spending by the various ministries, including examination of time limitations presently inhibiting the effective consideration of estimates; televising parliamentary proceedings to improve standards of debate and conduct; introduction of non-parliamentary Cabinet members to improve the quality of Cabinet, involving amendment of the Civil List Act 1950; improvement in conditions of work and rewards, to attract the best talent to Parliament; confining the parliamentary session to the hours of a normal working day; MPs' disclosure of financial and other interests which might create conflict between their own and the public interest.[25]

Some of these reforms are designed to improve conditions within the House, and might be expected to be of greater interest to MPs (who have to work there) than to the electorate. On the other hand, the citizen has a legitimate interest in seeing Parliament develop into a more efficient legislative body capable of effective deliberation on public issues. More significant reforms, however, seek to reverse the drift of power towards the executive, and seek to create in Parliament an institution equipped to provide creative legislation and independent scrutiny. This effort requires changes to Standing Orders which inhibit the development of a more vital legislative body.[26]

A reconvened Standing Orders Committee (or, preferably, an entirely independent body formed to inquire into parliamentary functions and procedures) might usefully review: S.O. 65, 68, and 69, giving precedence to Government in the Order of Business; S.O. 39, dealing with hours of meeting; S.O. 47, which permits 'urgency' to be taken on 'any Bill, matter, or other proceeding' in 'the public interest', a provision used for convenience by National to expedite the passage of its legislative programme; S.O. 89–92, limiting motions of adjournment to discuss public issues; S.O. 103, disallowing certain notices of motion; S.O. 87, disallowing certain questions to Ministers; Part XXI, setting forth the rules of debate; Part XXII, establishing the pattern of debate on public bills; S.O. 322, 324, and 325, restricting to Ministers the right to introduce proposals dealing with taxation and appropriation. As even the most innocuous proposals invariably involve some form of public expenditure, these Standing Orders entrench in the very rules of Parliament the absolute dominance of Cabinet over legislation. Parliamentary control over government is vitiated, and the opportunities for initiative by Opposition or even government backbench MPs are inhibited by rules such as these. At the same time, the Committee might usefully review provisions for dealing with alleged breaches of privileges (S.O. 427–432). This protection for MPs, providing them with immunity from prosecution for statements made in the House and designed to promote freedom of expression in parliamentary debate, has deteriorated into a partisan weapon used by MPs against one another in a retaliatory fashion.

Provisions for electing the Speaker (S.O. 5–15) might usefully be reviewed, to permit a person who is not an MP to preside over the affairs of the House. Alternatively, both parties should seek through prior consultation to select to preside over the House an MP (or MPs) enjoying the confidence of all parties. It would be desirable as well for Parliament to remove the enormous powers granted to it in S.O. 380–385, which state that any person judged guilty of contempt shall be 'dealt with accordingly'. Nor do S.O. 174, 181, 182 and 184, prohibiting 'unbecoming' references to the House or the Judiciary, the use of 'disorderly' or 'offensive' language, and 'disrespectful' references to the Queen or Governor-General, inspire confidence in the regard of MPs for civil libertarian principles. As U.S. Supreme Court Justice Louis D. Brandeis once observed:

> To justify suppression of free speech there must be reasonable ground to fear that serious evil will result if free speech is practiced. There must be reasonable ground to believe that the danger apprehended is imminent. There must be reasonable ground to believe that the evil to be prevented is a serious one . . . Prohibition of free speech . . . is a measure so stringent that it would be inappropriate as the means for averting a relatively trivial harm to society.[27]

While Justice Brandeis' opinion was directed towards the rights of citizens to express their political views, inhibitions and restrictions on the rights of the people's elected representatives are at least equally serious, and should be imposed (if at all) only in the gravest circumstances lest the entire debating process becomes (as it so often does in the New Zealand House) trivialised. Certainly enormous powers, which can be exercised for exceedingly vague offences of speech, are not calculated to promote vigorous and meaningful debate, either within or outside of the House. One consequence of Rules such as these is that *so much parliamentary energy is expended on alleged offences of language* and disregard for parliamentary courtesies–forms of 'victimless crime'. Nor does it seem very sensible, given the restrictive time limits on debate, for S.O. 163 to declare that 'A member shall not read his speech . . . '; perhaps more informative, coherent debates might emerge were this rule to be repealed. The unusual nature of the rule may be further appreciated by noting that the rule states that 'no member, other than Mr Speaker, shall interrupt a member who is speaking to suggest a breach of this rule . . . ' Thus it is a breach of Standing Orders to draw the attention of the Speaker to the fact that a member is violating Standing Orders by indulging in the forbidden vice of reading a prepared address.

Finally, given the detailed character of Standing Orders, the discretion available to the Speaker, and the dominance of the majority party leadership, S.O. 439, reproduced below, seems to be superfluous as well as excessive in its grant of authority:

439. Suspension of–(1) Any Standing Order or other order of the House may be suspended wholly or in part on motion with or without notice: Provided that such motion shall not be moved without notice unless there be 40 members present at the time of moving the motion.[28]

The prospects for parliamentary reform are meagre, however. There is little motivation for an entrenched executive to seek to devolve powers to the legislative authority. Nor is there much enthusiasm for a review of Parliament's role as a debating chamber–an arena–in which MPs succeed by sustained verbal aggressiveness, and where collective argument often resembles a collision between opposing armies of words, each ravaging the landscape of the English language in search of an idea. Parliamentary reform will only occur through public pressure which, in turn, can only be promoted by persuading the electorate that detailed reform proposals will produce policies of direct benefit to them. This is a case which, however, has yet to be made.

The Roles of an MP

The MP may have lost much in his capacity as a legislator, but if the parliamentary system continues to be as adaptable as it has been in the past, he may find new though secondary roles for himself in the light of modern conditions . . . as an intermediary between local governments and the central government . . . as a reflector of sectional interests when legislation which will affect localities in different ways is being considered.[29]

Riemer has identified four roles for a representative: as a *trustee,* answerable to their own conscience; as a *delegate*, representing their electorate; as a *partisan*, serving their party; as a *politico*, balancing needs, interests, and commitments according to circumstance.[30] Most MPs fit the 'politico' model, since they must balance duties to electors, Parliament, party, and their own conscience. Moreover, much parliamentary work occurs outside the debating chamber, involving service to constituents, party and committee work.

New Zealand MPs rarely vote free from party discipline. 'Free' votes normally occur on measures relating to liquor licensing, gambling, marriage and divorce, and, since 1975, homosexual law reform and abortion measures. One way for MPs to reconcile conflicts among complementary roles is to persuade themselves that all pressures point in the same direction. Thus, on the abortion issue, for example, MPs may persuade themselves that their own conscience, the wishes of the electorate (intuitively ascertained through sensitive political 'antennae'), the national interest *and* the fortunes of party all require the same action. Such reasoning eases the MP's burden, and makes some kind of decision possible. In general MPs believe that 'New Zealand is a working democracy. Our representatives in parliament do represent their electorates. They are accessible. They know what their constituents think and want–they hear from them'.[31]

Others may feel that New Zealand has yet to devise a parliamentary system that is responsive, efficient, effective, democratically organised, and equipped to attract and utilize persons of talent and imagination to the limits of their resources.

References

1. A useful biography of Prime Minister Atkinson places his career into perspective. See J. Bassett, *Sir Harry Atkinson 1831–1892*, Auckland: University of Auckland Press, 1975.
2. See L. Lipson, *op. cit.*, p. 75.
3. *Ibid.* These figures update those in Lipson, p. 253.
4. *Ibid.*, pp. 254–5.
5. See S. Levine and J. Lodge, *The New Zealand General Election of 1975*, Wellington: Price Milburn for New Zealand University Press, 1976, pp. 20–3, 27.
6. A.D. Robinson, *op. cit.*, ·p. 76.
7. *Ibid.*, pp. 85–6. See H. Nelson, 'Democracy's Dodo: The Back-Bencher' in H. Mayer and H. Nelson (eds), *Australian Politics: A Third Reader*, Melbourne: Cheshire, 1976. The British experience may be appreciated by looking at P. Norton, *Dissension in the House of Commons, 1945–74*, London, Macmillan, 1975.
8. M. Waring, *op. cit.*, p. 86.
9. R.N. Kelson, *The Private Member of Parliament and the Formation of Public Policy: A New Zealand Case Study*, Toronto: University of Toronto Press, 1964, p. 54.
10. See M.L. Logeman, 'Committee Structure and Parliamentary Function' in S. Levine (ed.), *New Zealand Politics: A Reader*, pp. 365–73.
11. See R.M. Alley, *op. cit.* An interesting account of an imbalance of power *against* the executive and favouring the legislative authority is found in W. Wilson, *Congressional Government: A Study of the American Constitution*, London: Constable and Company Ltd, 1914. A genuinely comparative study of legislative assemblies is contained in M. Ameller, *Parliaments: A Comparative Study on the Structure and Functioning of Representative Institutions in Fifty-Five Countries*, London: Cassell for the Inter-Parliamentary Union, 1962. An excellent study of the impact of the British Parliament on Government Bills is to be found in J.A.G. Griffith, *Parliamentary Scrutiny of Government Bills*, London: George Allen & Unwin Ltd, 1974.
12. See S. Levine, 'New Zealand Politics: Annual Review', *op. cit.*, p. 114.
13. P. Laundy, *The Office of Speaker*, London: Cassell, 1964, pp. 397–8.

14. *Journals of the House of Representatives*, Wellington: Government Printer, 1976, 1977, 1978.
15. See S. Levine, 'New Zealand Politics: Annual Review', *op. cit.*, p. 103.
16. M.J. Minogue, *op. cit.*; see L. Abse, *Private Member*, London: MacDonald, 1973.
17. *Ibid.*
18. Interview, TV1, October 1976.
19. See W.F. Stone, *The Psychology of Politics*, New York: The Free Press, 1974, especially Parts III and IV.
20. L. Carroll, *Alice's Adventures in Wonderland*, New York: Doubleday, 1961, p. 94.
21. See S. Levine, 'New Zealand Politics: Annual Review', *op cit.*, pp. 113–15.
22. J.S. Clark and other Senators, *The Senate Establishment*, New York: Hill and Wang, 1963, pp. 22, 132–33.
23. M. Minogue, *op. cit.*
24. J.S. Clark, *op. cit.*, pp. 132–3, 22. For further material on Procedural reforms and the structure of power in the United States Congress, see S.K. Bailey, *Congress in the Seventies*, New York: St Martin's Press, 1970.
25. See M.L. Logeman, *op. cit.*, pp. 365–7; the Alan D. Robinson Memorial Lectures, 1976, on the theme of Parliamentary Reform; A.D. Robinson, *op. cit.*, pp. 93–4.
26. See *Standing Orders of the House of Representatives, Relating to Public Business*, Wellington: Government Printer, 1975.
27. Concurring opinion in *Whitney v. California* (1927): see A.T. Mason and W.M. Beany, *op. cit.*, pp. 602–3.
28. *Standing Orders of the House of Representatives*, p. 113.
29. R.N. Kelson, *op. cit.*, pp. 130–1.
30. N. Reimer (ed.), *The Representative: Trustee? Delegate? Partisan? Politico?*, Lexington, Massachusetts: D.C. Heath & Co., 1969.
31. J.R. Marshall, Speech made to University of Auckland, 19 March 1969.

4 Political Parties

The Two-Party System

New Zealand's present two-party system emerged during the Depression with the election of Labour in 1935 and the formation of National out of the remnants of the decimated Reform and United parties.[1] As in other Western nations, the impact of widespread economic deprivation brought about a major, enduring realignment of political forces which has persisted to the present day. The subsequent emergence of the National Party as New Zealand's governing party for nearly three decades reflects the changing character of the electorate, although Labour has lost trade union support during the post-war period.[2]

In 1954, the Social Credit Political League began contesting general elections, although it has only won two parliamentary seats (in 1966 and in a 1978 by-election successfully defended in the 1978 general election). The Values Party, formed in 1972, contested half the European electorates in 1972 and every electorate in 1975 and 1978, but has thus far failed to win a seat. Certainly New Zealand's 'first past the post' electoral system has discouraged third parties and, with the exception of Social Credit's brief representation, neither third party has been able to become a durable parliamentary party participating in decision-making and resource allocation.

The Extra-Parliamentary Party

Within Parliament, party cohesion is maintained through the activities of the governing and opposition caucuses. However, outside Parliament both Labour and National have evolved a complex, integrated structure with distinct functions: policy-making; candidate selection; campaign organisation. Policy is developed at regular meetings and conferences, at electorate and regional levels. Policy incorporated into the Party's campaign manifesto, however, needs to be approved at the annual conference of the various political parties. Policy will also be shaped by the decisions of the parliamentary caucus on issues as they arise in Parliament; for the majority party, the decisions of Cabinet will also play a major role in shaping party policy.[3]

Procedures surrounding candidate selection are among the features supporting party discipline within the House. Party loyalty–obedience to the decisions of the party caucus, and conformity to the objectives of the party conference–is essential for renomination. Since party membership is crucial to electoral success, MPs contemplating rebellion, and an independent candidacy (should they fail to be renominated), may well feel that they are entering a political graveyard. The strength of party discipline in the House is based, ultimately, on the party's ability to deny renomination to dissident MPs. This power, in turn, rests on the MPs' inability successfully to challenge the decision of a party selection committee. The only alternative for such an MP is to seek to mount an independent candidacy which is almost certainly doomed to failure, given the system of party-based government and electoral behaviour. In one-party areas, *selection* by the dominant party is tantamount to election; thus the real choice for electors must occur within the dominant party, at selection meetings. Selection meetings, however, are open only to *enrolled party members*. The larger base of *party supporters and voters* have little opportunity to participate in the selection process.

While many reformers seeking to loosen the grip of New Zealand's two-party system over the electoral and political process have favoured proportional representation, a more far-reaching measure would involve the introduction of *a primary system* (as in the United States) to permit voters enrolled in a party (i.e. the 'grassroots' membership) the opportunity to confirm or alter the choice of candidate made by the party selection committee.[4] At present, it is very difficult for a sitting MP to be replaced at selection (except in rare circumstances). In 1978, 17 independent 'National Alternative' candidates and one independent Labour candidate stood as well, a further indication of the strains on party loyalty which may result when public participation in the nominating process is restricted. Of course the test of a true partisan is whether the voter will support their favoured party irrespective of the identity of the candidate selected. However, poor candidates may fail to appeal to uncommitted or 'floating' voters. Equally important, a local organisation disappointed with the choice of a selection committee will lack the enthusiasm to work for the candidate (some may choose to labour for candidates in neighbouring seats, or cease effective activity altogether). This effect will ripple through the party organisation, affecting not merely the vote in a particular poll but long-term recruitment of personnel, retention of support, and the development of programmes. A system of voter choice *within* the party system would democratise the nomination process, and permit voters dissatisfied with an MP an opportunity to support another candidate *within* the party of the voter's choice. At present, voters disenchanted with their party's candidate have the option of abstention, or of voting for another party (usually one of the two 'third' parties). A primary system would thus have two major functions: (1) to permit voters to challenge their party's choice of candidate; (2) to enable dissident MPs successfully to defy leadership and caucus pressures by securing renomination against the hostility of party selectors.

At the same time, the existence of such a system would seriously weaken party discipline in the House. MPs presently compelled by caucus pressures to support an unpopular policy might refuse to do so, if aware that the public would have the opportunity to deny them selection despite the preferences of local electorate committees. Indeed, MPs might become excessively obedient to public opinion, since the party could no longer provide protection against public demands. The erosion of party discipline could make the execution of a government's programme impossible.

It is likely that a choice exists between two goals: (1) a party system committed to programmes, disciplined within the House by caucus pressures (and within the Cabinet by the doctrine of collective responsibility), and supported outside the House by a selection system that precludes intra-party electoral choice; or (2) a party system encouraging intra-party democracy, but undisciplined and unprogrammatic, comprising shifting coalitions of support in the House and supported outside the House by a selection system seeking to maximise public participation in the nomination process.[5]

There may be contradictions involved in seeking to mould ideologically committed, disciplined parties which are *at the same time* open to direct participation in decision-making by party members and supporters. It is possible to strive for a system of disciplined parties, with a leadership powerful enough to impose sanctions on dissidents, *or* a system of loosely organised parties, encouraging independent decision-making by MPs and involvement by party supporters. It may not be possible, however, to promote *both* values simultaneously. New Zealand has thus far preferred a disciplined model of programmatic parties. Nevertheless, the absence of open political party structures must inhibit the full contribution of new social and political forces to the democratic process.

Party Membership and Organisation

A *mass-based party* is one which seeks to involve as large a proportion of the party's voters as possible. A *cadre-based party* is one which relies upon a small, unified core of committed activists to formulate programmes, select candidates and organise campaigns.[6] New Zealand parties seek to blend both features. The four major parties regularly attempt to enlarge their membership, particularly in election years, and they have been remarkably successful in persuading large numbers of voters to enrol. In practice, each party has developed an elite–a small and coherent group–which undertakes on a regular basis the management of party affairs.[7] Attempts to acquire a large party membership appear to be efforts aimed at identifying voters, securing funds, and obtaining campaign workers. Neither party seems prepared genuinely to involve the electorate in their deliberations, and no effort is made to recruit members into decision-making roles.

TABLE 4:1 *Party Membership and Voting: 1975 General Election*[8]

Party	Number of votes	Number of members	Number of branches	Proportion of members/votes	Number of electorates (of 87)
Labour	636,322	13,000 (excluding unions)	420	1:49	87
National	760,462	200,000	1,300	1:4	87
Social Credit	119,123	8,000	124	1:15	84
Values	83,211	3,600	71	1:23	71

Parties and the Political System

The functions performed by parties include: (1) co-ordinating the exercise of power; (2) organising elections; (3) identifying issues and proposing alternative policies: (4) promoting public discussion; (5) ensuring leadership recruitment. It has been claimed that

> The New Zealand party system promotes political consensus in the community. In a two-party system both parties are concerned with securing a majority. In order to do this they seek support from as many individuals and groups as possible. The system encourages compromise . . . and the development of moderate ideas through the influence of party identification. The logic of two-party competition also encourages non-ideological politics concerned with the solution of practical problems.[9]

More recent political events suggest that political consensus has broken down in many areas. Neither Labour nor National Party supporters appear to be reconciled to their adversary's leadership.[10] Voters for Social Credit and Values appear to be becoming permanently alienated from a system providing them with no prospect for political power.[11] Moreover, each party has developed an ideological basis which, however inarticulate, is nonetheless influential among MPs, party activists and voters.[12] National's ideology has as its core the promotion of 'freedom', and the avoidance of socialism. Labour is more committed to equality, and tends less frequently to emphasise 'freedom' as a primary goal.[13] Moreover, both Labour and National view New Zealand's place in the international community from an ideological perspective. National regards New Zealand as a bastion of anti-communism firmly based in the Western alliance, or 'free world', while Labour regards New Zealand as a South Pacific nation identifying with 'uncommitted', 'third world' nations.[14] However inconsistent various policies may be with these general tendencies, there are underlying ideological commitments which make for mutual distrust amongst the parties, and inhibit reconciliation and the promotion of consensus. In Parliament, the breakdown in consensus is reflected in the decline in standards of conduct, and the rapid repeal by National of so many major features of the Labour programme.[15] Social Credit and Values both benefit in the public view in that whatever their defects, neither party can be held responsible for present problems or past government misdeeds. While these parties have ideological identities that render them distinct and recognisable, each is characterised by a certain innocence associated with: (1) restricted access to official information; (2) the absence of formal responsibility for the exercise of executive power.

The National Party

When the National Party was formed, in 1936, its objects were clearly stated:

(a) To unite all men and women who are unswervingly loyal to His Majesty the King: who realise the immense political, financial, commercial and cultural advantages which accrue to New Zealand from close association with the other nations of the British Commonwealth, and who desire to promote the political and economic unity of the Empire.

(b) To maintain an efficient system of defence.

(c) To formulate and carry out policies designed to benefit the community as a whole, irrespective of sectional interests: particularly to bring about co-operation between country and city interests, and between employers and employees.

(d) To pursue a policy of progressive social and humanitarian legislation.

(e) To arouse and maintain interest in political matters, to advocate the policy of the Party, and to oppose subversive and other doctrines which are contrary to the principles and policy of the Party.

(f) To encourage and assist the candidature for Parliament of able and honourable supporters of the Party.

(g) To carry out educational and organising work in furtherance of the fore-going aims and objects.

(h) To keep in touch with and, as may be deemed practicable, to co-operate with other organisations which have similar aims.[16]

The 1975 Constitution and Rules maintain these commitments and include as well an emphasis on development of a property-owning democracy.[17] Despite changes in leadership and governing style, the major ideological themes of the National Party have remained fairly constant. Thus former Prime Minister J.R. Marshall expressed the party's philosophy quite cogently, in observing of National:

We are here today because 36 years ago the Liberal and Conservative political forces in New Zealand united to form the National Party to champion the rights of the individual and private enterprise and to oppose the socialists and red feds of the then resurgent Labour Party.

We are the heirs of the liberal conservative tradition, the heirs of the pioneers who settled this land and who adapted the art of government to deal with new problems and new situations, improvising as only New Zealanders can, seeking within the framework of their political philosophy, the pragmatic flexible policies best suited to their needs.

By right of succession the National Party carries on these traditions, adapting them to our times and our needs in the same flexible pragmatic way as the pioneers did in their day and generation. We stand for liberty, property, progress and security for all New Zealanders. These goals are safe in our hands but they are under attack from many quarters here and round the world.

From the socialists, the anarchists, the communists, and the radical left who, in these days raise a clamour out of all proportion to their size and importance but who, if they got the chance, would wipe out much that we stand for. In a little more subtle and insidious way the Labour Party which has its share of socialists, radical left wingers and militant trade unionists would be an untrustworthy custodian of liberty, property, progress and security as we see those basic objectives of our political policies.[18]

The change in leadership from Marshall to Muldoon was one of style and approach rather than underlying philosophy. As Jackson has noted, policy differences played no part in the leadership challenge.[19] Moreover, the party's *philosophy* has not been substantially altered in spite of the evolution of state *programmes* (such as National's development of a superannuation scheme). The differences which have

developed more recently in the party, however, reflect some estrangement from the Muldoon *style* of government. More significant
differences over philosophy have resulted from some National voters'
support for *conservative* economic policies and a *progressive* posture
towards moral issues.[20] Splits between the 'liberal' wing of the party
and those who regard National as the 'conservative' party of New
Zealand (and promote remits at conferences calling for harsher
treatment of prisoners, corporal punishment in schools and opposition
to sex education) surface regularly.

There are bound to be strains and tensions in a party that seeks
to be New Zealand's sole legitimate party, the only one representative
of people from all social classes and regions. This aspiration towards
one-party dominance would, if fulfilled, be short-lived, for no party
can represent all interests so long as political differences persist in
society. National would benefit momentarily from the electoral annihilation of its opposition, but neither it nor the country would benefit
from National becoming too large an organisation. There are limits
to which conflicts within a single party can be pushed, and indeed
these have been approached on occasion within the life of the Muldoon
government.

The conflict within the National Party between two ideological
camps, each seeking to shape New Zealand society into a particular
mould, presents perhaps the greatest threat to National pre-eminence.
Otherwise, National has been able to maintain power because of the
regular renewal of its membership and policies, and the reformulation
of its party organisation. National has engineered the development of
successive 'generations' of leadership teams capable of exercising
power for long periods, and generating enthusiasm throughout the
party. So long as an 'aging' party can periodically recreate itself, it
will avoid the decay which has beset entrenched parties in the past.[21]

The Labour Party

Labour's objectives in its 1975 constitution are clearly stated:

> The objective of the Party is to promote and protect the freedom
> of the people and their political, social, economic and cultural
> welfare; to educate the public in the principles of democratic
> socialism and economic and social co-operation; to elect competent
> men and women to Parliament and local authorities for the purpose
> of giving effect to the Party policy; and to ensure the just distribution
> of the production and services of New Zealand for the benefit of
> all the people.[22]

As Webber has noted, Labour abandoned in 1927 its commitment
to the control by the State of the means of production, distribution

and exchange.[23] Its more recent 'socialism' has involved little more than the belief in a 'co-operative' society. While some criticisms have been directed at the Rowling leadership for an 'intellectual' approach, and a deviation from the party's historic principles and commitments, the then Prime Minister, Norman Kirk, described Labour's philosophy in 1973 without mentioning 'socialism' once.

The stability of the home is the basis of the emotional stability of the family and society. The family is the basic unit of society. When the family does well, the nation does well. The family unit must be protected and strengthened, and our priorities must be reordered to provide for happy people and stable families. A nation is basically a family of families and the world a family of nations. To grow as a nation we need the same things a family needs for its growth. We must be a country that is fair to its own people, a country that seeks the expression of its nationhood in the strength of family life, social justice and steady progress. Our objective always has been social justice for all people in the sense that everyone is able to live decently without having to face constant hardships.[24]

Confusion over purposes has not helped a party demoralised by decline in membership, desertion by affiliated trade unions, an eroding electoral base, inadequate financial resources, uninspiring leadership, and an ineffective parliamentary performance.

TABLE 4:2 *Branch and Affiliated Membership of the Labour Party, 1916–1975*[25]

Year	Branch	Affiliated	Total	% Affiliated
1917–18	1,000	10,000	11,000	90.91
1925–26	5,278	40,399	45,667	88.46
1929–30	5,170	45,481	50,651	89.79
1934–35	6,554	24,663	31,217	79.01
1939–40	51,174	185,431	236,605	78.37
1944–45	20,340	136,923	157,263	87.07
1949–50	38,155	174,913	213,068	82.09
1954–55	38,261	135,941	174,202	78.04
1958–59	30,052	142,873	172,925	82.62
1964–65	17,812	167,602	185,414	90.39
1969–70	13,384	189,890	203,274	93.42
1974–75	14,247	184,656	198,903	92.84

Labour may be described as having three major 'wings': (1) the 'intellectuals' or 'academics', oriented towards socialist objectives and reform on 'social' or 'moral' issues; (2) the 'technocrats' dominant among the leadership, concerned with maintenance of power, incremental reform and economic management; (3) the 'trade union' group, distrustful of a non-working class leadership and parliamentary party, conservative on 'moral' or 'social' issues, and concerned almost exclusively with economic gains and the protection of organised union strength. These groups exist in uneasy alliance, and the tensions within the party may not be susceptible to resolution.

While the 'intellectual' wing of the party has successfully urged (at the Labour Party's 1977 Conference) a redefinition of 'socialism' and a renewed attention to this goal, the leadership might have preferred the public and the media to have identified Labour as something other than New Zealand's 'socialist' party. While trade union activity in and loyalty to Labour has been marginally restored by National's 1976 industrial relations legislation imposing penalties for 'political' strikes and requiring ballots on union membership, and the 1977–8 rise in unemployment, Labour has sought as well to bring the size of its branch membership closer to National's.

The 1975 election demonstrated that in politics, as in other fields, *professionalism* in the conduct of affairs is likely to promote success. While the professional management of electoral politics has become a full-time business in New Zealand, Labour has sought as well to revive its depleted membership. Over a period of thirty years–from the late 1930s through to the end of the 1960s–Labour Party membership declined from over 50,000 people to fewer than 14,000, and the number of branch organisations dropped from 630 to 307. The 1976–8 membership drive appears to have returned the party to its late 1930s peak of around 50,000, although in an electorate of much greater size. In addition to branch membership, fourteen national trade unions and sixty-nine provincial (district) trade unions are affiliated with the Labour Party. The combined membership of these unions is approximately 200,000 workers. While the unions are affiliated with the Labour Party, it is clear that *few union members are enrolled, subscribed, participating members* of the Labour Party. Considering that full membership (entitling the member to take an active part in the affairs of the Labour Party) involves a fee of $1.00 per annum, the financial burden entailed in full commitment to Labour is very slight indeed.[26]

Labour's goal–doubling its membership to 100,000 people by the 1978 election–seemed modest in relation to National's sustained position, yet was one which appeared to elude the party's grasp. The professionals of both parties, who seek to organise and mobilise the New Zealand electorate for their purpose (winning elections), may find that there are limits to the reach of their professionalism. To intensify participation in partisan politics requires the scope and meaning of political conflict to be widened and personalised. The

enlargement of public involvement in politics cannot be manipulated
into existence, but must emerge out of a renewed awareness of the
salience of politics, and of the existence of meaningful alternative
choices.[27] The promotion of mass membership by Labour, therefore,
is likely to be an artificial phenomenon, rather than one based on a
genuine public conviction that Labour represents an unambiguously
desirable choice.

Labour's 'new' philosophical basis has been forcefully articulated
in the party's internal newsletter, *Action Talk*.

The clear and complete answer to the question of whether it is
essential to the socialism of the New Zealand Labour Party to
advocate the abolition of the private ownership of the sixty-six
thousand privately owned farms which produce 80% of the export
income is NO. The socialism of the New Zealand Labour Party
is . . . the socialism adopted by the post-World War Two Socialist
International wherein it declared its principles as follows: 'Socialists
strive to build a new society in freedom and by democratic means.
Without freedom there can be no socialism . . .'

. . . the record of the New Zealand Labour Party reveals its
commitment to the ideal of democracy. It abolished the country
quota, a weighted electoral measure which hitherto was a built-in
constitutional bias against the city voter. It introduced broadcasting
of Parliament as a measure to off-set the bias of the New Zealand
press. Its Education Ministers, Fraser and Amos, formulated
education policy on the basis of public participation. It sought to
replace a rundown constitutional infra-structure by the creation of
strong regional Government with the prospect of devolution of
power, in the Local Government Act, 1974 (the regional provisions
of which have been emasculated by the National Government). It
freed electronic media broadcasting from Government control by
the creation of diversified and independent systems. It held longer
Parliamentary sittings and opened committee hearings to public
scrutiny. It legislated for openness in Local Government by the
compulsory publication of committee agendas.

Labour must vigorously market itself as the democratic party of
New Zealand politics. By demonstrating democracy in its own
procedures by openness, consultation, debate, respect for dissenters,
it can win the minds and hearts of the electorate . . .

There is an inter-dependence between the ideal of the Welfare
State and the ideal of democracy. Freedom and equality are the
twin foundations of Labour's philosophy. Therefore, Labour differs
in its premise that the community's resources should be used to assist
the self-fulfilment of each person in the community, thus demonstrating its fundamental attitude to the economy.[28]

At Labour's 1977 Conference, Frank O'Flynn (then ex-MP, Kapiti; now MP, Island Bay) emerged as one of Labour's major theoreticians. His definition of socialism won the support of delegates.

A modern socialist state is one in which all fundamental or important economic and social decisions are taken in the interests of the whole community and not in the interests of, or under, economic or other pressure from particular sectional groups.

Socialism involves complete and effective political democracy; full civic rights; full human rights; and above all the maximum economic justice that can practically be achieved. Socialism will not restrict individual or personal freedom. On the contrary, the economic justice that it will produce is essential to the practical and effective exercise of political and social freedom.[29]

Nevertheless it is clear that Labour has not solved the problem of developing a philosophy, an organisational structure, a programme, and a team of activists capable of inspiring mass support and overcoming widespread distrust. Whether it can do so is by no means certain. As Gustafson concluded:

Over a period of time a party created in response to specific socio-economic circumstances and aspirations must allow itself to be recreated and to co-operate in its own transformation if it is to survive . . .

The composition, demands, values, social relations, and technology of a society change; the changes are reflected in the composition and policies of a party; the party starts functioning informally in a different way; and finally, not without considerable ambivalence, tension, and frequent backward glances, the functional changes are recognised and accepted as irreversible, and endorsed and facilitated by alterations to the party's formal structure.

The major danger facing a Labour and Social Democratic party today is not that it will imitate its conservative rival but that it will fail to respond, programmatically and organisationally, to the challenges of . . . change . . . [30]

The Social Credit Political League

Social Credit philosophy adheres to the principle that the individual is more important than the state, and that systems should respond to the needs of man, not man to the dictates of a system.[31]

Social Credit has repeatedly sought to define its policies in clear language. Despite twenty-four years of participation in electoral politics, it has failed to persuade the electorate that it has a coherent programme and philosophy. The principles, purposes and policies of Social Credit, as outlined by the League itself, are reproduced below:

Tenets of Social Credit[32]

OUR PRINCIPLES

1—Our basic principle is the establishment of an economic and social order built on the foundations of brotherly love, truth, justice and honest endeavour.

2—We believe that what is physically possible and desirable for the betterment of mankind should be made financially possible.

3—We believe that the individual is more important than the state and that systems should be made for man, not man for systems.

4—We believe that restrictive forms of political and financial dictatorship, monopoly and bureaucracy should be strenuously opposed.

5—We believe in competitive and co-operative enterprise and that state-owned businesses should conform to the same conditions as privately owned concerns. We believe that the function of Government is to set fair rules.

6—We believe that the only proper purpose of production is consumption and that labour saving is the proper purpose of labour-saving inventions.

7—We believe that the first necessity in establishing our principles is to reform our present un-Christian monetary system which is dishonest and unjust and is the basic cause of many other evils.

OUR PURPOSE

1—To secure to the people of New Zealand the beneficial use and control of their own credit and currency.

2—To establish an economy where the people will be able to develop and expand the country's real wealth without mortgaging their own and their children's future.

3—To restore and stabilise the purchasing power of money, thereby enhancing and protecting the value of wages, pensions and savings.

4—To encourage the introduction of all forms of automation, thereby increasing production and the standard of living.

5—To encourage skill in all fields of endeavour by ensuring that skill is justly rewarded.

6—To promote the speedy introduction of labour-saving devices, both industrial and domestic.

7—To ensure that, in an age of increasing automation with machines progressively taking over the work of more and more men, incomes will nevertheless be maintained so that all may share in the benefits of automation.

8—To increase the opportunity for engaging in, and facilities available for, educational, cultural and recreational activities.

9—To recover complete control of New Zealand's economic affairs and establish greater political independence.

POLICY—FIRST STEPS

1—We will introduce the Bill of Rights for New Zealand, to limit the power of Government and safeguard the individual against the invasion of rights and liberties.

2—We shall secure to the people of New Zealand the ownership of their own credit by setting up a National Credit Authority, responsible to Parliament, in which will be vested the power to authorise and control the issue of all credit and currency. The National Credit Authority will be charged with the duty of preparing proper statements of the National Accounts, including a National Balance Sheet showing the true wealth and financial position of the country.

3—We shall eliminate internal Government borrowing and progressively redeem the internal national debt. External debt will be repaid as circumstances permit.

4—We shall reduce taxation.

5—We shall increase pensions and other benefits to ensure that the recipients are able to maintain a reasonable standard of living comparable with other sections of the community.

6—We shall restore subsidies on essential commodities and gradually extend them to cover a far wider range of consumer goods.

7—We shall provide from the National Credit Account finance for approved public and local body works at cost of issue.

8—We shall substantially increase the proportion of the national resources allocated to education.

9—We shall enter into bi-lateral and reciprocal trade agreements on diversified markets.

The financial measures contained in these first steps will lower the whole cost structure, increase the purchasing power of the dollar, restore individual incentive and stimulate production.

Despite documents such as these, few people seemed to take much notice of Social Credit prior to 1977–8, and consequently its performance as 'the third force' of New Zealand politics has been unimpressive. Social Credit has been represented in Parliament on two occasions only. Its one-term MP for Hobson (Mr Vern Cracknell) was defeated for re-election in 1969, and in 1977 its leader Mr Bruce Beetham was elected in a by-election in Rangitikei, an electorate in which it had finished second behind National in 1975. Nevertheless, its vote totals at general elections prior to 1978 have not reflected that slow, steady accumulation of strength characteristic of a party climbing towards success.

Third parties, when new, often arouse expectations and attract support not only from persons approving of their programme but from people disillusioned entirely with 'the system'. Moreover, there are always persons sympathetic to a party with little prospect for success, as well as those upholders of a special sort of equity anxious to give *any* new group 'a fair go'–which, in this case, means an opportunity to experiment with the exercise of public power. While other parties have quarrels or divisions, Social Credit has 'schisms'. In 1972, when Bruce C. Beetham became leader, a walk-out by 'loyalists' to original doctrine produced the moribund New Democrats. Such behaviour reflected an atmosphere in which disagreements over policy were regarded more as 'heresies' than reasonable differences of opinion.

Social Credit's rationale for continued existence has been regularly questioned by the news media. While its party conferences attract the media, the attention of broadcasters and journalists has tended to focus on the League's persistent futility. Social Credit is not yet a party, and proposals formally to change its name to reflect its participation in general elections (among the traits Social Credit shares with political parties) are resisted by the membership with the passionate suspicion of the unsullied confronted by inventive temptation.

Social Credit continues to field candidates at general elections because its leadership shares the conviction that Social Credit offers alternatives to the New Zealand public not provided by any other political force. According to the League, its membership at the time of the 1975 General Election comprised 8,000 persons, down from its 1966 peak of more than 9,000 members but a substantial and healthy climb from its 1972–3 decline to 2,000 persons. Its rise in support during the 1977-8 period was accompanied by a significant growth in membership and financial resources. There are branches or organisations of Social Credit in each of the 88 European electorates, and in addition Social Credit has numerous sub-branches operating within some of these electorates. Social Credit's campaign to recruit new members had as its goal 12,000 members by the end of 1976 and 24,000 members–a trebling of Social Credit's near-record 1976 strength–by the 1978 elections.

Attempts by Social Credit to persuade Parliament to enact a proportional representation system have not made much progress. Another Social Credit stratagem has involved proposals for an electoral 'accommodation' (in Mr Beetham's words) with the Labour Party. However, Social Credit's suggestion that it engage in 'co-operative' electoral arrangements with the Labour Party–with Social Credit and Labour candidates not standing against each other in selected seats, and thus not dividing the so-called Opposition vote–ultimately was received by Labour like an All Black at an Organisation of African Unity meeting. However, many Labour *voters* formed (in effect) their own coalitions with Social Credit in 1978, deserting Labour to support Social Credit when the League's chances to defeat a National candidate seemed superior to Labour's. Whether Labour informally aided such an effort by selecting 'weak' candidates in seats in which Social Credit appeared strong is difficult to establish.

How can Social Credit hope to present itself as a credible alternative to the major parties? Despite attempts to create a more positive image and to broaden its appeal, Social Credit remains–after over twenty years of organising–an enigma to most voters[33]. Most voters have been unable clearly to distinguish what the party stands for, and consequently have had no strong feelings towards Social Credit one way or the other. Some voters associate the party with some monetary reform policy, but this is usually a label (or, occasionally, an epithet) applied by them to a phenomenon which they cannot understand. This has been a great pity for Social Credit, because it has been indicative of its inadequate effort to communicate its message to the electorate in a manner which voters can understand. It has been a misfortune for the New Zealand public as well, which has been deterred by Social Credit's monetary policy from looking into some of the other areas of public policy on which Social Credit has developed alternatives.

In 1978, the enormous growth in support for Social Credit was *not* based on widespread understanding and approval of the League's monetary policies. Rather the movement to Social Credit reflected Mr Beetham's own appeal and enhanced credibility as an MP, disillusionment with the major parties and their leaders and a feeling among some anti-National and anti-Muldoon voters that a return to Labour was premature after the 1972–5 experience. Thus the League won support *in spite of*, rather than because of, its economic policies, although ridicule of them was deterred by the disappointing character of Labour and National policies developed from more orthodox sources of economic theory. Whether a protest vote based more on aversion to the main parties can evolve into a positive and sustained enthusiasm is the challenge that remains for Social Credit.

Shrunken political parties, repeatedly rejected by the voters at the national level, may maintain and rebuild their strength through participation in elections below the national level. Despite the success of Bruce Beetham in being elected Mayor of Hamilton in 1976, Social Credit has rejected this strategy largely because 'Social Credit believes that New Zealanders should keep party politics out of local body affairs.' Yet the challenge of developing viable policies at the local level is by no means an insignificant one; in Social Credit's case, it has a special urgency. Social Credit's major obstacle has been the ridicule which otherwise potentially sympathetic voters have erected against it. This can best be overcome through its candidates gaining the confidence of New Zealanders, by acquiring the experience of elected service as Social Credit representatives in communities around the country.[34]

The Values Party

Values' programme and philosophy is clearly distinct from the other parties, for its concerns are those of the 1970s: environment; population growth; moral issues. A 1975 campaign brochure established Values' orientation with great clarity.

An Alternative Future[35]

Voters:

Are you confused and dissatisfied with the present lack of integrity of our major political parties?
Do you feel that New Zealand is suffering from a depression in human values?
Are you more interested in preserving the standard of life rather than the standard of living?
Are you concerned about your childrens' future heritage?
If your answer is 'YES' to any of these questions, you have something in common with the members of the New Zealand Values Party.

We Believe:

That people are becoming tired of listening to promises and worn out cliches of politicians.
That people are more important than material values.
That people are becoming 'dehumanised' by the pressures of modern living and the rapid expansion of economic growth.
That people want more time to enjoy their heritage in New Zealand and take stock of their environment.

We would introduce:

* ZERO POPULATION GROWTH as a means to increase social stability, reduce the need for economic growth and urban sprawl and advance the arrival of the four day working week.
* A STRONG ENVIRONMENT POLICY involving tough anti-pollution measures, conservation of natural assets, beautification of cities and restrictions on the use of cars in congested city streets.
* An extensive JOB IMPROVEMENT PROGRAMME to increase job satisfaction and reduce industrial unrest.

* Changes in education curricula to meet the more relevant needs of the modern child;
  Decentralisation to ease the control of Education from Wellington;
  Increased spending to reduce class sizes;
  Phasing out of national examinations in favour of internal assessment in schools.
* Sex education in schools, increased availability of contraceptive advice and facilities. Abortion Law Reform.
* Equal pay for women and greater attention to the needs of the working mother and the stay at home mother.
* Increased aid for pensioners.

We also Believe:

* That there should be a greater representation of youth in the Government.
* That our Foreign Policy should be more independent and not dictated by Foreign Powers.
* That we should channel our financial resources from the production of unnecessary consumer goods to more urgent needs such as pollution control and increased overseas aid.

VOTE VALUES
To Preserve the Quality of Life

As Mr Muldoon has dominated the New Zealand political scene during 1975–8 when viewed from the perspective of power, so too it had seemed for a time that the Values Party had come to hold an intellectually vital place in New Zealand politics quite out of proportion to its strength in terms of voting figures.

> . . . the future of our major parties is intimately bound up with the future of the Values Party, for Values can be regarded as a response to the intellectual failings of our MPs generally, and an indication of the desire of many New Zealanders to debate politics at a higher level. So long as the two established political parties fail to take up the role that Values has constructed, we can expect this third party to continue to grow in appeal.[36]

Clearly the 'role' of Values has been that of mover of ideas; of the major parties, Values sought to occupy a strategic position in the intellectual life of the community. When new ideas have been encountered, or new policies proposed, it is the Values Party which has seemed their natural home. It is easy to dismiss this tendency as a form of political dilettantism, or to explain it away as a function of middle-class Marxist juvenalia. It is nevertheless apparent that the

Values Party, whatever its faults or weaknesses may be, has had an interest in *ideas* as well as power. This attraction for ideas makes the party distinctive in appeal and interesting to observe. It renders Values in this sense the driving force of New Zealand politics, without which New Zealand politics might become mired in a miasma of vacuousness and fatuity.

Politicians' interest in the Values Party is confined almost exclusively to its role as a danger to electoral success. It is exclusively as an electoral threat that Values remains alive to Labour and National. During 1972 and 1975 Social Credit's strength was known and predictable, so that the League could be taken into account, and dismissed. However, the *unpredictability* of the Values vote in these two general elections was a source of disturbance for major party strategists. In 1978, in this respect, Values and Social Credit reversed electoral positions and intellectual roles. Labour and National spokesmen made allusions to financial reform and had some kind words for Social Credit policy and intent, while Values, discounted as a threat, found neither major party taking an interest in its proposals or point of view.

Among Values' more obvious strengths are its willingness to adopt forthright and unambiguous positions on issues of urgent social importance, such as nuclear power. A comparison of Values' statements on nuclear power, or abortion law reform, for example, with those of National and Labour, underscores the clarity of Values' position. In 1975, National and Labour sought mandates for ambiguity. On the other hand, Values left the voters in little doubt about its commitment to certain ideas, and undertook the obligation to defend these ideas with enthusiasm and vigour. In 1978, Values continued to articulate its views on controversial 'moral' issues more forthrightly than is common, yet there was a failure to communicate these views with sufficient urgency, or to disseminate them with the necessary organisational skill. Moreover, Values failed to recognise that the concerns and anxieties of voters in 1978 were very different from those of 1972 and 1975, so that at a time of unemployment and emigration, Values' strictures against conspicuous consumption seemed to have only the most oblique relationship to voters' needs and fears. Finally, Values' introduction of an additional layer of policy objectives, concerned with virtually confiscatory taxation of wealth and land and the compulsory maintenance of a very restricted range of personal income, failed to attract additional support to the party from working-class voters.

Thus while in 1975 Values overtook Social Credit in all 8 Christchurch electorates, and most of the electorates in Wellington, Auckland and Dunedin to become New Zealand's 'third party' in the major urban centres, in 1978 Social Credit outpolled Values by huge margins in every electorate in the country. During 1978 there had been little discussion of the possibilities of Values' supplanting Social Credit, and it appears that the desertion of Values voters to Labour was a major factor in the party's decline. Parties such as Values may be more likely to prosper against Labour-led governments, for while they may attract those disillusioned with the left, this disappointment is likely to be momentarily suppressed in a desire to oust a conservative National government.

In many ways, Values' ideas and values suggest a 'tendency to look simultaneously backwards and forwards, showing nostalgia for earlier patterns of working life and yet aspiring towards a more just and harmonious society in the future'.[37] This inner tension in the party makes it at the same time philosophically the most reactionary of New Zealand's parties, yet programmatically the country's most radical in terms of the measures envisaged in the domestic and international sphere. While Values' mistrust of state power and centralisation makes the party somewhat 'anarchist', its goal of an 'integrated, non-fragmented life' based on the life of the people in a 'true community' is reminiscent too of the nostalgic elements in fascist ideology, with its cultural precursors among the German Romantics. There are resonances between a reactionary politics of nostalgia and certain emotive strains underpinning Values policies. Moreover, the attitude which Values communicates towards economic policies reveals a lack of sympathy for the everyday 'ordinary' concerns of most New Zealanders.[38] Until the party can transcend its relatively narrow base of support, it is likely to remain committed to policies unsympathetic to the concerns which most New Zealanders share for an improvement in the material bases of social and personal life. At present, Values members appear to be a highly educated, committed, intense and imaginative group of people intolerant of optimism, scornful of the joy and happiness 'ordinary' people experience from 'ordinary' pleasures. It is a great pity, but nevertheless true that in the anti-bourgeois rhetoric of Values there is a politics of contempt antagonistic to the 'values' of co-operation and goodwill the party is pledged to uphold.

Like Social Credit, Values has been ambivalent about being a political party at all. At times, its leaders have openly discussed the possibility of becoming an 'interest group' seeking to influence the major parties but not contesting parliamentary elections. This ambivalence, reflecting an aversion towards politics, is reflected in the party's extremely diffident attitudes towards political leadership. While seeking to 'lead' New Zealand towards new values, the party has been unwilling or unable in its internal structure to decisively promote leaders who can communicate self-confidence to the public, and sustain party morale. It appears that Values is unable to recognise that political leadership can be *authoritative without becoming authoritarian* (an essentially degenerative form), and this has interfered with the party's efforts to obtain the necessary broad base of public support. It is to Values' credit, however, that it has been willing to involve its members in local body electoral activity, and its founding leader (Mr A.J. Brunt) has served as an elected Values candidate on the Wellington City Council. In the long run, Values–if it persists as a party–should be able to accumulate political strength (if only because of the age composition of the party) through the conscientious involvement of its members in community politics. To attain political success at the national level, its leaders, organisers and voters will need to commit themselves to a long struggle, while demonstrating an increased willingness to alter the presentation of Values' essential messages into a more electorally competitive form.

Future Prospects

It is common to regard electoral politics as corresponding to a 'pendulum'; one party is elected to be replaced, inevitably, by the other. So long as the electoral system and selection processes remain unaltered, a predominantly two-party system may be expected to endure. That these two parties will continue to be Labour and National, as presently organised, is less certain. While Roberts regards Labour as the dynamic force of New Zealand politics–a 'value-creating' party[39]–the pre-eminence of National throughout the postwar years despite considerable change in the composition of New Zealand society has been impressive. However, the growth of the 'uncommitted' vote, the decline in the proportion of the electorate voting, the rise of Values and Social Credit, the difficulties Labour has had in maintaining support nation-wide, and the conflicts faced by National voters alarmed at the style of leadership or the growth in the power of the state under a 'free-enterprise' party committed to personal freedoms, are all factors which are indicative of the gradual collapse of the alignment of political parties initiated in 1935 and characteristic of the 1935–78 period. Robinson's conclusion remains appropriate:

> In accounting for the persistence of the two-party system the most important factors have been the strength of party loyalties and the image each party has in the public mind of being associated with a major and permanent set of economic interests. Both major parties have a large reserve of support in the electorate whatever might happen. Third parties have a difficult task to win over voters while a victorious party at the most can win only a few extra seats. Party loyalties thus provide stability for the present party system.

> But there is nothing inevitable about an alternation of the parties

in a two-party system. One party might win all or most elections over a long period of time. For example, by 1969, the National Party had been in office for 17 of the previous 20 years. Long periods of office are the rule rather than the exception in New Zealand history . . . there is no guarantee that a party which has lost office will always retain its place as one of the two major parties . . . Failures in political management, the opening up of deep social or ideological fissures in the community, possibly a consequence of economic depression, could produce either a multi-party situation or the gradual replacement of one of the existing parties by a new party. The possibility of change of this kind cannot be excluded.[40]

Seemingly only a capricious set of electoral results could propel one of the third parties into a decisive role in Parliament. However, certain features of political life may so endure that they seem permanently rooted. It used to be argued, for example, that no government in New Zealand could permit substantial unemployment and hope to survive a general election, yet the National Party was returned to power in 1978. That New Zealand must have its politics dominated by two parties, and that these two parties must be Labour and National, is neither obvious nor inevitable. A multi-party system already exists, in terms of the alternatives presented to the voters. The structural obstacles inhibiting the full reflection of this political diversity in Parliament have been powerful, yet once overcome the weakening of the 'wasted vote' argument may see multi-party representation develop into a more permanent feature of the political system. Alternatively, a major realignment of parties around new issues, groups and ideological perspectives may develop, leading once more to a two-party system involving a new set of contenders. A *genuinely* democratic politics involves the continuous exploration of political alternatives as these emerge from our personal experience of government, our neighbours and ourselves. New Zealanders need to ensure that the political expression of this experience remains as vital and as represent-ative as it can be.

References

1. See L. Lipson, *op. cit.*, also R.S. Milne, *Political Parties in New Zealand,* Oxford: Clarendon Press, 1966.
2. See D.C. Webber, *Trade Unions, The Labour Party and The Death of Working-Class Politics in New Zealand.* University of Canterbury, Department of Political Science, M.A. Thesis, 1975.
3. A.D. Robinson, *op. cit.*
4. A useful discussion of the American party system can be found in C.G. Mayo and B.L. Crowe (eds), *American Political Parties: A Systemic Perspective*, New York: Harper and Row, 1967.

5. R.L. Rubin, *Party Dynamics: The Democratic Coalition and the Politics of Change*, New York: Oxford University Press, 1976.
6. See M. Duverger, *Political Parties: Their Organisation and Activity in the Modern State*, London, Methuen, 1964.
7. R. Michels, *Political Parties: A Sociological Study of the Oligarchic Tendencies of Modern Democracy*, Glencoe, Illinois: The Free Press, 1949.
8. S. Levine and J. Lodge, *op. cit.*, p. 7 for voting data; data on membership and distribution of branches obtained from representatives of the parties.
9. A.D. Robinson, *op. cit.*, pp. 50–1.
10. See S. Levine, 'The Nelson By-Election: Politics in a New Zealand Community' in S. Levine (ed.), *Politics in New Zealand: A Reader*, pp. 222–240.
11. The figures for Values and Social Credit voters on the item measuring perceptions of difference between National and Labour are suggestive in this respect. See S. Levine and A.D. Robinson, *op. cit.*, p. 143.
12. For the expression of these ideological tendencies in the party manifestos, see S. Levine, 'Values and Politics: A Content Analysis of Party Programmes' in S. Levine (ed.), *New Zealand Politics: A Reader*, pp. 115–24. The contrasting ideological commitments of Labour and National MPs are explored in P.R. Watson, *Ideology and the New Zealand Parliamentarian*, University of Canterbury, Department of Political Science, M.A. Thesis, 1977.
13. S. Levine, 'Values and Politics: A Content Analysis of Party Programmes', *op. cit.*
14. This is revealed in the *Annual Reports* of the Ministry of Foreign Affairs, and it would be especially useful to compare those of Prime Minister Norman Kirk (who was Minister of Foreign Affairs as well) with those of National's Deputy Prime Minister (and Minister of Foreign Affairs) Brian Talboys. Also see N.E. Kirk, 'New Zealand: A New Foreign Policy', and W.P. Reeves, 'The "New" Foreign Policy: A Dissenting View', in S. Levine (ed.), *New Zealand Politics: A Reader*, pp. 428–437, R.M. Alley 'Prime Ministers and New Zealand Foreign Policy: A Comparison Between Holyoake and Kirk'. Address to the Auckland Branch of the New Zealand Institute of International Affairs, 22 July 1974.
    A poll conducted by the New Zealand Foundation for Peace Studies prior to the 1975 general election, sampling attitudes towards foreign and defence-related issues, found significant differences in orientation amongst National, Labour Social Credit and Values candidates for Parliament. The differences between National and Labour MPs and candidates, in particular, seemed broader and deeper in terms of underlying attitudes than the more marginal differences of tone and emphasis in the two party's election manifestos.
15. See W.K. Jackson, 'Government Succession in New Zealand', in S. Levine (ed.), *Politics in New Zealand: A Reader*, pp. 1–21.
16. M.J.S. Nestor, *A History of the National Party*, Wellington, New Zealand National Party, 1969, p. 4.
17. *Constitution and Rules of the New Zealand National Party*, Wellington: New Zealand National Party, 1969, pp. 1–2.
18. J.R. Marshall, Speech to the National Party Conference, 22 July 1972, Wellington.
19. See W.K. Jackson, 'Political Leadership and Succession in the National Party' in S. Levine (ed.), *Politics in New Zealand: A Reader*, pp. 161–181.

20. See S. Levine and J. Lodge, *op. cit.*, pp. 30–1; S. Levine and A.D. Robinson, *op. cit.*, Chapter 14, and various issues such as abortion and homosexual law reform, and sex education reported in Chapters 2–10.
21. This point is developed by W.J. Luff, 'The Historical Significance of the 1972 General Election Reconsidered in the Light of the 1975 General Election', mimeographed paper, 1977.
22. Constitution of the New Zealand Labour Party, p. 3: *Constitution and Rules, New Zealand Labour Party,* 1975, Wellington: New Zealand.
23. D.C. Webber, 'Trade Unions and the Labour Party: The Death of Working-Class Politics in New Zealand' in S. Levine (ed.), *Politics in New Zealand: A Reader,* pp. 182–195.
24. N.E. Kirk, 'The Philosophy of the Labour Party' in S. Levine (ed.), *New Zealand Politics: A Reader,* p. 144.
25. New Zealand Labour Party, *Annex to the Annual Reports of the National Executive, 1926–48; Delegates Attending Annual Conferences, 1949–1975.* See D.C. Webber's thesis for further details about trade union and branch membership in the Labour Party.
26. See D.C. Webber's article in *Politics in New Zealand: A Reader* for further discussion on the implications of party membership for Labour's electoral prospects.
27. The socialisation of political partisanship is explored effectively by E.E. Schattschneider in *The Semi Sovereign People: A Realist's View of Democracy in America,* New York: Holt, Rinehart and Winston, 1960.
28. J.C. Jeffries, 'It's Time to Think: A Contribution to the Philosophy Debate of the New Zealand Labour Party', pp. 23–7. Jeffries' paper was a contribution to Labour's internal debate on the meaning and relevance of socialism to the contemporary Labour party.
29. F. O'Flynn, 'Labour Restates Socialism for the Seventies', *The Dominion.*
30. B.S. Gustafson, *Social Change and Party Reorganisation: The New Zealand Labour Party Since 1945,* London: Sage Publications, 1976, p. 55.
31. Social Credit Political League, *The Little Green Socred Book,* Palmerston North: Orion Publications Ltd., 1972, frontispiece.
32. Social Credit Political League, 'Tenets of Social Credit', 1972.
33. See S. Levine, 'The Nelson By-Election: Politics in a New Zealand Community', *op. cit.,* for a discussion of voters' attitudes towards Social Credit. These results were consistent with those found in the six-electorate study by S. Levine, N.S. Roberts and G.A. Wood, in which knowledge of the League and its candidates was minimal. Interviews by telephone with 100 Wellington voters, selected at random, found ignorance, confusion, amusement and lack of interest to be the dominant attitudes towards Social Credit in 1975.
34. Further study of Social Credit in S.L. Dickson, 'Social Credit and Class Voting in New Zealand', *Political Science,* vol. 21, pp. 31–41, 1969, and in Dickson's M.A. thesis on Social Credit completed in 1969 for Victoria University of Wellington, Department of Political Science; J.R. Barnett, 'Regional Protest and Political Change: Social Credit in New Zealand', 1954–1972, in R.J. Johnston (ed.), *People, Places and Votes: Essays on the Electoral Geography of New Zealand,* Armidale: University of New England, 1977; S. Levine and J. Lodge, *op. cit.,* pp. 13–14, 32–4; S. Levine and A.D. Robinson, *op. cit.,* passim.
35. Joan Beaufort Introduces 'The New Zealand Values Party, An Alternative Future', Campaign brochure, 1975.

36. K. Ovenden, 'Prospect: On The Absence of Political Ideas' in R. Goldstein with R.M. Alley, *Labour in Power: Promise and Performance*, Wellington: Price Milburn for New Zealand University Press, 1975.
37. S. Levine, 'The Paradoxical Values Party', *The Week*, vol. 1, no. 13, 17 September 1976, p. 9.
38. This antipathy appears to be recognised by voters themselves; see the comments of voters about Values in S. Levine, 'The Nelson By-Election: Politics in A New Zealand Community', *op. cit.*
39. S. Levine, 'Labour After Nine Months: An Interview with John L. Roberts' in S. Levine (ed.), *New Zealand Politics: A Reader*, p. 426.
40. A.D. Robinson, *op. cit.*, p. 51.

5 Elections and Electors

Sources of Party Support

The sources of support for the New Zealand parties have been well established by recent empirical research. These studies included: (1) a postal survey of voters selected on a random basis from the electoral rolls of each electorate, conducted immediately after the 1975 general election;[1] (2) interviews with persons in homes selected on a 'random walk' basis in six electorates, during the fortnight preceding the 1975 general election;[2] (3) a postal survey of voters in one electorate (Nelson), selected on a random basis from the electoral rolls.[3] These three separate studies relied upon different samples (i.e. representative populations) and distinct methods of sample selection; in each case, moreover, different survey instruments (i.e. sets of questions) were used, and the methods of obtaining information included both the interview and written questionnaire.

While there is some distrust of public opinion polling in New Zealand, nevertheless one valid principle of research has been well established in the conduct of survey research. Multiple methods of verification provide a more secure basis for determining the truth or falsity of propositions about voting behaviour (for example) than reliance upon one technique. Each method has its limitations; however, when different measures used with respect to distinct samples produce similar results, confidence in those results can reasonably be expected to increase. With respect to electoral behaviour, each of these studies has revealed similar patterns of electoral support for New Zealand's parties. Moreover, in spite of recent 'landslide' fluctuations during general elections, the pattern of support for Labour and National has proved remarkably durable.

The consequence in terms of the geographical distribution of votes is that National is strongest in rural and small-town areas and in higher-income suburbs, while Labour is strongest in central city areas and in lower-income suburbs. Marginal seats are to be found in medium-sized towns (20–50,000 people) and in moderate income or mixed high/low income city areas.[4]

The class basis of the parties is fairly clear. Farmers and wealthy urban voters are pitted against manual workers.[5]

Support for different parties may also be determined by other features of an individual's background. Younger voters, rather than their elders, have been more disposed to support Values for example. Labour has tended, more than National, to receive the support of Roman Catholic voters, although this may have been attributable to their working-class position. Maori voters have tended to give their support to Labour, and Pacific Islanders have tended to do so as well. While many non-church goers support Labour and National, they constitute a particularly large proportion of the Values vote, a further reflection of the youthful character of the party's appeal. The distribution of support for each party, ascertained by one study, analysed by voters' educational background, is described in Tables 5:1 and 5:2:[6]

TABLE 5:1 *Political Party Preference by Educational Background**

Formal education	Party			
	Labour	National	Values	Non-voters
	%	%	%	%
Primary school only	14.8	13.1	4.2	7.7
1–2 years secondary	20.6	17.6	6.3	15.4
3 years secondary	27.0	15.0	8.3	26.9
4 years secondary	10.6	12.4	25.0	15.4
5 or more years secondary	8.5	11.8	6.3	15.4
Attended tertiary institution	13.8	23.5	43.8	19.2
Other	4.7	6.6	6.3	—

TABLE 5:2 *Political Party Preference by Educational Qualifications Obtained**

Qualification	Party			
	Labour	National	Values	Non-voters
	%	%	%	%
None	56.6	41.8	16.7	46.2
School Certificate	6.3	8.5	14.6	11.5
University Entrance	5.3	13.7	18.8	15.4
Bachelor's degree or university diploma	1.1	6.5	8.3	7.7
Graduate degree	0.5	1.3	6.3	—
Teacher's, nursing or professional certificate; polytechnic certificate	11.1	13.1	20.8	7.7
Apprenticeship or trade qualification	7.4	4.6	6.3	—
Other	11.7	10.4	8.4	11.5

* Social Credit support excluded due to the small numbers of the party's voters in the survey.

The class basis of Labour and National is suggested by the higher formal attainments of National voters, for educational achievement, type of occupation, income levels and social class tend to be related together. The exceedingly high educational levels of Values voters, in relation to the other parties' voters and to the country as a whole, underscores further the party's problems. One of its strengths rests with the talents and energies found amongst its vigorous and talented membership. One of its weaknesses is precisely that the party is so unrepresentative, so unusually constituted, that it may fail to secure the support of those who perceive the party as 'elitist' whether justifiably or not and feel excluded from it.

The implications of New Zealand's class-based system of party politics are susceptible to a variety of interpretations. While the National party spokesmen tend to deny the relevance of social class to New Zealand, preferring to describe their party as a 'broad spectrum' party representative of all New Zealanders, former Prime Minister J.R. Marshall on at least one occasion adopted that perspective with some interesting results.

> The individualists and the private enterprisers, those who have arrived and those with enough faith in themselves to believe they can and will succeed, are with the National party. They are the ones who want equality of opportunity, not equality of rewards. The idea of state interference, restriction or control is not to their liking.
>
> Looking again at the sources of support of the two parties, we find that by and large the owners and managers and administrators of the means of production are with the National party, both in farming and manufacturing industries . . . A National Government sees more clearly the need and the means for increasing the production of wealth as the way to increasing the standard of living. The Labour party concentrates more on the redistribution of the national wealth through the agencies of the welfare state. But it is the producers of wealth who provide the life blood of the welfare state.[7]

While politically self-serving, Marshall's analysis sought to establish a firm link between the policies and philosophies of the parties, the capacities and experience of the party members and leaders, and the sources of electoral support for the parties.

On the other hand, the balance between Labour and National in marginal electorates, and in the country as a whole, is held by a largely middle-class group of 'independent' or "floating" voters. Certainly both parties strenuously seek the support of these voters, to the point where their more loyal supporters may feel neglected. The attempt of Labour to appeal to this 'floating' vote thus leads to some resentment from trade union groups, while some of National's policies provoke periodic expressions of complaint from farming organisations. While New Zealand has a 'one-man, one-vote' system, in which all votes are of equal value, the goal of major parties–the winning of elections–makes inevitable the attempt of party strategists to capture the 'floating' vote. In particular, both Labour and National have sought in recent years to mould policies likely to attract 'swing' voters away from the 'protest' parties, Social Credit and Values. While there appears to be some discontent with the major parties' efforts to converge upon the political centre, accusations that the parties resemble 'tweedledum and tweedledee' (or 'tweedledumb' and 'tweedledumber') tend to be confined to ideologues, purists and supporters of third parties. Most voters appear to believe that Labour and National represent reasonably distinct alternatives, and that electoral contests are consequently meaningful affairs. Whether voters believe that these parties can fulfil the promises made during campaigns is another matter. In any event, the implications of the 'floating vote' for policy-making have been cogently expressed.

In any country where both parties need to appeal to the same class, the differences between their platforms tend to decrease, but not to the point of becoming unimportant. The opposition party, needing to steal some of the government's party's votes, is forced to steal some of its platform . . . A government with a narrow majority knows that it must at all costs appeal to the floating vote, and if necessary it will disappoint its steadfast supporters. It would be most unlikely they would rally to the opposition party.

The floating vote is the regulator of the whole system, indicating to the party in office how it must balance the interests of the classes. Its power of making and breaking governments on election day is spectacular, but does less to mould the political system than the indirect power it wields between elections by holding out carrots to the government of the day. A government cannot govern solely in the interests of the class it represents, for that would be certain to alienate most of the floating vote; and a government knows that it cannot afford to do that, and that it can afford up to a point to offend its steadfast supporters. Its motive may be to cling to office; the consequence is likely to be good government, establishing a fair reconciliation of sectional interests.[8]

It is important to recognise that there is a strong (and growing) regional basis to New Zealand politics. This is revealed in several ways: (1) there has been a substantial shift of population, and political and economic power, to the Auckland area; (2) other urban centres have sought to develop bi-partisan support from their parliamentary representatives for assistance from government; (3) the South Island has developed a distinctive orientation towards the North Island, and the government, in reaction against perceived neglect and a decline in political influence and economic prospects. This became so pronounced during the 1978 campaign that Mr Beetham proclaimed that the election was about the continued 'unity of the country', and a South Island independence movement of indeterminate strength was formed. More intense feelings on the West coast of the South Island led to formation of the West Coast party, which finished within 200 votes of second-place National in the Labour-held West Coast electorate. Nevertheless, this regional basis is not entirely new, and an appreciation of this dimension seems necessary in electoral interpretation.

It seems erroneous, for example, to suggest that recent general elections have been won or lost in Auckland. It seems evident that, from a geographical point of view, Labour won in 1972 because it captured the provincial centres, and the 'small town and semi-rural electorates' (as defined by the Electoral Office) of the North and South islands; that National won in 1975 not because it 'won' Auckland (for only four seats changed party in that city) but through its recapture of the rural, small town and smaller urban areas. Thus some of the vital electorates to be fought over by the parties include: (1) Hamilton East, Hamilton West and New Plymouth, which went to Labour in 1972, returned to National in 1975 and remained there in 1978; in contrast to (2) Hastings, Gisborne, Palmerston North and Taupo, which swung to Labour in 1972, back to National in 1975, and again to Labour in 1978.

In 1978, Labour failed to secure the anti-government 'swing' (partially due to Social Credit competition) in all of the areas that it gained in 1972, and thus could not quite dislodge National from its position as the governing party. In particular, the small town and semi-rural electorates of the South Island failed to go to Labour (as they had in 1972), despite the anti-government feeling prevalent during the campaign. While a number of electorates could be described as 'indicator' electorates–as seats which voted National in 1969, Labour in 1972, National in 1975 and National once more (but more narrowly) in 1978–it may be possible (in the interests of predictive brevity, and mindful that in the United States the 'As Maine goes, so goes the country maxim' became 'As Maine goes, so goes Vermont' in the wake of the 1936 Democratic landslide) to declare on the basis of the last four elections: 'As Invercargill goes, so goes the country.'

Of course the number of factors influencing a person's vote, and the outcome of an election, are clearly quite large. Little wonder that predictions are so frequently wrong, or imprecise. The variables in an election range from elements peculiar to a voter to those affecting whole groups of voters. Even the weather can be a factor, affecting voter turnout (and voter disposition) so significantly that campaign organisation–the ability to identify supporters and bring them to the polls–can ultimately be crucial. The variety of factors cited in electoral interpretation prompted one commentator to observe:

> All these explanations are, I suggest, partly true. But don't they contradict one another? Labour, it would seem, lost power because of post-war economic conditions quite beyond its control; because it did control them, to the real or fancied detriment of the farmer and the white collar worker; because it did not control them enough to satisfy the trade unionist; because it antagonised the middle classes and because it forgot its 'working class principles'. There are two answers. First, that politics are not as simple as they seem, and that the most useful generalisation about this or any election is the inadequacy of most generalisations about it; secondly, that 'the people' who 'speak' or 'give mandates' have no existence: there are only Bill Jones and Jack Smith and Mary Brown, who speak in different voices, and often enough contradict themselves as well as one another.[9]

Thus in 1972, Labour won because: (1) it had the more forceful leader; (2) National chose an ineffective 'team' approach; (3) Labour devised an attractive regional development programme; (4) the voters were bored with twelve years of National rule; (5) the voters were enthusiastic over the prospect of a third Labour government; (6) National changed the colour of its campaign material from blue to orange; (7) National changed its leadership too close to a general election; (8) Labour pledged to abolish conscription; and so on.[10] Similarly, in 1975, National won because: (1) it had the more forceful leader; (2) Labour chose an ineffective 'team' approach; (3) National devised an attractive superannuation programme; (4) the voters were frightened after only three years of Labour government; (5) the voters were eager to see a National government restore 'New Zealand's shattered economy'; (6) National changed its campaign colours back to blue; (7) the transition of Labour leadership, in mid-term, gave too little time for Mr Rowling to establish a clear image to voters; (8) National pledged to repeal the Labour programme, to obliterate the third Labour Government in all but memory (and its member's memoirs); and so on.[11]

In 1978, the Prime Minister's prediction (at the outset of the campaign) of 'a substantial majority . . . a little bit better than we've been' failed to be realised because: (1) there was a reaction by persons voting National in 1975 against the Prime Minister's abrasive style of leadership; (2) Social Credit made strong inroads into National support in many electorates; (3) Labour developed a vigorous campaign; (4) National waged an uninspiring and complacent campaign; (5) National failed to convince many voters of the accuracy of its major campaign theme ('we're keeping our word'); (6) voters were disturbed about unemployment, emigration, massive overseas borrowing and the government's failure successfully to manage industrial relations. On the other hand, the ambiguous outcome for Labour–a narrow and, therefore, glorious defeat for a party whose demise had been cheerfully (but prematurely) predicted by the Prime Minister and National party candidates–may be attributed to a variety of factors. Labour did well because of: (1) Mr Rowling's emergence during the campaign as a confident, assertive and forceful leader; (2) the skilful packaging of a programme brimming with ideas and promises; (3) the considerable improvements introduced to the Labour campaign and party organisation during the 1976–78 period; (4) the failure of many otherwise National voters to support the government in protests ranging from specific issues to the behaviour of the Prime Minister. Labour failed to become the government because: (1) many voters disillusioned with National nevertheless were unwilling to return Labour to power; (2) Social Credit deprived Labour of anti-National support in certain electorates; (3) the magnitude of Labour's promises, in its pledge 'To rebuild the nation' (the theme of its manifesto), persuaded some voters that Labour could not be trusted to manage the economy responsibly; (4) certain Labour candidates were uninspired choices (as conceded during the campaign by Deputy Leader of the Opposition Mr R.J. Tizard), unable fully to exploit the anti-National sentiments in their electorates; (5) the redistribution of electoral boundaries, implemented for the 1978 general elections, gave a slim advantage to National just sufficient to overcome the Labour challenge.

Social Credit achieved remarkable success in 1978, more than doubling its share of the vote (with 16.4%, and one seat), surpassing the League's previous best performance (in 1966, when it received 14.5% of the vote, and one seat). The growth in Social Credit support was a consequence of: (1) disappointment with the recent performance of both National and Labour; (2) the increasing confidence and assurance of the Social Credit leader, Mr B.C. Beetham; (3) the decline in standards of conduct in Parliament, leading to an antipathy towards 'the system' and the dominant parties; (4) the deterioration of New Zealand's economic position. Yet Mr Beetham's prediction –'Social Credit is going to do exceedingly well . . . I'm certain we're going to win 3 or 4 seats'–failed to be fulfilled, although the narrowness of the outcome in the country as a whole, and in certain seats in which Social Credit outpolled Labour to approach National, nearly gave the League that most valued prize for a third party: the balance of power in Parliament. Ultimately, though, Social Credit's objectives were not satisfied because: (1) some anti-National voters in certain electorates supported Labour rather than Social Credit to increase the chances of defeating the government, and thus not 'waste' their vote; (2) many potential Social Credit voters remain confused about the League's economic and financial policies; (3) the 'first past the post' system discriminates against third parties, so that even with support from 1 in 6 voters, the League could only secure one seat; (4) Social Credit failed to reach 18–20% of the popular vote, the probable threshold for the League to overcome in order to acquire significant parliamentary representation.

Few of these generalisations are entirely accurate, nor would the many more plausible points which can be cited provide a complete explanation. The difficulty is that all these factors interact with one another; none of them operate on the electorate in isolation, and the almost insuperable challenge for the psephologist, therefore, is one of *measurement*, to determine the importance of particular factors for different groups of electors.

Politics and Marriage

It is often claimed, in effect, that women are the political ciphers of their men. There are assertions in the political socialisation literature, for example, that daughters acquire the political orientations of their fathers and, subsequently, that wives adopt the political loyalties of their husbands. In the voting behaviour literature, wives are often assigned a social class position based on the income and social class of their husband. Moreover, interpretation of the voting behaviour of women has not been consistent. For example, one author has noted that women are *less* likely to 'float' because of their 'natural conservatism'. Thus, women are *more loyal* to their traditional partisan attachments. Another commentator, however, has observed that 'phenomena such as political loyalty may be viewed as activities on their own and as exhibiting the male bond'. When women 'float', this demonstrates their inherently 'fickle' nature, the irrational basis of their support and the promiscuous ease with which they will transfer their political affections. When men 'float', however, this is usually regarded as the exercise of rational, discriminating political judgement in its highest form, indicative of the democratic process at its most perfect.[12]

Very little evidence has been presented in support of these generalisations, and little systematic work appears to have been done to test the effect of the contemporary women's rights movement on the voting behaviour of spouses. If accurate, of course, the notion that women change their policies to coincide with the preferences of their husband suggests a new and not insignificant form of 'floating vote'. Presumably, among the many divorces and remarriages occuring annually, there are many instances of women marrying men whose political loyalties are different from those of their previous husband. Perhaps these situations tend to cancel each other out, with the number of female Labour voters remarrying National men approximately equal to the number of female National voters remarrying Labour men. On the other hand, perhaps research might explore the possibility that the family that votes together, stays together.

The following tables seek to explore the extent to which husbands and wives do, in fact, vote for the same party in New Zealand.[13] At the same time, these tables indicate the difficulty involved in obtaining reliable information about the political behaviour of husbands and wives. Political researchers must rely upon secondary information, since the secret ballot quite properly would exclude the direct observation by spouses of each other's voting behaviour.

In the Nelson by-election study, voters were asked: 'If you are married, do you think that your wife or husband voted the same way as you did in this by-election?' The same question was asked with respect to the preceding November general election. The responses are summarised below:

TABLE 5:3 *Husband's Perceptions of Wife's Vote**

Perception of Wife's Vote	Male Labour voters		Male National voters		Male Values voters	
	By-el. %	Gen. el. %	By-el. %	Gen. el. %	By-el. %	Gen. el. %
Voted for same party	70.6	69.6	75.1	73.8	43.4	52.2
Voted for different party	8.6	8.7	10.1	10.0	21.7	21.7
Don't know	3.3	4.3	3.8	6.3	4.3	—
Not married, other	17.5	17.4	12.0	19.9	30.6	26.1

TABLE 5:4 *Wife's Perception of Husband's Vote**

Perception of Husband's Vote	Female Labour voters		Female National voters		Female Values voters	
	By-el. %	Gen. el. %	By-el. %	Gen. el. %	By-el. %	Gen. el. %
Voted for same party	57.3	53.1	61.4	60.0	48.0	64.0
Voted for different party	9.4	13.5	12.8	14.3	40.0	24.0
Don't know	2.1	3.1	1.4	1.4	—	—
Not married, other	31.2	30.3	24.4	24.3	12.0	12.0

* Social Credit data excluded due to the small number of the party's voters in the survey.

The responses indicate the difficulty involved in measuring this phenomenon. What is involved is sampling the *speculation* of husbands and wives about their spouses' political behaviour. This matrimonial conjecture may be subject to the same confusions, distortions and errors of judgement as other features of husband–wife relationships. Nevertheless, several patterns seem to emerge from the data. It is obviously an over-generalisation to suggest that women *always* vote the same way as their husbands. To attribute a vote for the same party as the *consequence* of the husband's influence, in the absence of supporting data, is similarly unwarranted. For the major parties, at least, husbands appear to be more confident than wives about their spouses' support for their own political party preference.

Of married male Labour voters, for example, 1 in 9 thought that their wife voted for a different party; a comparable figure describes the male National Party voters. However, 1 in 5 married female Labour voters thought that their household had been politically divided during the elections, while 1 in 6 female National voters were of a similar opinion. The small sample of Social Credit voters makes generalisation impossible, but it would seem that politically 'split' households are more common for third parties. Values, in particular, may be developing a new 'wasted vote' phenomenon, in which husbands and wives may be partially cancelling out each other's influence at the ballot box.

The discrepancy in figures between wives' and husbands' perceptions may suggest a greater realism amongst the women, who may be more willing to accept that their spouse may develop political judgements independent from their own. Table 5:5 provides some support for the view that a marriage must endure for a reasonably long period of time, before politically harmonious judgements develop amongst husbands and wives.

TABLE 5:5 *Perception of Spouse's Political Behaviour: New Voters*

Perception of spouse's vote	New voters	
	By-election	*General election*
	%	%
Voted for same party	31.6	34.2
Voted for different party	10.5	7.9
Don't know	—	—
Not married, other	57.9	57.9

Alternative hypotheses are possible: (1) changing attitudes may mean that younger married persons will be more willing to tolerate political 'deviance' from their spouses than has been previously true; (2) people who have been married only a short period have yet to develop an enduring marriage relationship, which may in turn depend, at least to some degree, on their ability to evolve compatible perspectives towards the political world.

Whether non-voting is a trait shared by husbands and wives has been measured as well. This data may test the notion that the family that stays together, stays home together.

TABLE 5:6 *Perceptions of Spouse's Political Behaviour: Non-voters*

Perception of spouse's vote	Non-voters	
	By-election %	General election %
Both did not vote	38.4	34.6
Only respondent did not vote	11.5	15.4
Don't know whether spouse voted	—	3.8
Other, not married	50.1	46.2

Clearly non-voters tend to believe that their spouse similarly abstained from participation in the electoral process. Finally, an attempt has been made to discover whether the 'floating vote' is an entirely individual phenomenon, or by contrast whether husbands and wives flee together from the party of their previous electoral choice.

TABLE 5:7 *Perceptions of Spouse's Political Behaviour: The Floating Vote*

Perception of spouse's vote	Type of voting change	
	Changed to Labour since General Election %	Left National for Labour, Social Credit or Values since General Election %
Husband and wife both 'floated'	48.1	27.3
Only respondent 'floated'	14.8	36.3
Don't know	7.4	—
Other, not married	29.7	36.4

In the Nelson by-election, at least, a move towards the main Opposition party–Labour–away from National (in most cases) was one *shared* by both husband and wife. This disaffection, predominantly based on a negative evaluation of the government's performance since taking office (and its management of economic affairs), was one affecting the household. However, voters 'floating' from National to *other* parties (predominantly Values) did not tend to do so for economic reasons, and it would seem that in most cases their change of vote was not endorsed by their spouse. Thus, whether husbands and wives 'float' together may depend on the kind of factors motivating a change of voting preference.

Rationality and Public Opinion

The model of the rational voter assumed that political consent (to governing authority) required prior rational inquiry into the merits and demerits of opposing arguments.[14] However, the attempt of survey research to discover the political beliefs, attitudes and values of voters makes no such assumptions. Consequently, debate about public opinion research often fails to centre on the objectives of such research, for individuals and groups dissatisfied with the pattern of orientations uncovered may assert that the results reveal the ignorance of the electorate. For example, the Report of the Royal Commission on Abortion, Contraception and Sterilisation in New Zealand asserted: 'It is difficult to know whether the opinions expressed on these issues are based on an adequate knowledge of the relevant facts or a full appreciation of the issues involved.'[15]

Of course this statement is self-evident, but the implications, in the context of the Commission's report, were quite surprising. This sort of objection can be advanced against *any* measure of public opinion irrespective of its accuracy or purpose. Indeed the Commission's objections, literally applied, would extend even to New Zealand's triennial measurement of public choice. For in an election no less than a public opinion poll, 'it is difficult to know whether the opinions expressed . . . are based on an adequate knowledge . . . or a full appreciation of the issues involved'. Indeed public opinion research in New Zealand and elsewhere suggests that in most cases, 'knowledge' *is* less than adequate, and 'appreciation' *is* less than full. If the Commission sought to exclude the relevance of public opinion polls, on these grounds, such an attitude could logically be extended to discount the collective judgement of the voters as expressed in general elections.

The Commission's reasoning on this point was profoundly alien to the democratic values on which New Zealand political institutions have been founded. For what the Commission was really arguing was that public opinion is *unnecessary* to the formulation of public policy. If public opinion coincides with the preference of policy-makers, then public opinion is *superfluous*, adding nothing not already known. If public opinion does not so coincide, then public opinion can be ignored as misguided and ill-informed. In effect, the Commission concluded that, by and large, public opinion research involves the study and measurement of erroneous opinion.

The relevance of public opinion is often at the centre of political controversy. Certainly pressure groups often appear to believe that if they can demonstrate a preponderance of public support for *their* position, that Parliament would have an 'obligation' to legislate their group's preferences. Yet pressure groups have a fall-back position as well. An intended 'tyranny of the majority' can be denounced for seeking to interfere with basic rights which no majority, no matter how clear-cut, can legitimately take away. Had the Royal Commission stated that public opinion had no bearing on these issues because they dealt with rights so basic that majorities could not take them away, it would have been arguing on familiar grounds about which there are legitimate differences of opinion amongst democratic theorists.

The position of survey researchers on these matters is clear. Professionalism compels a concern with discovering and communicating the way the public feels about political issues,[16] irrespective of the preferences of the researcher, the delicacy of the issue, the claims of sectional interests or the views of policy-makers. As the Director of the National Research Bureau observed: 'We try to find out what the public thinks. It is not our job to criticise people as ignorant or misinformed'.[17]

The Complexity of Electoral Choice

The act of voting is not without its stresses and burdens. The voter is compelled to make decisions, often on the basis of limited information. Non-participation may be one way of avoiding such stress. In local body elections, in which the system has been less helpful in simplifying voter choice, non or partial-participation (voting for fewer than the full slate of city council candidates, for example) is virtually the norm.[18] General elections present their own dilemmas. While the voter is only required to select a candidate for Parliament, this choice is inextricably bound up with attitudes towards the party leader, who becomes the next Prime Minister if the voter's choice is duplicated by a plurality of voters in a majority of electorates. In fact, voters are required to balance a number of assessments simultaneously in arriving at a 'rational' voting choice, including: (1) the qualities of the respective candidates for MP; (2) the qualities of the respective party leaders; (3) the programmes and philosophies of the competing parties; (4) the qualities of the party leadership teams, the future executive (Cabinet) of the country; (5) the needs of the electorate. What constitutes a 'rational choice' is not always easy to determine. In Dunedin North in 1975, for example,[19] habitual Labour voters *wanted* a Labour government, *expected* a Labour government, wanted Mr Rowling as Prime Minister, yet deserted their party in sufficient numbers to elect a National MP (Richard Walls). It was their expectations that Labour would be elected the government anyway, and therefore did not need Dunedin North, that freed these voters (who continue to identify themselves as supporters of the Labour Party) to vote for a National MP. In other words, these Labour voters thought that they could simultaneously obtain both a Labour government, *and* their preferred candidate. That they were wrong does not invalidate their electoral choice, nor their experience of politics as citizens.

Is it 'rational' to vote for the more competent candidate of a party for whom one may feel little sympathy? On the other hand, is it 'rational' to vote for a candidate whom one regards as less able, because of his membership in the party of one's choice? Is it 'rational' to vote for or against a candidate because of one's attitudes towards the leaders of the major parties? Is it 'irrational' to vote for a candidate, or a party, because of a strong preference for one of the policies in the potpourri found in any manifesto? Given the compression of alternatives into a single voting act, it is difficult to avoid a general conclusion about the use of terms like 'rationality' and 'irrationality'. These terms may be nothing more (nor less) than labels which some people use to describe the behaviour and experience of other people, according to criteria reflecting their own behaviour and experience.

One frequent argument *against* the use of the referendum in politics is that the voters are unequipped to cope with the task of arriving at difficult policy choices.[20] However, given the complexity of New Zealand elections imposed by the parliamentary fusion between the executive and legislature, and the disciplined party system, the use of referenda may in fact *decrease* the complexity of electoral decision-making.[21] The separation of issues in special polls, conducted at the time of the general election, imposes minimal expense and may significantly *reduce* the costs of decision-making for voters. Moreover, the results of general elections may serve as a more unambiguous guide to public preferences, if they are supplemented regularly by referenda on important issues in dispute amongst the parties.[22] The voters of other political systems (Australia; many of the American states) have possessed a sufficient literacy to 'cope' with exercising a preference towards issues of public policy. In Great Britain the referendum has won favour in the 1970s to measure opinions on the transcendent political issues of British membership in the European Community, and devolution of powers to assemblies in Scotland and Wales. In New Zealand, the voters have been polled irregularly in the past on various proposals, including one involving the extension of the parliamentary term[23] and another on the introduction of compulsory military service.[24] Moreover, voters have participated in numerous local referenda on liquor licensing questions, while no fewer than fifteen nation-wide referenda have been conducted on three liquor licensing alternatives.[25]

TABLE 5:8 *Results of Nation-wide Liquor Licensing Referenda, 1960–1978*

Voting issue	1960	1963	1966	1969	1972	1975	1978
For national continuance	765,952	791,767	817,760	903,962	931,778	1,094,445	1,054,336
For State purchase and control	138,644	157,581	176,946	242,499	244,003	235,374	252,496
For national prohibition	255,157	235,959	198,859	176,055	203,791	250,640	374,518

TABLE 5:9 *Results of Referendum on the Length of the Parliamentary Term, 1967 (23 September)*

Support for present maximum 3-year term	678,960
Support for maximum 4-year term	317,973

TABLE 5:10 *Results of Referendum on Conscription, 1949 (3 August)*

For compulsory military training	568,427
Against compulsory military training	160,998

There is little basis for suggesting that the New Zealand electorate is incapable of expressing an independent judgement towards other issues as well. It should be possible for an independent commission to frame questions assessing public attitudes towards more urgent issues of public controversy. If Parliament is unwilling to place questions on the ballot, through its own efforts or those of an independent commission, it ought to be possible in law for the voters themselves to take action to secure referenda on issues of public importance. In Switzerland and in many American states, for example, questions are placed on the ballot when petitions secure a sufficient number of signatures as provided by law. Such legislation encourages citizen participation, and in New Zealand could contribute to the resolution of problems too politically sensitive for government to confront squarely. The results of referenda, however organised, could serve as a guide to policy-makers which would significantly alter parliamentary debate. So often such debate involves conflicting claims, intuitively developed, about public attitudes, claims which nearly always coincide with the preferences of the MP holding the floor. A creative use of referenda can contribute to the parliamentary process of decision-making, and can enhance the character of democratic politics in New Zealand.

This was recognised in 1978 by the Labour party, which pledged to hold a referendum on the abortion issue. This followed the refusal of Parliament to amend rather than repeal the Abortion, Contraception and Sterilisation Act, despite a petition which gained 321,119 signatures (the third largest in New Zealand's history). Similarly, Social Credit (particularly on local issues and ratepayers' demands) and Values have from time to time expressed support for a more widespread use of referenda. Mr Beetham (Social Credit, Rangitikei) unsuccessfully sought to amend the legislation governing local body referenda following the Wellington City Council's rejection of a petition calling for a poll on the Council's programme to construct a new town hall. Perhaps more significantly, the 1978 campaign witnessed a remarkable (though largely unsuccessful) effort by branches of the Womens Electoral Lobby to persuade voters *to regard the referendum on liquor licensing as a referendum on the abortion laws!* Since Parliament had refused to repeal the abortion laws, or to authorise a referendum on the subject, voters were urged to transform the only referendum that was available (and one which travestied the referendum process, for no doubt existed about the outcome) and remake it into one that suited their own purposes. Thus voters were urged to vote for prohibition, partially to demonstrate to legislators some of the guilt and anxiety that might be involved in seeking to procure a prohibited service, and partially to 'punish' the government for its failure to repeal the abortion laws by depriving it of needed revenues obtained from the sale, manufacture and distribution of liquor in New Zealand.

Of course the pro-Repeal group assumed that a substantial increase in the vote for prohibition over its expected level, based on the recent referenda, would be interpreted as a vote for repeal rather than prohibition, and that therefore repeal of the abortion laws rather than prohibition of liquor would be the consequence. Paradoxically, the pro-repeal prohibitionists returned the women's movement to its source, by involving itself in the temperance issue, but with a quite profoundly altered emphasis. For its part, the groups advocating prohibition did not welcome this unexpected and unusual coalition of support. Moreover, some advocates of a 'single-issue' vote concentrating on defeating parliamentary candidates (regardless of party) supporting the present abortion laws withheld their approval for the initiative, describing it as 'dishonest'. Yet this may be viewed as a dishonesty arising out of the government's refusal to adopt procedures to widen opportunities for the direct expression of sentiments by the voters on major issues. Clearly citizens ought not to be compelled to fashion such desperate efforts, out of utter frustration with a political system of surpassing structural inflexibility. It is critically important that the present referendum on liquor licensing–a superfluous measure, since it provides information about public attitudes when these are not in doubt–should be augmented, if not replaced, by referenda more responsive to the needs and concerns of the public.

By-Elections

In New Zealand, these contests are far less frequent than in Britain, for example, a function of the far smaller House of Representatives and the significantly shorter parliamentary term. Thus, in Britain it can be expected that during the nominal five-year term of the government, there will be a fairly sizeable number of deaths and resignations occurring within the House of Commons. A government's term of office will be peppered by a series of haphazardly scheduled by-elections. In most cases, each by-election is approached by the parties, the media and, apparently, the voters themselves (for the most part) as a mini-general election. Each contest is a miniature public opinion poll on the government's performance in office and on the credibility of opposition alternatives. The sample is complete, involving all participating enrolled voters in the electorate in which the by-election is being held. The researcher can augment the by-election, by obtaining information from voters on the reasons for their voting choice. The by-election itself, however, attracts enormous attention as a reliable measure of support for the government and the opposition parties. Moreover, by-election results can have a politically significant effect in a number of ways in Great Britain: (1) they can alter the timing for the next general election, encouraging the government to move a general election closer or cautioning the government to delay a general election until its prospects become more favourable; (2) they can alter political influence within the parties, as various factions seek to claim credit or apportion blame for the outcome; (3) they can alter the character of parliamentary life, by changing Opposition tactics depending on whether the government emerges as one in precipitous decline, or, by contrast, one secure in the public estimation.

None of these features has assumed very much significance within New Zealand. Governments usually serve out their full term. Since 1946 only one early election (in 1951) has been called, and this was not a consequence of by-election results. Parliamentary parties are relatively small; for the governing party, a large proportion of its members will be serving in Cabinet while the rest may expect, in time, to do so if the party remains in power (and they can keep their seats). Factions are small, few and not institutionalised (unlike the Tribune Group in the British Labour party, or the Democratic Study Group in the U.S. House of Representatives, which have their own regular caucuses and leadership structures). New Zealand by-elections rarely affect, except momentarily, the life of a Parliament. MPs withdraw from Wellington to campaign in the electorate, and this may affect committee work and the conduct of parliamentary business but not in a politically vital manner.

The number of by-elections per parliamentary session has ranged since the general election of 1908 from a low of none (in the 1963–6 session) to a high of fourteen (in the extended 1914–19 session coinciding with the First World War). The mean number of by-elections during the 1908–77 period has been four, although in normal circumstances it may be expected that there will be between one and three by-elections during a parliamentary term.[26]

TABLE 5:11 *Number of By-elections per Parliamentary Term, 1908–1977*

Number of by-elections during parliamentary term	*Number of terms*	*Dates of parliamentary terms*
0	1	1963–1966
1	4	1935–1938; 1949–1951; 1969–1972; 1972–1975
2	3	1925–1928; 1954–1957; 1957–1960
3	3	1911–1914; 1922–1925; 1946–1949
4	2	1951–1954; 1975–1978
5	3	1908–1911; 1931–1935; 1943–1946
6	1	1966–1969
7	3	1919–1922; 1928–1931; 1960–1963
9	1	1938–1943*
14	1	1914–1919
Totals: 92 by-elections	22 parliamentary terms	

* Vacancies occurring in 1943 in Northern Maori, Pahiatua and Kaipara were not filled until the general election.

It is unclear that voters approach the by-election as a 'referendum' on the performance of the government, or as a mini-general election. Recognising that much less is at stake, the voters (in smaller numbers than at general elections) appear to act out their habitual voting patterns. There tends, however, to be a 'swing' against the government, although its range is confined to limited proportions; few seats change from one party to the other, although in rare instances the party holding a seat may lose it in a by-election. Of forty-six by-elections held in the 1936–78 period, this has happened only five times. In Bay of Plenty (26 November 1941), and Raglan (5 March 1946), seats held by the governing Labour Party were lost to the National Opposition. In Palmerston North (2 December 1967) and

Marlborough (21 February 1970), seats held by the governing National Party were captured by Labour candidates, and the loss in Marlborough, in particular, seemed to make the Labour victory in 1972 more likely. In Rangitikei (18 February 1978), the Social Credit leader, Bruce Beetham, won a by-election from National following the death of the Speaker, Sir Roy Jack, in an election characterised by a weak Labour performance and in an electorate subject to substantial boundary changes in the general election less than twelve months later. Despite this performance, Social Credit has never done especially well in by-elections. It might be assumed that with control of government not at stake, voters might feel that votes for a third party would be less likely to be 'wasted'. Of course in a Parliament in which the government clings to power with a 1-seat majority, a by-election in a seat held by the governing party would involve high stakes indeed—but this circumstance has not thus far occurred in New Zealand. Nevertheless, prior to the Rangitikei victory Social Credit's best performance was in Sydenham (2 November 1974) when it obtained 16.8 per cent of the vote. However, National did not contest that by-election which followed the death of Labour Prime Minister Norman Kirk, and marked the entrance into Parliament of his son, John. Otherwise, the Social Credit vote has never been higher than 15.3 per cent in Palmerston North (2 December 1967) and 15.0 per cent in Eastern Maori (12 August 1967). The Values Party has contested five by-elections, and its best performance was in Nelson (28 February 1976) when it captured 1,524 votes (8.8 per cent). While swings against the government are the norm, therefore, they tend to benefit the main opposition party rather than the third party. In only four of thirty-two by-elections since the Second World War has there been a swing towards the government: in Hutt (3 August 1968), Eastern Maori (12 August 1967), Northern Maori (16 March 1963) and Clutha (18 January 1958). In each of these cases, however, the seats were retained by the major opposition party's candidates.

New Zealand by-elections are enormously significant in one vital (and neglected) respect: *recruitment of political leadership*. For example, Labour Prime Ministers first entering the House as a result of a by-election include Peter Fraser, Walter Nash and Wallace ('Bill') E. Rowling, while for National Sir Keith Holyoake was first elected to Parliament in a by-election held in Motueka in 1932. Many other major political leaders in New Zealand's history have been elected to the House in a by-election, including Robert Semple, former Labour Leaders of the Opposition Henry E. Holland and Arnold Nordmeyer, Deputy Prime Ministers (Labour) Hugh Watt and Robert J. Tizard and Cabinet Ministers of both parties, including: (for Labour) H. May; M. Connelly; M. Rata; F. Colman; Sir Basil Arthur; (for National) P. Allen; L. Adams-Schneider; H. Pickering; E.S.F. Holland.

It is not entirely clear why this phenomenon should have occurred. However, given the infrequent character of New Zealand by-elections, it is extraordinary that so high a proportion of its major political figures should have first entered Parliament by this relatively uncommon path. It may well be that when selection is limited to only one electorate, the parties take special efforts to ensure that their candidate is one able to represent the party as a whole. With the focus of the media and the country on a single electoral contest, the party clearly is motivated to ensure that its candidate will be of superior quality. In 1977, the Mangere by-election results led newspapers already to cite the Labour winner, David Lange, as a 'future Prime Minister', and he quite quickly became Labour's second most popular MP in a nation-wide public opinion poll. Similarly, the successor to Sir Keith Holyoake in Pahiatua, John Falloon, emerged from a keenly fought selection contest to widespread expectations about his future role within the National Party. A 'safe' seat such as Pahiatua, of course, is likely to attract persons of talent interested in the opportunity of a parliamentary career likely to be secure from the vicissitudes of electoral competition.

By-elections have also played a role in introducing women into the New Zealand House of Representatives. Of the fifteen women who have entered the House of Representatives, seven have been elected initially in a by-election: Mrs McCombs (Labour); Mrs Dreaver (Labour); Mrs Grigg (National); Miss Howard (Labour); Dame Hilda Ross (National); Mrs McMillan (Labour); Mrs Tirikatene-Sullivan (Labour). *

It seems clear, however, that the pattern of women entering the House has undergone some transformation indicative of a maturing political culture. Initially, women entering Parliament did so through extraordinary circumstances: (1) by standing in a by-election; (2) securing nomination through relationship with previously active MPs. Thus Mrs McCombs succeeded her husband (and was, in turn, succeeded by her son in what was, for a time, a family fief); Mrs Grigg succeeded her husband (unopposed); Miss Howard was the daughter of a former MP; Mrs Ratana succeeded her husband, who, in turn, had succeeded his brother; Mrs McMillan was the widow of a former MP; Miss Tirikatene succeeded her father. This pattern of entry into political life is similar to that found in other political systems: Mrs Ghandi succeeded her father as Prime Minister of India; Mrs Bandaranaike succeeded her late husband as Prime Minister of

---

* Women MPs first elected at general elections include: Mrs Ratana (Labour); Mrs Tombleson (National); Mrs Stevenson (National); Mrs Jelicich (Labour); Mrs Batchelor (Labour); Miss Waring (National); Miss Dewe (National); Mrs Hercus (Labour).

Sri Lanka; Mrs Peron succeeded her late husband as President of Argentina. However, more recently in New Zealand, women have been able to establish themselves in Parliament without being anchored (at least at the outset) to an established male reputation. The last five women MPs, and seven of the last eight, have not been related to previously active husbands or fathers who enjoyed political careers.

The Maori Seats

The evolution of the Maori seats has been examined recently by McRobie.[27] From a temporary measure, these seats have evolved into a form of permanent ethnic representation for New Zealand's indigenous, or pre-European, population. Successive amendments to the Electoral Act have examined the basis of representation with a view towards partisan advantage. Labour sought to provide for an increase in the number of Maori seats, in anticipation of an increase in the number of persons registered on the separate Maori electoral rolls. By contrast, National effectively restored the previous legislative position, fixing the number of seats at four.

Tabacoff has identified the functions of the Maori MPs within a systems framework: (1) as an articulator of the community's demands, the MP expresses the needs and interests of the Maori people; (2) as an aggregator of demands, the MP organises those issues and policies affecting the Maori people within a larger political programme; (3) as a participant in the law-making process, the MP seeks to ensure that the special needs of the Maori people are not neglected.[28] Tabacoff concludes that:

> . . . it must be noted that at present there is still a special department dealing with Maori affairs and special laws dealing with Maori land. As long as there is a need for special regulations regarding the Maori population, there will still be a need for a separate group of legislators to protect Maori interests when conflicts arise. The Maori MP has shown that the function of legislator for a separate ethnic community can be performed within the national political system.[29]

However, there are unmistakeable indications of public displeasure with the Maori seats.[30] Many people appear to resent the seats, which seem to them to provide an unfair advantage to a group already receiving special benefits from the government.[31] On the other hand, these services are provided because of the disadvantaged position of the Maori in many areas, and in recognition of the special place of the Maori people in New Zealand society and culture.[32] Discussion of the Maori seats in Parliament is not free from emotion; moreover, debate centres on the principle of equity, which is not easily interpreted on this issue. Is it 'fair' to other disadvantaged minorities to maintain separate representation, indefinitely, solely for the Maori? Is it 'fair' to the majority to maintain a *guaranteed* representation for one ethnic group? Is it 'fair' to the Maori community to apportion the number of MPs to which they are entitled by a measure different from that used to apportion the number of MPs provided for the non-Maori population? The majority of New Zealanders, at least in the abstract, would appear to favour the abolition of the Maori seats rather than a rectification of their basis of apportionment.[33]

TABLE 5:12 *Attitudes of New Zealanders Towards Abolition of the Maori Seats, 1975*

Would you agree with the view that 'the separate Maori seats in Parliament ought to be abolished'?		
	No. of respondents	%
Disagree	436	27.2
Agree	1030	64.1
Other	54	3.4
Don't know	65	4.1
No answer	19	1.2

Much political debate resolves itself into calculations of electoral advantage. In some ways, it may be ironic that Labour has favoured the retention and, indeed, the expansion of the Maori seats, while National has struggled to maintain them in their present form. The relatively low participation of Maori voters in these seats may be attributed to impediments to voting[34] and, perhaps more significantly, to their one-party character. Voting studies elsewhere have discovered that, in general, constituencies lacking in meaningful electoral competition (i.e. 'safe' seats) have lower rates of voter turnout and political participation than constituencies where the outcome is less predictable. The Maori voters have been more sympathetic to Labour than any of the other parties for a long period. Many Maori voters reside in inner-city electorates in major urban centres vital to Labour. Other Maoris continue to live in rural areas that have been firmly National. The abolition of the Maori seats might be ultimately more favourable to Labour, which might become more secure in urban centres and begin to present a credible alternative in rural areas. The latter prospect would be helpful to *all* residents, for the needs of people in many 'safe' seats may often be neglected by parties whose leaders can take their support for granted. Democratic politics depend for their vitality on vigorous competition amongst parties with genuine prospects for electoral success. Finally, the disappearance of the Maori seats would encourage a fuller participation by Maoris in the 'dominant' political system, and might enable them to secure a more significant share of societal rewards than has thus far proved possible.

Proportional Representation and Parliamentary Size

Proportional representation (P.R.) has been proposed as a solution to the grip of the two-party system on New Zealand political life.[35] Mr Beetham's petition for P.R., launched with the hope of gaining more signatures than any previous petition in New Zealand history, failed to attain its objective. Submitted to Parliament in August 1977, it is impossible to determine whether this failure was the result of public opposition to or lack of interest in P.R., an unwillingness on the part of voters to become involved in a Social Credit-promoted scheme, or Social Credit's weak organisational structure and lack of resources.

One rally cry for Social Credit and other electoral reformers might have been: 'Remember 1911'. In that year, the Liberal Party won a plurality of the popular vote, by a considerable margin over its nearest opposition. Yet the Reform Party, with far fewer popular votes, won six more seats than the Liberals in the House of Representatives. In 1978, for the first time in more than half a century and in the first instance involving Labour–National competition, this very critical outcome has again occurred. Certainly an electoral system which can permit a party to secure power, despite having been defeated by another party in the popular vote, has a time bomb ticking away at its centre. Whether people will respect, or regard as legitimate, a government so formed may be questioned. There is little doubt that inside and outside of Parliament, a government's entire term will be beset by criticisms of its minority, 'undemocratic' character. A system which risks a serious erosion of support, by providing an opportunity for a party to be preferred by more New Zealanders than any alternative yet be defeated, is involved in a dangerous flirtation with instability and political paralysis.

New Zealanders have become accustomed to their winning party receiving less than an absolute majority (i.e. 50.1 per cent) of the votes, but that the country would accept a *genuine minority govern-ment*–one elected to govern despite obtaining fewer popular votes than its main opponent–remains to be determined. Certainly such an electoral outcome must produce a most unruly parliamentary session, one straining the remaining bonds of consensus considerably. It is indicative of the absence of political memory amongst New Zealanders that the 1911 election had not been cited in any way by P.R. reformers. In the United States, by contrast, every cycle of electoral reform proposals brought before Congress hearkens back to several presidential elections held *prior to 1900* to support the need for a more 'democratic' system! The 1978 outcome should increase interest in and support for P.R. in several respects: (1) the election of National despite Labour's slim popular-vote victory; (2) the disproportion between Social Credit's vote totals and its parliamentary representation; (3) the controversy over the errors, omissions and duplications in electoral rolls, arising in part out of a massive redistribution of electoral boundaries (affecting 83 electorates) which nevertheless failed to provide electorates of reasonably equal voting population by polling day. Under P.R., the disruption in rolls and boundaries occasioned by the present system could be avoided.

While proportional representation might reduce or eliminate altogether the need for massive electoral redistributions, there are some measures which could alleviate some of the problems in the present system while preserving its 'first past the post' character. Re-enrolment on the electoral rolls could be carried out through the Post Office, which has the detailed knowledge of addresses and locations and the personnel to do the job efficiently. Moreover, the time lag now existing between census and enrolment can be significantly reduced, so that re-enrolment could be undertaken through enrolment cards distributed through the Post Office in the July preceding a November election. A main roll so constructed ought to reduce the likelihood of errors and the suspicion of voting irregularities, and should reduce the number of special votes which need to be cast by persons omitted from the rolls.

The fundamental principle to be followed in devising and implementing any electoral system is the requirement that such a system be recognised as equitable by all parties and by the general public. Practices which can lead to misinterpretation, and undermine the confidence of the public in the fairness and honesty of the electoral outcome, represent a very real danger which, if not remedied, must threaten the political system in a range of subtle ways. It would be helpful, for example, if significant minor parties could be represented along with Labour and National on the Representation Commission to scrutinise and comment upon suggested boundary changes. Similarly, scrutineers from all parties ought to be represented (if they so wish) when decisions about the validity of special votes are made.

In 1978, the number of special votes greatly exceeded the majority won on election night by a significant number of candidates. Given the closeness of the over-all outcome, the refusal of the Leader of the Opposition to concede defeat, the preceding months-long controversy over the electoral rolls (and the threat to the voting rights of members of the public), and the deep divisions in the community over the Prime Minister's approach to government, New Zealand could ill-afford the spectacle of several weeks of uncertainty about the identity of its government over the next three years. Considering the prevailing disenchantment with Parliament, politicians and the major parties, it could scarcely have been desirable for voters to feel that the outcome of the election could be determined by decisions (over the validity of special votes) made in the office of the Chief Electoral Officer, or by Returning Officers (each using their own criteria to rule on the validity of special votes) in electorates won by small majorities.

Certainly P.R. would stimulate electoral competition throughout the country. Under P.R., it would be profitable for parties to compete vigorously in every part of the country, since every vote would 'count', and a plurality of the votes in an electorate might no longer become the overriding objective. Minor parties might be expected to accumulate increased strength, for voters preferring them would no longer be compelled to make a calculated, 'smart' vote. No votes would be 'wasted', and voters could act on their genuine preference without feeling that they had been 'irresponsible'.

> Under a system of proportional representation, Social Credit would indubitably win some seats, but it is precisely the succour such a scheme would provide to the third parties which assures that neither National nor Labour will permit its adoption.[36]

As on the issue of parliamentary reform, it is clearly not realistic to expect the dominant parties to restructure an electoral system which works to their benefit. Nor is there any reason *necessarily* why Parliament should adopt an alternative voting system, such as P.R. Its adherents have not made a conclusive case, other than to suggest that minor parties would be more likely to obtain representation in the House. The argument that voters do not have representation because the candidate or party of their choice has been defeated can not be sustained, yet it is made all the time. The Social Credit and Values voters, and the voters for Labour and National candidates who have been defeated in their electorates, are represented in the House by an MP. That the MP was not the one for whom they cast their vote does not mean that these voters are 'not represented', or that democratic procedures have been violated. One might equally argue that Acts of Parliament not passed unanimously are undemocratic. The MPs of one party were outvoted so that the people whom they represented were, by extension, deprived of their preference.

Persons seeking P.R. would be on more secure ground were they to demonstrate that positive consequences would flow through the political system by the adoption of such an electoral programme. The present system is both democratic and representational. However, its operations tend to stifle political competitiveness and to discourage political participation by interested voters. Moreover, certain voters–Social Credit, Values, and 'losing' voters in safe, one-party seats–become permanently excluded from and cynical towards a system in which their chances of political success are virtually nil.

Persons permanently excluded by a system have little reason to feel loyalty towards it, and neither a withdrawal from public affairs nor the development of a bitter, mistrustful attitude towards the 'system' are features which an electoral system ought to be promoting.[37]

Critics of P.R. often claim that it leads to unstable government. As Lipson has commented:

> On the figures, then, proportional representation seems to have a strong case . . . What believers in 'P.R.' usually overlook is the effect of their schemes on the working of the legislature. Ideally from the electoral point of view it is desirable to have a legislature which is truly representative. To be so, Parliament must embody the various shades of opinion and must reproduce each in its precise quantitative strength. Yet never was political truth more evident than that a legislature so constituted could not legislate effectively, could not reach decisions without wrecking its principles by half-hearted compromise, and could not be organised to maintain a stable government. 'P.R.' holds out hypothetical electoral salvation with one hand and positive legislative damnation with the other . . . 'P.R.' encourages a multiparty Parliament, and that is often the parent of weak government.[38]

Yet more recent analysis, examining the experience of seventeen Western political systems from 1918 to 1974, suggests that stable and responsive government may be attained in multi-party *or* majority party parliaments. Observing that 'the mystery of parliamentary government . . . baffles and fascinates the political analyst', Dodd claims that there is a 'myth of multipartism':

> (1) governments in multiparty parliaments must be minority cabinets, coalition cabinets or both; (2) by their very nature, minority cabinets and coalition cabinets are quite transient; (3) multiparty systems are consequently undesirable since they produce transient governments.[39]

Indeed, James Callaghan, the present British Prime Minister, once rejected the possibility of a coalition government in Great Britain with these words: 'A coalition is like a mule. It has no pride of ancestry and no hope of posterity'.[40]

Yet stable, authoritative and representative government need *not* be based upon a two-party model involving majority party government and a single-member district, plurality 'first past the post' electoral system. As Dodd's brilliant study concludes:

> It is conceivable that too few parties are just as detrimental in particular settings as too many parties. Perhaps Lord Bryce was wrong when he wrote that since 'there must be parties, the fewer

and stronger they are, the better'. If a party system fails to provide broad representation of citizens' views, society may disintegrate because of (rather than despite) the existence of majority party rule.[41]

Questioning whether democracy is well served by 'a system forcing public opinion into two moulds', Dodd argues that

Political choice among several minority parties need not undermine political stability; quite the contrary, a party system reflecting a moderately diverse range of views conceivably could integrate the citizenry through open recognition of and competition between competing minority perspectives, activating the instinct for community by the development of widespread appreciation of and commitment to democratic processes.[42]

New Zealand voters have been given the opportunity in the past to vote, in a referendum held simultaneously with a general election, on a significant feature of their electoral system: the length of the parliamentary term.[43] This was an issue lacking the complexity of the debate over alternative electoral systems, but one nevertheless of fundamental importance within the democratic process. It would be desirable for a paper to be prepared setting forth the arguments for competing electoral systems, to be printed and distributed at government expense through the Post Office. Such a booklet, containing contributions from individuals and groups favouring different systems, would provide the basis for a discussion and debate of this issue prior to a general election, at which time a referendum on the subject might usefully be held.

Table 5:13 describes a range of electoral systems available in democratic polities.

Each system involves different kinds of consequences. Because the kind of system used structures voters' behaviour, it may be misleading to simply transpose electoral results produced under one system into the framework of another system. Therefore, it is difficult to determine what would have happened in a previous election under a particular electoral system. However, Social Credit can be expected to assert that its share of the vote would have 'entitled' the League to more than a dozen seats during the 1978–81 term. Under preferential voting, however, it is likely that in 1975 Values would have been the second choice of many Labour and National voters, although this position might have been surrendered to Social Credit in 1978. The practical effects of such preferences are uncertain, however. Under a preferential voting system in which the voters for minor parties have their second choice assigned to other parties when no candidate secures a majority within an electorate, it would normally have been Values or Social Credit voters who would have had their second choice allocated amongst Labour or National candidates. In 1978, however, in certain electorates the second choice of Labour voters would have been allocated, and in those instances in all probability the Social Credit candidate would have edged past the National candidate. In rural electorates in which Labour has fallen into third place behind National and Social Credit, therefore, the effect of preferential voting might be to enable Social Credit to acquire additional seats and a balance-of-power position in Parliament (and, possibly, Cabinet).

Since the Labour and National parties are incapable of considering this issue dispassionately, a referendum on proposals for electoral reform (including P.R.)–an issue which cuts across conventional lines of political difference in the community–would be a useful way of determining public sentiment in a binding manner. In particular, were the voters to favour *the present system* over any of the alternatives, this result might deprive citizens presently alienated from the two-party system of the opportunity of claiming that their parties had been deprived of representation through an 'undemocratic' conspiracy amongst the major parties' elites.

Proposals for P.R. are often associated with the argument that New Zealand requires a larger House of Representatives. It has been asserted that an increase in the size of Parliament would enlarge the pool of potential Cabinet Ministers, and ease the burden on over-worked MPs. Moreover, it is clear that the size of the New Zealand Parliament has not kept pace with population growth, although there is no inherent reason why it should do so. The size of the U.S. Congress, for example, has remained constant for a very long period (with the exception of the admission of new states), and the size of Congressional districts (rather than their number) are adjusted to correspond with shifts in the size and distribution of population.

The relationship between a country's population and its legislative size has not been resolved by political scientists.

> Countries which have populations below twenty million tend typically to have chambers of between one hundred and two hundred and fifty members; countries which are very small–one or two million, or less–tend to have chambers of only fifty members or less.[46]

Moreover, Dahl and Tufte observe: 'Although population is not the only explanation of parliamentary size, it is by far the most powerful . . . Population size is clearly the most important describing variable; taken alone it describes 76 per cent of the variation in parliamentary size.'[47]

TABLE 5:13 *Types of Electoral System*[44]

Electoral unit	Type of ballot	Consequences	Advantages	Disadvantages
Single member district	Candidate(s) with most votes wins (win), whether or not they have a majority of the vote ('first past the post'). Single vote cast; system can be altered to permit run-off ballots until absolute majority (50.1%) obtained.	Produces majority winner. Narrows voter choice to probable winner. Favours best-organised electoral forces.	Simple; short ballot paper; single member to represent constituency; usually ensures one party has parliamentary majority.	Minorities under-represented (unless geographically concentrated); composition of legislature does not reflect national voting figures; party may have parliamentary majority with only small minority of the vote; gerrymandering and population shifts can produce inequities in value of vote between districts.
Multi-member district; single-member district	Voter has chance to express second choice, either in the same or on another ballot, if no candidate(s) has (have) absolute majority on the first ballot.	*Preferential system* permits representation of minority candidates; may result in either majority or minority representation, with tendency towards latter.	Simple; short ballot paper; single-member seats possible; candidates can stand without fear of splitting vote for right or left and so letting in minority opponent.	Results may be as disproportionate as in 'first past the post' system; system may require extra ballots and trips to the polls by voters; system may depend on electoral 'deals' amongst competing parties.

| Multi-member district | Seats shared by parties; all candidates elected according to parties' share of the vote. List system requires voter to cast one ballot for entire party list. Single, transferable vote (STV) allows voters to rank candidates in order of preference, with seats allocated by successive choices. | *Proportional representation* permits representation by minority parties, and reflects most accurately the parties' share of the total vote. One-party majority in Parliament unlikely. | Fewer wasted votes; composition of legislature reflects voting figures; minorities represented. STV gives most choice to voters and loosens party grip on elections; list system easier for voters to use. | Results depend on different formulae used to allocate seats; constituencies are usually large and ballot papers long and complex. STV requires long ballot paper; list systems require larger electorates and lead to strong party control. |

FIGURE 5:1 *Population Growth in New Zealand 1840–1978*[45]

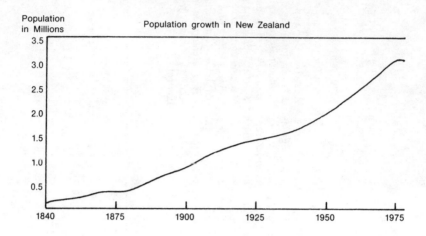

FIGURE 5:2 *Number of Members of House of Representatives and Legislative Council 1853–1978*

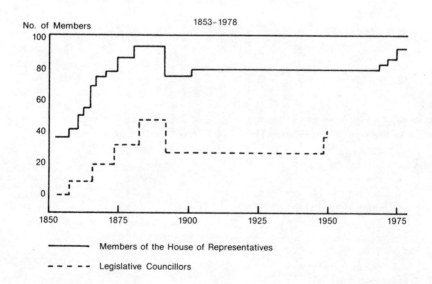

FIGURE 5:3 *Total Number of Members of Parliament, 1853–1978*

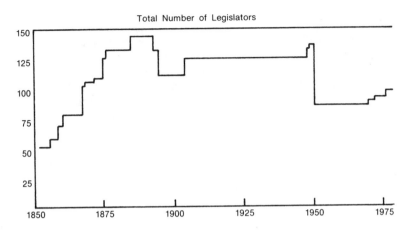

Total Number of Legislators

*Legislative Council abolished in 1950.

Partially because of its unicameral legislature, New Zealand (by world standards) has a very small legislative assembly in relation to its population. Yet New Zealand's early parliamentary life was characterised by inconsistency in the size of its House of Representatives. From 1853 to 1902, there were *eleven* alterations in the size and composition of the House of Representatives, which ranged from 37 MPs in 1853 to 95 in 1881. In 1902, with a population of under one million, the size of the House was fixed at 80, and remained so until 1969 (when it was enlarged to 84). The 1965 Electoral Act, however, allocated a minimum quota of seats to the South Island (25), and made provision for successive increases in the size of the House following each census.[48]

Recent proposals, however, have sought more extensive increases in the size of the House. The 1974 Labour Party Conference endorsed a remit calling for the 'Government to increase Parliamentary electorates to a minimum of 120 after the 1976 census and in time for the 1978 General Election'. Of thirty-two MPs interviewed in one study, nearly 80 per cent agreed that an increase was desirable, although only a third of National MPs favoured enlarging the House. As one National MP observed: 'I'm not absolutely convinced a sudden increase is going to work miracles; the situation is not nearly as bad as it is made out to be'.[49] Many MPs felt that improvements in conjunction with an increase in parliamentary size would need to be made to effect an improvement in parliamentary performance. Without procedural reforms, most of the proposals advocated for increasing the size of the House would not markedly reduce the pattern of demands made on MPs by constituents. At present, MPs represent fewer than 40,000 constituents; increasing parliamentary size to 100 would mean a constituency of about 30,000, scarcely likely to result in a significant decrease in demands on MPs.

Committee work would also be affected by increasing parliamentary size. An increase to 120 members would enlarge the personnel available to man committees by over one-third, and reduce MP's present committee commitments by over one-quarter, while a membership of 130 would bring about even more significant results. In addition, an increase of some magnitude would provide a healthier balance between Cabinet and caucus. At present, the large number of Ministers in proportion to total caucus size can lead to Cabinet domination of caucus. Increasing the size of the House to either 120 or 130 could significantly alter this power balance; a larger caucus could enable caucus to play a more forceful, independent role as a 'check' against executive power. Of course, this may be one factor behind opposition to an increase in size; as one former National Minister commented: 'The only advantage I can see is in a more independent back-bench who can thumb their noses at the party over major matters.'[50] However, 'if the M.P. is [not only] overworked, but also working ineffectively,'[51] because of a House that is too small for the system's requirements, an increase in parliamentary size should become part of a comprehensive programme of institutional regeneration.

References

1. S. Levine and A.D. Robinson, *The New Zealand Voter*, involved a study of voting behaviour and an examination of New Zealanders' attitudes towards selected political issues.
2. This study, in preparation, is a collaborative work undertaken by S. Levine (Victoria University of Wellington), N.S. Roberts (University of Canterbury) and G.A. Wood (University of Otago) to explore the 'personal vote' in New Zealand. The study is primarily concerned with measuring voters' attitudes towards and knowledge about candidates for parliament and leaders of the New Zealand parties, although sufficient data on the background of voters has been obtained to permit measurement of the sources of party support.
3. This study was an attempt to examine voting behaviour in a New Zealand by-election, at which the consequences of voting choice are different from those following a general election. The study examined voters' perceptions of issues, candidates, party leaders, the parties themselves and the needs of their community, and is analysed (in part) in S. Levine, 'The Nelson By-Election: Politics in a New Zealand Community' in S. Levine (ed.), *Politics in New Zealand: A Reader*, pp. 222–240.

4. A.D. Robinson, *op. cit.*, pp. 44–5.
5. K.J. Scott, 'The Floating Vote in New Zealand', *Landfall*, vol. 4, March 1950, p. 63.
6. See S. Levine, 'The Nelson By-Election: Politics in a New Zealand Community', *op. cit.*, for discussion of methodology and analysis of additional features of the study. The figures from the Nelson study have been used because the nation-wide figures have been published in *The New Zealand Voter*, and this will permit further comparison and documentation of the sources of political partisanship in New Zealand to be made. At the same time, the use of these figures augments the data reported in *Politics in New Zealand: A Reader*. Interesting comparative data on voting behaviour and the sources of political partisanship can be found in D. Butler and D. Stokes, *Political Change in Britain: Forces Shaping Electoral Choice*, London: Macmillan and Company Ltd., 1974; H.R. Penniman (ed.), *Britain at the Polls: The Parliamentary Elections of 1974*, Washington, D.C.: American Enterprise Institute for Public Policy Research, 1974; D. Aitkin, *Stability and Change in Australian Politics*, Canberra: Australian National University Press, 1977.
7. J.R. Marshall, speech to the University of Auckland, 1969.
8. K.J. Scott, 'The Floating Vote in New Zealand', *op. cit.*, pp. 60–1; 65.
9. D.H. Monro, 'Some Thoughts on the General Election', *Landfall*, vol. 4, March 1950, p. 78.
10. 'Why Labour won' (or 'why National lost') can be found in N.S. Roberts, 'The General Election of 1972', N.E. Kirk, 'The Philosophy of the Labour Party', T. Simpson, 'Huey Long's Other Island: Style in New Zealand Politics' and S. Levine, 'An Interview with John L. Roberts: Labour After Nine Months' in S. Levine (ed.), *New Zealand Politics: A Reader*; B. Lockstone and W. Page, *Landslide '72*, Dunedin; John McIndoe, 1973; J. Eagles and C. James, *The Making of a New Zealand Prime Minister*, Wellington, Cheshire, 1972; B. Edwards (ed.), *Right Out: Victory '72–The Inside Story*, Wellington: A.H. and A.W. Reed, 1973. The colour of National's campaign material was cited by K. Comber (MP for Wellington Central) in 'The National Campaign in Wellington Central' in S. Levine (ed.), *New Zealand Politics: A Reader* and by R.D. Muldoon (then Leader of the Opposition) in *The Rise and Fall of a Young Turk*, Wellington: A.H. and A.W. Reed, 1974.
11. 'Why National won' (or 'why Labour lost') can be found in N.S. Roberts, 'The New Zealand General Election of 1975', *Australian Quarterly*, vol. 48, no. 1, March 1976, pp. 97–114; G.A. Wood, *Why National Won*, Dunedin: John McIndoe, 1975; S. Levine and J. Lodge, *op. cit.*; S. Levine and A.D. Robinson, *op. cit.*, especially Chapters 12 and 14; C. Wilkes, 'The Great New Zealand Melodrama' in S. Levine (ed.), *Politics in New Zealand: A Reader*, pp. 207–221.
12. M. Goot and E. Reid, *Women and Voting Studies: Mindless Matrons or Sexist Scientism*, London: Sage Publications, 1975.
13. Analysis is based on data obtained in the Nelson survey.
14. See A. Downs, *An Economic Theory of Democracy*, New York: Harper & Row, 1957; S.J. Brams, *Paradoxes in Politics: An Introduction to the Nonobvious in Political Science*, New York: The Free Press, 1976.
15. *Report of the Royal Commission on Abortion, Contraception and Sterilisation in New Zealand*, Wellington: Government Printer, 1977, p. 231.
16. See B.D. Murphy's concluding comments in 'Public Opinion Polling in New Zealand' in S. Levine (ed.), *New Zealand Politics: A Reader*.

17. *Evening Post* (Wellington), 10 July 1977.
18. See J. Halligan and P. Harris, *op. cit.*; J.C. Blydenburgh, 'Innovation in New Zealand Local Government Election Campaigns' in S. Levine (ed.), *New Zealand Politics: A Reader*; J.C. Blydenburgh, 'The Effect of Ballot Form on City Council Elections', *Political Science*, vol. 26, 1974, pp. 47–55.
19. See the forthcoming Levine, Roberts and Wood study of six electorates.
20. This view was expressed forcefully at the 1977 National Party Conference in Dunedin, where a remit was defeated (narrowly) calling for a referendum on the abortion issue.
21. For a comparative view of the use of the referendum to augment decision-making, see G. Smith, 'The Referendum and Political Change', *Government and Opposition*, no. 3, Summer 1975, pp. 294–305.
22. See S. Levine and A.D. Robinson, *op. cit.*, Chapter 14. Moreover, voters appear to endorse a more frequent use of referenda held to sample voter opinion towards a variety of issues of controversy. See the figures for questions examining attitudes towards the use of referenda in S. Levine and A.D. Robinson, *op. cit.*, pp. 103–8. Voters of all parties supported abolition of the liquor referendum and its replacement by referenda on more topical issues.
23. See *New Zealand Official Yearbook* 1976, p. 930.
24. *New Zealand Gazette*, vol. 2, 1949.
25. *New Zealand Official Yearbook* 1976, p. 930.
26. Sources for all by-election data are: the Chief Electoral Officer, Department of Justice, Wellington; *Appendices to the Journal of the House of Representatives*.
27. See A.D. McRobie, 'Ethnic Representation: The New Zealand Experience' in S. Levine (ed.), *Politics in New Zealand: A Reader*, pp. 270–283.
28. See D. Tabacoff, 'The Role of the Maori MP in Contemporary New Zealand Politics' in S. Levine (ed.), *New Zealand Politics: A Reader,* pp. 374–83.
29. *Ibid.*, p. 382.
30. The National Party, sensitive to public opinion on some issues, clearly decided that there was electoral mileage to be gained by making an issue out of Labour's changes to the electoral laws to provide for increases in the number of Maori seats. National's repeal of these changes reflects the party's view that the Maori seats are not popular with non-Maori voters. For an interesting debate on the government's measure carrying out 'a manifesto commitment', see *N.Z.P.D.*, pp. 2845–56, 1 October 1976; pp. 3074–83, 13 October 1976.
31. See S. Levine and A.D. Robinson, *op. cit.*, pp. 95–9.
32. See A.D. McRobie, *op. cit.*; D. Tabacoff, *op. cit.*, pp. 381–2.
33. S. Levine and A.D. Robinson, *op. cit.*, p. 97.
34. McRobie accounts for some non-participation in this way. See A.D. McRobie, 'Ethnic Representation: The New Zealand Experience', *op. cit.*
35. B. Beetham, 'The Case for Proportional Representation' in S. Levine (ed.), *Politics in New Zealand: A Reader*, pp. 284–287.
36. S. Levine and J. Lodge, *op. cit.*, p. 34.
37. See E.E. Schattschneider, *op. cit.*, especially Chapters 6–8.
38. L. Lipson, *op. cit.*
39. L.C. Dodd, *Coalitions in Parliamentary Government*, Princeton, New Jersey: Princeton University Press, 1976, p. 10.
40. Quoted in L.C. Dodd, *op.cit.*, p. 29.

41. L.C. Dodd, *op. cit.*, p. 242.
42. *Ibid.*, pp. 243–4.
43. See *New Zealand Official Yearbook* 1976, p. 930. How New Zealanders feel on this question at present is discussed in S. Levine and A.D. Robinson, *op. cit.*, pp. 99–101.
44. See A. Leiserson, 'Elections, Groups, and Parties: The Representation of Political Interests' in B. Brown, A.N. Dragnich and J.C. Wahlke (eds), *Government and Politics: An Introduction to Political Science*, New York: Random House, 1966, pp. 434–5; 'The Road to Electoral Reform', *The Economist*, 2 August 1975, pp. 13–23; 'How Elections Elect', *The Economist*, 6 December 1975, pp. 24–25; 'Electoral Systems', *International Encyclopedia of Social Sciences*, New York: Macmillan, 1968; S.E. Finer (ed.), *Adversary Politics and Electoral Reform*, London: Antony Wigram, 1975. For an interesting proposal involving the enlargement of Parliament through creation of a second tier of larger electorates chosen through special electoral procedures, see A.D. Robinson *et al.*, 'An Alternative Voting System: Submissions to The Electoral Act Committee of the House of Representatives', 1974 in J.R. Marshall (ed.), *The Reform of Parliament, op. cit.*
45. The source for these figures (updated) is J.M. Hundleby, *op. cit.*
46. J. Blondel, *An Introduction to Comparative Government*, New York: Praeger, 1969, p. 374.
47. R.A. Dahl and E.T. Tufte, *Size and Democracy*, California: Stanford University Press, 1973, p. 81.
48. See 'Entrenched Sections of the Electoral Act and Amendments' in L. Cleveland and A.D. Robinson (eds), *Readings in New Zealand Government*, Wellington: A.H. and A.W. Reed, 1972, pp. 297–300.
49. Quoted in J.M. Hundleby, *Parliamentary Size*, University of Canterbury, Department of Political Science, 1974, p. 73.
50. *Ibid.*, p. 82.
51. S.P. Cottrell, *op. cit.*, p. 53.

6 Interest Groups and Politics

The Necessity of Groups

On so many issues in New Zealand politics, the activities of pressure groups converging on decision-makers and dominating the media appear to evoke alarm and dismay. Pressure group politics is inevitable in a democratic society yet, paradoxically, fatigued politicians and citizens alike often feel angry and frustrated by these groups' conflicting and paralysing demands and claims. In many ways a fear of pressure groups represents an aversion to *politics*, a displeasure with the slow, often tedious, complex process by which the needs and aspirations of different groups and interests become reconciled. Sometimes the impatience of politicians leads to short-sighted recommendations, as in the suggestion of National's Attorney-General (Mr Thomson) that members of groups such as HART (Halt All Racist Tours) or CARE (Citizens Association for Racial Equality) should be liable to prosecution for comments made outside New Zealand which might be detrimental to race relations. Clearly this recommendation was intended, if enacted into law, to intimidate pressure group activity of a more vocal nature, and would have had a 'chilling' and inhibiting effect on freedom of expression.

In his Maiden Speech in Parliament as a Member for Tamaki, in 1961, Mr Muldoon observed:

> Over the years there has been a growth of pressure groups of various sectional interests. They follow a typical pattern of making press statements of a somewhat extravagant nature on matters affecting them. They hold annual conferences preferably attended by a Minister of the Crown so that they can beat more drums and get more free publicity, but any fair-minded man will discount their arguments substantially.[1]

Williams has described the opposition of CARP (Citizens Against Rising Prices) to 'secret' involvement in decision-making. One of CARP's objectives has been to open up the processes of government, to share information and alternatives with the public, and to avoid

124

becoming co-opted into the prevailing system of reciprocal manipulation between pressure groups and government. By contrast, Mr Muldoon went on to argue in his Maiden Speech that: 'Surely it is better to have groups meeting around a table in a reasonable manner to solve their problems for the good of us all. The policy of the Government is directed towards that end, because the Government believes that is a better and more reasonable way.'[2]

As a backbench MP, Muldoon was expressing a preference for *quiet, orderly policy-making* between groups and government, based upon a belief in their mutual reasonableness and an acceptance of shared objectives. It is precisely this absence of consensus, however, which precludes groups such as CARE, CARP and HART from disavowing public agitation in preference for participation in a framework of managed decision-making. The distrust of pressure groups, however, is not limited to the present Prime Minister. Many people appear to feel that there is something politically *unclean* about *private* organisations seeking to concentrate their collective powers for the achievement of public purposes. Certainly some of the suspicion directed towards trade unions is related to this theme.[3] There is resentment of the power of a group unelected by the majority, but which nevertheless seeks to exert major influence on public policy-making. The hostility many New Zealanders feel towards the more publicly active groups thus transcends opposition to the purposes which such groups seek to advance. There is an added antagonism towards these groups for their temerity in challenging the government, and opposing its judgement, will and public 'mandate'. In doing so, these groups are suspected of being inherently 'undemocratic', for their purposes are to overturn the preferences of the majority as expressed in government policy.

This suspicion of pressure group activity is never far below the surface in New Zealand and other Western democracies, and it is an underlying attitude which successive governments can exploit without much difficulty. For many people see the activities of these groups, and their members, as part of the atmosphere of decay and dangerous disorder captured in Yeats' verse:

> *Things fall apart; the centre cannot hold;*
> *Mere anarchy is loosed upon the world,*
> *The blood-dimmed tide is loosed, and everywhere*
> *The ceremony of innocence is drowned;*
> *The best lack all conviction, while the worst*
> *are full of passionate intensity . . .* [4]

These fears have a long history in democratic thought. For example, the theorists of the American constitutional system suggested that 'factions' would subvert the unity of the nation, rendering the exercise of responsible power by government a less predictable enterprise.

'Factions'–our modern-day interest groups–were 'this dangerous vice', whose consequence was that 'the public good is disregarded in the conflict of rival parties.' Factions were 'adverse to the rights of other citizens, or to the permanent and aggregate interests of the community'.[5]

In similar vein, contemporary New Zealand politicians argue that pressure groups interfere with the process of long-term planning, and in advancing their own claims disturb efforts to protect and promote the 'national interest'. However, while pressure groups may be irksome, they are not easily banished from the political realm.

There are two methods of curing the mischiefs of faction: the one, by removing its causes; the other, by controlling its effects. There are again two methods of removing the causes of faction: the one, by destroying the liberty which is essential to its existence; the other, by giving to every citizen the same opinions, the same passions, and the same interests.[6]

It should be clear that pressure groups arise out of a political climate which permits citizens to enjoy freedom of expression, and to co-operate together for the achievement of common purposes.[7] Certainly these groups may be divisive, endangering a unity which silence would preserve intact. Were these groups *not* permitted to form, or were New Zealand parties and institutions utterly unresponsive to their claims, the New Zealand political system would be considerably less democratic than it is at present. New Zealand political parties themselves may be viewed as clusters of interests, for each of the major parties appeals to separate, identifiable groups of people and each depends on competing pressure groups for their support and sustenance. New Zealanders' freedom of association permits like-minded persons to join together for common objectives, and to openly express themselves as a collective body on political issues of interest to them.

Liberty is to faction what air is to fire, an ailment without which it instantly expires. But it could not be less folly to abolish liberty, which is essential to political life, because it nourishes faction, than it would be to wish the annihilation of air, which is essential to animal life, because it imparts to fire its destructive agency.[8]

Since the rise of interest groups (and political parties) is inevitable in a free society, liberty will be protected *not* by seeking to discourage their activity but rather through the widest possible proliferation of such activity.

The smaller the society, the fewer probably will be the distinct parties and interests composing it; the fewer the distinct parties and interests, the more frequently will a majority be found of the same party; and the smaller the number of individuals composing a majority, and the smaller the compass within which they are placed, the more easily will they concert and execute their plans of oppression. Extend the sphere, and you take in a greater variety of parties and interests . . . [9]

Ultimately, Madison argued that 'the increased variety of parties' would make the emerging American democracy more secure, and the rights and liberties of its citizens more protected, than any alternative programme. A similar view has prevailed in New Zealand, for the most part, although it has not always been securely rooted amongst either country's citizenry. Nevertheless pressure groups by their existence and activity promote individual liberties and more responsive government. The more numerous the groups, and the more vigorous their public activity, the more secure is the democratic process within which these groups contend and compete.

Types of Interest Groups

Robinson defines a pressure group as: ' . . . a privately organised group which seeks to influence government policies mainly by means other than that of seeking political office. It differs from a political party which is mainly concerned with obtaining or retaining political office.'[10]

Both interest groups and political parties serve as 'input structures' for the political system, in that each serves as a channel for the transmission of political demands to the government. While parties nominate candidates for elective office, group activity (in the electoral process) attempts to influence party policies and to promote parties and candidates sympathetic to their objectives. Another way of describing interest groups is 'as private concentrations of power devoted to the achievement of goals that may not necessarily be shared by the majority of the population'.[11]

This formulation may help to explain the overtones of disapproval so widely adopted in relation to interest group activity. While Robinson notes 'ambiguities in the meaning of "interest" '[12], Beer's definition seems useful: 'By interest we mean here simply a disposition to act to achieve some goal.'[13]

Political scientists commonly distinguish between types of interest groups. The more enduring pressure groups are *protective* groups, with an economic or sectional basis. While these groups tend to become part of the policy process, and to vigorously defend the interests of their members, they tend (with notable exceptions) to be less 'visible' than *promotional* (or *cause*) groups, formed to achieve certain purposes relating to particular (often controversial) political issues. More transient, these groups tend to receive the most publicity, largely because their lack of political influence with decision-makers requires them to adopt a strategy concentrating on the media to reach a wider public.

Beer distinguishes between special-interest groups and general-interest groups. 'The goal of the special-interest group is primarily a benefit to itself; that of the general-interest group primarily a benefit to others.'[14]

However, since most groups persuade themselves that satisfaction of their own interests will promote the interests of everyone else, this distinction requires too subjective an assessment of the 'benefits' of group activity to be very useful.

It has been further argued that *all* political conflict is *group* conflict, and that the process of politics invariably involves antagonism between, and the ultimate resolution of, group demands by the political system. Politics, rather than a struggle between the organised and the unorganised in which the former always wins, emerges from this perspective as a contest amongst organised interests, in which each set of interests obtains something from the system in exchange for loyalty and support.[15] Bentley claimed that: 'The great task in the study of any form of social life is the analysis of these groups . . . When the groups are adequately stated, everything is stated. When I say everything I mean everything. The complete description will mean the complete science, in the study of social phenomena, as in any other field'.[16]

Bentley's blunt study of group activity set forth his terms with force and clarity. 'There is no group without its interest. An interest . . . is the equivalent of a group . . . There exists only the one thing, that is, so many men bound together in or along the path of a certain activity . . . The society itself is nothing other than the complex of the groups that compose it.'[17] Truman described interest groups as '. . . any group that, on the basis of one or more shared attitudes, makes certain claims upon other groups in the society for the establishment, maintenance, or enhancement of forms of behaviour that are implied by the shared attitudes . . . The shared attitudes, moreover, constitute the interests'.[18]

It is noteworthy that Madison asserted that 'factions' tended to have an economic basis. In other words, attitudes tended to follow interests, which in turn reflected economic position. ' . . . the most common and durable source of factions has been the various and unequal distribution of property'.[19] From this point of view, an individual's opinions and passions serve mainly to justify their economic position in society. Interest groups emerge primarily as the defender of economic claims and social position.

The term *pressure group* 'carries a load of emotional connotations indicating selfish, irresponsible insistence upon special privileges . . .

the word 'pressure' suggests a method or category of methods.'[20] However, groups vary in their tactics and strategies, and moreover it is useful for analysis to avoid terms and concepts which are imprecise and carry 'emotional connotations'. For these reasons, it is preferable to use the term *interest group* to refer to associations of persons seeking to achieve common purposes, whether of a protective or promotional character.

There are two main foci for research into interest group behaviour in the political process: *membership; activities.* The first kind of inquiry seeks to discover the motivations of different people for joining interest groups. Ultimately, such research seeks to discover why some people may join a particular group while others may not. As in voting studies, such research is not limited to the reasons provided by the individual; the analyst seeks to discover the existence of attributes shared by people of similar political orientation.

The second kind of research attempts to trace the *consequences* of interest group activity for the political process. Such research may examine the interactions of groups in the parliamentary setting, seeking to influence legislative outcomes. Another focus of research may scrutinise the efforts of groups to influence budgetary allocations.

In New Zealand, political science research into these two dimensions of interest group behaviour has been growing in the past decade. Studies of membership include analysis of CARE,[21] WEL (Women's Electoral Lobby),[22] and OHMS (Organisation to Halt Military Service).[23] Few studies have been made of the role of groups in the policy process, although the activities of the Federation of Labour, Federated Farmers, the Employers Federation and the Public Service Association regularly receive considerable attention from the news media.[24]

Groups in the Policy Process

In the United States, efforts to 'pressure' or 'lobby' may be made against any and all aspects of the political system. The 'pressure points' of the system are legitimately expected to include the judiciary, the bureaucracy and the executive as well as the legislature, and group activity is vigorous not only at the national level but at the level of state and local government as well. Indeed, often pressure may be applied simultaneously to various branches and institutions of government, with the hope that efforts which may fail with respect to one institution may succeed with another. In New Zealand, however, interest groups will make only limited use of judicial avenues of appeal, given the sharply circumscribed participation of the courts in the policy-making process.[25] Moreover, while public servants have considerable powers of discretion, nevertheless norms of neutrality and proper conduct preclude much serious lobbying effort being directed towards the public service[26] (except in instances in which the Public Service Association itself becomes involved in public dispute, acting as a professional association providing representation for its members). Thus most attempts to exercise influence in order to obtain favourable outcomes will be directed towards MPs, Parliamentary Committees and Ministers. Of course the strategies of interest groups will vary according to numerous factors: the extent of policy change sought; the group's size and position; the resources (including information) available to the group; the group's leadership and internal cohesion.[27] Many groups are unable to mobilise their membership effectively, either because of poor organisational efforts or because of the limited involvement of the membership. The phenomenon of 'overlapping membership' refers to the involvement of individuals in many different groups, and their consequent inability to fully participate in all of the groups in which they are members.[28]

Lipset has argued that:

A stable democracy requires a situation in which all major political parties include supporters from many segments of the population. A system in which the support of different parties corresponds too closely to basic social divisions cannot continue on a democratic basis, for it reflects a state of conflict so intense and clearcut as to rule out compromise.[29]

There are signs that New Zealand's political system may have evolved towards one in which *the political parties and interest groups correspond closely to basic divisions of sex, social class, race and political orientation.* Thus rather than being a society with 'cross-cutting' cleavages, New Zealand may be one in which, increasingly, the same groups of people find themselves opposed to one another on one issue after another. In other words, the lines of difference appear to be reasonably similar on a range of conflicts, and thus the political system seems to be one in which 'cumulative' cleavages rather than 'cross-cutting' ones may be predominating. This may be a crucial change (if indeed it does reflect a move away from an earlier period when intergroup conflict was more fluid, for empirical data about membership in voluntary associations is not copious), for Truman argues that: 'Overlapping membership among organised interest groups . . . is . . . the *principal* balancing force in the politics of a multigroup society . . . its impact . . . can scarcely be exaggerated . . . '[30]

If, however, the lines of conflict reinforce each other, and consolidate into basic social cleavages, then the intensity of political conflict will increase (and the likelihood of political compromise will lessen). As Huntington observes, 'a modern political system requires cross-cutting

cleavages to prevent it from being torn apart by . . . struggle . . . '[31]
Thus, the related propositions that: (1) most New Zealanders do not
participate regularly in politically active organisations, and (2) such
group participation and membership as does occur may *reinforce* other
differences, rather than blur them, are of considerable importance. If
differences are aggregated rather than eased through the supplementary system of interest groups, analysts will have discovered yet another
potential source of weakness and instability in New Zealand's decep-
tively fragile political consensus.

Moreover, Truman has observed:

> Perhaps the outstanding characteristic of American politics . . . is
> that it involves a multiplicity of co-ordinate or nearly co-ordinate
> points of access to governmental decisions. The signficance of these
> many points of access and of the complicated texture of relationships
> among them is great. This diversity assures a variety of modes for
> the participation of interest groups in the formation of policy, a
> variety that is a flexible, stabilising element.[32]

In New Zealand, however, this diversity of modes for political
participation is less plentiful, and the consequent inflexibility in the
policy process is an unhealthy element. Restricted opportunity for
participation is an important feature of the political system, for the
aspiration for self-government has been the revolutionary feature of
the democratic ethos. Modern politics in New Zealand and other
Western societies has evolved less romantic styles of political action
within a democratic framework. In the contemporary setting the search
for political sovereignty by the powerless transforms the quest for
'liberty' into a more mundane search for an 'access point', an entry
into the passage-ways of the powerful.

Many people probably do not recognise themselves in discussions
of group-based democracy. Indeed, the proportion of people regularly
involved and politically active with an interest group may be less
numerous than has been assumed. Trade unions may not be the only
organisations with memberships at least partially 'passive', grudging,
uninvolved. Moreover, many individuals are not members of *any* group
with an active involvement in the policy-making process. These people
may resent the claims and activities of pressure groups. Their non-
participation suggests a weakness in the view that democracy is well
served by a system of group participation in policy-making, for some
sectors of society may remain excluded.

Since every member of society has an economic position within
society, and may be expected to hold political opinions of one kind
or another, theorists have developed the concept of 'unorganised
interests' to describe the circumstances of persons whose interests are
not served by membership in an organised association. It is likely that

TABLE 6:1 *Types of New Zealand Interest Groups*

Type of interest group	Basis of membership	Objectives	Political influence	Examples
Economic	Occupation	Protect membership; influence budgetary allocations; secure economic benefits	Considerable; participate regularly in the policy process	Trade unions; Federation of Labour; Manufacturers Association; Federated Farmers
Environmental	Ideological (may involve local residents and ratepayers in certain disputes)	Protect environment; preserve natural features; oppose pollution; support stringent planning of economic development	Sporadic and irregular; depends on issue and extent of public involvement in *ad hoc* issues	Ecology Action; Action for Environment; Environmental Defence Society
Moral	Ideological (may involve affected persons or organisations)	Promote particular structure of values; urge government support to ensure desired pattern of values is implemented; oppose incompatible programmes	Sporadic and irregular; depends on issue and extent of public involvement; elite membership may be decisive	SPUC; ALRANZ; NOW: Women's Liberation; Gay Liberation; SPCS; Concerned Parents
Racial	Ideological; racial	Protect membership; ensure that government policies are not prejudicial; influence government's foreign policies to support non-white 'third world' struggles	Considerable at local level; irregular at national level; depends on issue and extent (and content) of media coverage	CARE; HART; Nga Tamatoa; Polynesian Panthers

in New Zealand, the concept of 'unorganised interests' may best describe *most people, on most issues, most of the time.* Thus a group-based politics fails to integrate most New Zealanders (despite their reputation as a 'nation of joiners'), leading to an anomic politics of resentment, the sullen anger the 'unorganised' feel towards the organised. This phenomenon may be one of the sources of the considerable hositility felt by non-union members towards trade union organisations, a seemingly inexhaustible emotional well from which politicians can draw as the 'need' arises. The 'faceless' mass, therefore, is to be found not merely in urban centres or large bureaucratic institutions but, perhaps more significantly, in large numbers of politically unorganised non-participants.

The most prominent occupational organisation in New Zealand is the Federation of Labour, an organisation of affiliated trade unions. The rise to dominance of the FOL, as the spokesman for what its leaders are fond of describing as 'the trade union movement', has coincided with the transformation of workers from a reasonably homogeneous, self-conscious aggregation of persons into a disparate gathering of heterogeneous, 'unself-conscious' persons. The working class, a 'latent' interest, is nowhere visible; it has been replaced by a large-scale interest group. The objectives, political style, influence, type of membership and composition of leadership of trade union organisations is entirely different from those associated with working-class groups. In other words, while contemporary New Zealand politics involves well-publicised and often controversial un-ion activities, nevertheless these are appropriate to interest group politics. Working-class politics is a much more marginal affair in New Zealand. Ironically, the voters can still be stirred by images of trade union activity drawn from working-class political stere-otypes. The FOL participates quite comfortably in the policy-making process irrespective of the governing party (though its influence under Labour is much greater), and its leadership discourages more profound alienation from and opposition to the institutional framework. As its President, Sir Thomas Skinner, observed on more than one occasion during 1976, in speeches to workers: 'Confront the government? What do you mean, confront the government? We can't have a confrontation with a democratically elected government. What do you want, a revolution?'[33]

The Rise of New Zealand Interest Groups

Most groups in New Zealand are formed for the achievement of non-political purposes. Many of these associations, however, will find that their activities impinge on the political process at some stage. Their resources may become inadequate, for example, and the group may follow a well-established New Zealand tradition by seeking to obtain financial support from the government for their activities.[34] A good example of this sort of pattern would be the relationship between numerous 'arts' groups–dramatic societies, film-makers, groups of artists–seeking support from the Queen Elizabeth II Arts Council.

Other groups may find political involvement thrust upon them by circumstance. The most recent vivid example of an interest group 'dragged kicking and screaming' into the political arena has been the New Zealand Rugby Football Union (NZRFU). Although never entirely 'apolitical', given the place of rugby in New Zealand culture and the resources available to rugby organisations, recent events have required the NZRFU to become an unwilling participant in public debate. Despite their claim that 'we only want to play rugby', it has proven impossible to separate their sporting interests from political controversy. Thus the NZRFU has been compelled repeatedly to attempt to justify their intention to maintain sporting ties with South Africa.

An examination of the rugby issue reveals another cause of pressure group formation and activity: the existence of other pressure groups. The effort of HART and CARE to bring about a cessation of sporting contacts between New Zealand and South Africa prompted the formation of another group, WARD (War Against Recreational Disruption). WARD was formed specifically to counter the threats of HART and CARE members to disrupt the proposed 1973 rugby tour of New Zealand by the South African team, the Springboks, a tour cancelled by the Labour Government. A general proposition descriptive of interest-group activity is that the existence of sectional or partisan interest groups tends to stimulate an opposite (though not necessarily equal) reaction from groups with diametrically opposed objectives or representing entirely separate sectional interests. Among other examples of this 'law' of political dynamics would be the following polarities: ALRANZ (Abortion Law Reform Association of New Zealand)/SPUC (Society for the Protection of the Unborn Child); Federation of Labour (FOL)/Employers Federation; Manufacturers Association/CARP (Campaign Against Rising Prices); RSA (Returned Servicemen's Association)/OHMS (Organisation to Halt Military Service); Tenants Protection Agency/ Landlords Association.

Robinson asserts that the rapid development of interest-group activity at the national level has been the consequence of several stimuli: (1) the impact of fluctuations in New Zealand's overseas markets, leading to unified requests for action at the national level and the submergence of provincial and local loyalties; (2) the specialisation of labour in the economy, leading to the self-conscious creation of professional associations based on occupation;

(3) improvements in communications and transportation, enabling local organisations to amalgamate more easily; (4) the widening range and scope of state involvement in society, leading to requests for special services and the entry of 'private' issues into the political arena for settlement by the government.[35]

In the course of New Zealand history political participation has taken three dominant forms in succession. In the nineteenth century up to about 1890, the dominant pattern of political activity was that of local pressure from groups and individuals upon local members of Parliament, largely for the purpose of securing more local public works. From 1890 onwards the pattern evolved of nation-wide conflicts between large sectors of economic life. Competing groups sought control of parties in order to control the machinery of the State. The peak of party development was attained in the nineteen-thirties and forties with two highly disciplined and programmatic parties facing each other in Parliament and the electorate. The period of the nineteen-fifties and sixties has seen the rise of national pressure group politics concerned with altering or defending details of the administration of the controlled economy and the welfare state. The patterns of local pressures, party competition, and pressure group demands combine to make a complex pattern of political participation.[36]

The rapid growth of Auckland as New Zealand's major urban centre is likely to have an effect on this pattern, however. Already there has been discussion of the need to counter an 'Auckland lobby' in Parliament–approximately a quarter of MPs represent voters from the greater Auckland area–through the co-operative activities of MPs of both parties to secure resources for their region. Thus 'Wellington' and 'Christchurch' lobbies may be evolving in Parliament and outside (in the formation of associations of economic organisations, including unions and employers), to enable these centres to compete for government support with the Auckland region.[37] Earlier pressures for regional development, however, from Dunedin and the South Island generally, foreshadowed these sorts of 'lobbies' representing geographic interests. While interest-group activity often has a national basis, some centripetal influence–a movement away from the centre–may be discerned as well.

Pressure groups in New Zealand have frequently been aligned with the major parties. For example, the Labour Party and trade unions have traditionally been closely linked, although recent studies have traced the attrition of union support for and membership in the Labour Party.[38] At one time, the leadership of the FOL and the Labour Party held formal meetings to co-ordinate policy, but the Joint Council of Labour gradually fell into disuse until, during the third Labour

Government, it ceased to meet at all. The National Party has maintained close ties with Federated Farmers, the Employers Federation and the Chambers of Commerce, but has never developed formal organisational ties with these groups. Nevertheless, it is useful to regard the political parties as constellations of interests, and consequently formal distinctions between parties and groups can be extended too far.

Despite public distrust, the contributions made by interest groups to the system can be distinguished; groups provide: (1) information to policy-makers essential for the administration of existing programmes and the development of new ones; (2) a form of representation for *functional* interests parallel to but distinct from the *geographic* or *community* interests serving as the basis of parliamentary representation; (3) a 'check' upon the government, as a means for individuals to respond to oppressive or distasteful government action; (4) a source of political leadership, by training individuals in the bargaining processes essential to modern government.

The most common model or image of the political process is one of 'the government', in contradistinction to groups, parties or individuals. However, the government is not a monolithic entity, and it is more useful to conceive of 'the government' as a collection of interacting groups each seeking to advance their own interests. These interests include a veto over policy commitments and a share of the resources available to and allocated by decision-makers. In other words, the interest-group model of political behaviour can appropriately describe the strategies of bargaining and pressure which occur *within* political institutions. These group conflicts may occur between and within departments and agencies of government, and mirror the dynamic process of group conflict which occurs among 'private' associations of interests.[39]

Sources of Political Participation

Interest group membership may be a consequence of many factors: age; occupation; sex; education; marital status; place of residence; religion; attitudes towards authority. Most studies of interest-group activity reveal some pattern of shared background characteristics among the members. Thus, irrespective of their purposes or their activities, groups as *social formations* tend to exhibit the characteristics of their members.

In New Zealand, political activity in cause groups tends to be more common among young, middle-class persons living in the main urban centres (i.e. Auckland, Wellington, Christchurch, Dunedin) as well as university settings (the main centres, Hamilton and Palmerston North). The phenomenon of 'middle-class' radicalism, perhaps superceding the 'working-class' radicalism of earlier social and economic movements, appears to sustain and nurture many groups (and at least one political party, Values).[40] It would appear that persons joining political groups may be more politically self-confident than those who do not. That is, people who join groups are those who think that groups can accomplish things that individuals, acting alone, cannot.

The search for generalisations about the sources of group membership may lead analysts to ignore the impact of unique 'situational' influences on individuals. The subjective experience and political behaviour of individuals, affected by an inherently unreplicable situation, unique in its details to them, has been noted by Brock (with respect to CARE members), Keir (in her study of WEL members) and Atwood (in a study of the changing attitudes of a group of young women towards sex roles).[41] First-person accounts of interest-group activity often stress the impact of a single event on the individuals conerned, although some persons may be more 'vulnerable' to the influence of an event than others exposed to nearly identical stimuli.[42] In discussions with members of OHMS, for example, the role of ideas, propagated in written form as well as through face-to-face contact with peers (other members faced with the prospect of military service), was repeatedly stressed to account for decisions to become non-compliers (or resisters). As one OHMS member put it:

I remember lying on the shooting mound, firing away at wooden targets with pictures of soldiers coming running towards me, pretending that they were enemy and we had to shoot them down. With a sudden shock, I realised how effective my army training had been. It wouldn't make any difference to me if those targets were real men . . . This experience led me to question more deeply just why I was having to serve in the army, and being forced to fit into the military machine.[43]

The influence of ideas on motivations for political behaviour has similarly been neglected, which suggests an attempt to diminish the 'rational' basis of political behaviour. Finally, it seems clear that individuals become most ready to join an interest group when their own interests become directly affected by government action. While politics and government impinge on the lives of individuals in society all the time, nevertheless it is only when individuals feel *directly* threatened by government action that organised political activity becomes appropriate to them. This general explanation for group activity describes active membership in both cause and promotional groups, and makes *politically-induced anxiety* the major driving force behind decisions to join (or form) an interest group and engage in political behaviour.

References

1. *N.Z.P.D.*, vol. 326, 27 June 1961, p. 65.
2. *Ibid.*
3. See S. Levine and A.D. Robinson, *op. cit.*, pp. 76–7, 83–6.
4. W.B. Yeats, quoted in A. Schlesinger, Jr., *The Vital Center; The Politics of Freedom*, London: Deutsch, 1970, frontispiece.
5. J. Madison, 'The Federalist Number 10' in R.P. Fairfield (ed.), *The Federalist Papers*, New York: Doubleday and Company, 1961, p. 17.
6. *Ibid.*
7. See, for example, the United States Supreme Court's reasoning in *Palko v. Connecticut* 302 U.S. 319 (1937).
8. R.P. Fairfield, *op. cit.*, p. 17.
9. *Ibid*, p. 22.
10. A.D. Robinson, *op. cit.*, Chapter 6.
11. S. Levine, 'Introduction to Part 5' in S. Levine (ed.), *New Zealand Politics: A Reader*, p. 199.
12. A.D. Robinson, *op. cit.*, p. 52.
13. S.H. Beer, 'The Analysis of Political Systems' in S.H. Beer and A.B. Ulam (eds), *Patterns of Government: The Major Political Systems of Europe*, New York: Random House, 1962, p. 52.
14. *Ibid.*, pp. 57–9.
15. This theory has been developed by R.A. Dahl, *Pluralist Democracy in the United States: Conflict and Consent*, Chicago: Rand McNally, 1967.
16. A.F. Bentley, *The Process of Government: A Study of Social Pressures*, Evanston, Illinois: The Principia Press of Illinois Inc., 1908, p. 208.
17. *Ibid.*, p. 211.
18. D.B. Truman, *The Governmental Process*, New York: A.A. Knopf, 1951, pp. 33–4.
19. J. Madison, *op. cit.*, p. 18.
20. A.D. Robinson, *op. cit.*, p. 52.
21. J.F. Brock, 'Christchurch CARE: An Analysis of Middle-Class Radicalism' in S. Levine (ed.), *New Zealand Politics: A Reader*, pp. 213–224.
22. M. Keir, 'Women and Political Action: The Women's Electoral Lobby, 1975' in S. Levine (ed.), *Politics in New Zealand: A Reader*, pp. 310–320.
23. S. Levine (ed.), *The Politics of Resistance: Accounts of Objectors Against Compulsory Military Service in New Zealand*, Wellington, 1973.
24. A description of interest group activity in New Zealand is found in L. Cleveland, *The Anatomy of Influence*, Wellington: Hicks Smith, 1972.
25. For example, see *New Zealand Official Yearbook, 1976*, pp. 234–44. For further material on the courts and civil liberties, see W.J. Scott, 'Civil Liberties in New Zealand'; '*Police v. Germaine Greer*: A Charge of Indecent Language'; 'The HAIR Case: Summing up of McMullin, J.'; R.K. Patterson, 'New Zealand Law and Political Dissent', in S. Levine (ed.), *New Zealand Politics: A Reader*, pp. 481–507; K.J. Keith (ed.), *Essays in Human Rights*, Wellington: Sweet and Maxwell, 1968.
26. See T.B. Smith, *The New Zealand Bureaucrat*, Wellington: Cheshire, 1974, for a study of the public service based on interviews with public servants. Also T.B. Smith, 'Politics and the Bureaucrat' in S. Levine (ed.), *New Zealand Politics: A Reader*, pp. 406–411; R.S. Milne (ed.), *Bureaucracy in New Zealand*, Wellington: New Zealand Institute of Public Administration, 1957.
27. See A. Holtzman, *Interest Groups and Lobbying*, New York: Macmillan, 1966.

28. A good discussion of the phenomenon of 'overlapping membership' is found in V.A. Pestoff, *Voluntary Associations and Nordic Party Systems: A Study of Overlapping Memberships and Cross-Pressures in Finland, Norway, and Sweden,* University of Stockholm: Department of Political Science, 1977. Pestoff meticulously examines Scandinavian survey material to come to the conclusion that hypotheses about 'overlapping membership', widespread interest group involvement and the presence of interest groups whose members come from varied social and political backgrounds 'are at best operative at the level of theory construction'. See Pestoff, pp. 142–7.

29. S.M. Lipset, *Political Man,* New York: Doubleday and Company, 1963, pp. 12–13.

30. D.B. Truman, *op. cit.,* pp. 158, 520.

31. S.P. Huntington, *Political Order in Changing Societies,* New Haven: Yale University Press, 1968, pp. 416–17.

32. D.B. Truman, *op. cit.,* p. 519.

33. This theme was reiterated frequently in speeches and interviews reported on New Zealand television during the first year of the National Government.

34. For comparative analysis of this phenomenon, see I.L. Horowitz, *Foundations of Political Sociology,* New York: Harper and Row, 1972, Chapter 23.

35. A.D. Robinson, *op. cit.,* p. 52.

36. *Ibid.,* p. 53.

37. See S. Levine and A.D. Robinson, *op. cit.,* Chapter 10, for relevant data on attitudes towards the growth of Auckland and the implications of this evolving issue.

38. See B.S. Gustafson, *op. cit.;* D.C. Webber, *op. cit.,* pp. 182–195.

39. See, for example, D. Easton, *A Framework for Political Analysis,* Englewood Cliffs, New Jersey: Prentice–Hall, Inc., 1965, especially Chapter 7.

40. See S.M. Mackwell, *Radical Politics and Ideology in the Coming of Post-Industrial Society: The Values Party in Perspective,* University of Canterbury, Department of Political Science, M.A. thesis, 1977, for a discussion of survey data obtained from a significant proportion of Values party members.

41. See J.F. Brock, *op. cit.;* M. Keir, *op. cit.;* N. Atwood, 'Feminism as an Alternate Life Style' in P. Bunkle, S. Levine and C. Wainwright (eds), *Learning about Sexism in New Zealand,* Wellington: Learmonth Publications, 1976, pp. 65–88.

42. This proposition formed the basis of an extensive study of student radicalism, reported in S. Levine, *Political Socialisation, Student Radicalism, and American Political Science,* Tallahassee, Florida: The Florida State University, 1970. See S. Levine, 'Introduction to Part 4' in S. Levine (ed.), *New Zealand Politics: A Reader* for further elaboration of the influence of 'unique, idiosyncratic circumstances' on individual political development. This may be exemplified to some extent by the personal accounts in G.R. Woolford, 'Recollections on Resistance', and A. Vooren-Hesp, 'No Commitments for Me, Please', in S. Levine (ed.), *New Zealand Politics: A Reader,* pp. 185–92.

43. G.R. Woolford, 'On Learning the Military' in S. Levine (ed.), *Recollections on Resistance,* p. 53.

7 Political Socialisation and Political Culture

Political Socialisation

There is no doubt that images about political reality may be formed very early in life. This has always been true, but has become more pronounced with the emergence of television as the major source of political information for New Zealanders.[1] As one child was overheard to comment upon the conclusion of a news report featuring the Prime Minister, 'I hate Mr Muldoon. He's not coming to my birthday party. If he comes to my house, I won't let him play with any of my toys.'[2]

Once established, an image can become very difficult to displace, and will have a profound influence on behaviour.

Behaviour depends on the image . . . as the child grows . . . he begins to perceive himself as an object in the midst of a world of objects. The conscious image has begun . . . as the child grows, this image of the world expands; he sees himself in a town, a country, on a planet. He finds himself in an increasingly complex world of personal relationships. Every time a message reaches him his image is likely to be changed to some degree by it, and as his image is changed his behaviour patterns will be changed likewise.[3]

The study of political socialisation is 'concerned with the personal and social origins of political outlooks'.[4] Political socialisation research has its main objective *explanation*. Researchers seek to explain differences between people in their outlook towards political phenomena. Perhaps most significantly, researchers seek to ascribe differences in political orientations to differences in social origins, environmental influences and psychological predispositions.

Political socialisation refers to 'the processes through which an individual acquires his particular political orientations–his knowledge, feelings, and evaluations regarding his political world'.[5] Political socialisation involves the development of political relationships, and research in this field seeks to trace the process by which people become socialised to, and acquire expectations about, the political system.[6] Earlier chapters have briefly discussed two kinds of professional

140

socialisation experience: for political scientists;[7] and MPs.[8] The study of political socialisation commences with the recognition that 'the political self is made. It is not born or innate'.[9] Thus the process refers to an evolving awareness about political phenomena. Researchers have traced this development to several 'agents' of political socialisation. These sources of political orientations include: the family; the educational system; communication media; peer groups; situational influences.[10] While early childhood experiences (including authority patterns at home and in school) have received considerable attention, perhaps owing to efforts to apply psychoanalytic approaches to political science, it is not assumed that political orientations, once formed, are immutable.[11] Nevertheless, an individual's political beliefs and attitudes become part of their approach to the world, so that ideas acquire an emotional basis and are functionally supportive for an individual's personality. Encouraging change in a person's political beliefs, therefore, can present enormous difficulties, for a considerable emotional investment may have been made in a set of political commitments.[12]

Socialisation will certainly be influenced by authority patterns in family, school and work place. There is an expectation that these relationships tend to undermine the sense of civic competence and to reinforce allegiance towards authoritarian figures. Lack of participation and decision-making in these settings can be deemed crucial in the shaping of political behaviour patterns.[13]

Political Culture

The democratic model formed long ago in Athens was articulated by Pericles in an idealised form.

> Our citizens attend both to public and private duties, and do not allow absorption in their own various affairs to interfere with their knowledge of the city's. We differ from other states, regarding the man who holds from public life not as 'quiet' but as useless; we decide or debate carefully and in person, all matters of policy, holding not that words and deeds go ill together, but that acts are foredoomed to failure when undertaken undiscussed.[14]

Few New Zealanders would classify individuals not participating in politics as *useless*. New Zealand, like the other Western democracies, has deviated in this respect from the model of direct participation in public affairs. Few New Zealanders, in their appreciation for the pragmatic, appreciate that the New Zealand political system has a theoretical basis. Yet it is possible to identify a succession of democratic models depicting the 'ideal' relationship between the individual, the community and the state. The Athenian model suggested a direct relationship between the individual and the government. Under this model, the formulation of the community's laws required, at least abstractly, deliberation and participation by each citizen. That a system designed to govern a city-state, with a confined geographical area and a small population, can serve as the basis of government for a continent (as in the United States, or Australia) or a multi-cultural community on two islands (as in New Zealand) has not been demonstrated. Certainly the system which has evolved in New Zealand does not rest upon direct democracy, with its stigmatisation of the apathetic and the apolitical. What has emerged instead is a system of representative democracy, in which all that is expected of the citizen is that a vote be cast every three years.

> New Zealanders are not . . . positively socialised to express themselves as political creatures. The voting act is one imbued with authoritarian overtones; rather than a calculated act of choice, in which the deliberate creation of social policy is celebrated, electoral participation in New Zealand is truly a matter of manners, dictated by consciously-fostered social pressures.[15]

The citizen may be regarded as *useless* if there is a failure to engage in the minimal participation involved in casting a ballot. Indeed, within the New Zealand political culture, citizens are often regarded as worse than useless–as positive irritants–if they seek more intensively to participate in the political system, through participation in pressure groups or public expression of dissent. Thus New Zealand has evolved a system of representative democracy, sustained by a culture which expects and rewards limited, restrained participation.

> When an investigator turns his attention to the political culture of any society he is likely to concentrate upon those political cultural orientations that are *widely shared*, on the assumption that they are most likely to influence the political process because they affect the behaviour of large masses.[16]

Political culture refers to the beliefs, expectations, attitudes and values of a given population towards the political system. As in socialisation research, analysts seek not merely to discover the *content* of political culture, but to trace as well the *process* by which distinctions and differences are formed, and patterns are developed and communicated.[17] The New Zealand political culture has not been the subject of very much formal, systematic empirical research.[18] Consequently discussions of political culture tend to take an impressionistic and subjective form. Not infrequently, discussions of what New Zealanders feel about politics become blurred, until they merge with what the author thinks New Zealanders are 'really like'.[19] Not uncommonly, such narratives tend to be the work of non-New

Zealanders seeking either to express their appreciation or, more frequently, to dissipate their resentment that New Zealand failed to measure up to their idealised preconceptions.[20] These discussions of New Zealand character and personality tend to be composed by disenchanted intellectuals. Perhaps people well integrated into the community have less inclination to write analytically about the sources of their satisfaction.

Contributions by political scientists to the study of New Zealand political culture have been indirect. Several studies have indicated what New Zealanders have felt about various topical political issues, and attitudes towards parties and political leaders have also been measured. Information about participation in groups and parties is available, although not abundant.[21] However, more basic research, identifying more enduring beliefs, attitudes and values, has yet to be undertaken. Speculation about the New Zealand political culture cannot rely very heavily, therefore, upon verified propositions developed through empirical research.

The sorts of propositions which research into the New Zealand political culture would seek to establish are clear. Table 7:1 outlines seven categories of orientation, and propositions related to them, which would need to be explored in any meaningful, comprehensive inquiry.

In some political cultures, seemingly non-political phenomena may acquire political meanings and overtones. Thus a willingness to join with people holding politically opposed views on non-political tasks may be considered politically significant, while a more widespread social separation corresponding to politically partisan divisions will similarly be noteworthy. Indeed, even the extent of resistance to a politically 'mixed' marriage–measured by a question (to a National voter) along the lines of 'Would you object to your son or daughter marrying a member of the Labour Party?'–may be a researchable topic.

Robinson has observed that: 'Compared with most other countries New Zealand has a very homogeneous culture . . . The degree of consensus in the New Zealand political culture possibly exceeds that in any other country'.[23]

However, the enormous distrust separating Labour and National voters suggests that consensus on political values and beliefs may be fragmenting. The rise of new social issues, concerned with the promotion of particular values and the moulding of the community's life-style, are further indications of *dissensus*. The re-emergence of Maori culture, with its distinctive beliefs and symbols, restricts impressionistic generalisations about New Zealand political culture still further.[24] That a basic consensus amongst groups and parties has formed about the proper *ends* of state action–the uses to which the state may legitimately be put–and the *means* by which these should

TABLE 7:1 *The Measurement of Political Culture*[22]

Orientation	Operational definition
Political identification	Nation of citizenship Political units and groups toward which one feels positively or negatively Political units and groups with which one is most often involved
Political Trust	Willingness to collaborate with various groups in different types of social action Group memberships Rating of groups in terms of trustworthiness, political motives, type of membership, etc.
Regime Orientations	Belief in the legitimacy of the regime Feelings toward, and evaluations of, major political offices and regime symbols Involvement in political activity supporting or opposing the regime
'Rules of the Game'	How one feels political opinions should be expressed Concepts of political obligations for oneself and others Concepts of how political decisions should be made by government Attitudes toward political deviation and dissent
Political Efficacy	Belief that government is responsive to one's opinions Belief in importance of civic activism and participation Belief in possibilities of political change
Political Competence	Frequency of voting and other types of political activity Knowledge of political events and their influence on oneself Interest in political affairs
Input–Output Orientation	Satisfaction with governmental policy Knowledge of how political demands are made on government Belief in effectiveness of policy inputs and outputs

be achieved–the 'rules' of the political game–is by no means apparent from recent electoral behaviour and parliamentary sessions.

Other generalisations, once valid, may perhaps no longer be so. That 'government in New Zealand is . . . intimate government and government highly responsive to public opinion'[25] 'is an observation which needs to be qualified. Comparison with some countries may suggest a greater 'intimacy' than has in fact been achieved; that one can telephone a Cabinet Minister, and obtain an appointment quite readily, does not necessarily demonstrate the existence of a 'responsive' government. In fact, the facade of genial accessibility may mask a reality of indifferent seclusion.

> What people believe about themselves may be as important in any attempt to discover the national ethos as what they do, for their beliefs serve to give them a sense of national identity and provide motivations for their actions.[26]

The New Zealand political culture involves the manipulation of emotional symbols, yet, paradoxically, knowledge of certain major symbols–the flag, the national anthem (God Save the Queen), and the national song (God Defend New Zealand)–appears not to be widespread.[27] Certainly, despite New Zealand continuing to be a 'nation of immigrants' (with the sources of immigration no longer confined to Great Britain),[28] the government has refrained from developing a programme ensuring the acquisition of knowledge about and favourable attitudes towards major national symbols. Nor is New Zealand characterised by the ostentatious symbolic display to be found not merely in 'new' states of the 'third world', but in the United States as well. While the power of certain symbols–such as the Treaty of Waitangi–may grow over a period of time, others–the Crown, ANZAC Day–may surrender entirely their dwindling emotional hold. Nevertheless there is a latent sense of collective pride, which can be stirred by the evocation of particular values–independence; freedom; equality. Politicians who can persuade the electorate that their policies will find New Zealand 'once again leading the world' are assured of political success. Despite the emotional arousal which such appeals can engender, the New Zealand political culture tends to be one characterised by a curious amalgam of qualities: apathetic partisanship. That is, most adult New Zealanders are intensely partisan, with Labour or National partisans seeing little of merit in their adversary's policies or philosophies (though more recently concessions about party leaders or particular candidates may be expressed). There may be a willingness to see positive features in the third parties, but their adherents in turn tend to take a very strong interest in political events. At the same time, many New Zealanders appear to lack confidence in their ability to promote political change. The 'system', or even entirely external or overseas forces, may seem too overwhelming to challenge. Thus there is not so much a conventional sort of apathy as a lack of confidence in the necessary personal political competence to effect meaningful change.

The Egalitarian Myth

The American capacity for myth-making is enormous though not unlimited; while we may scorn myths (particularly those of other nations), we ought not underestimate their strength.[29]

New Zealand has its own myths, less easily scorned except by the chronically cynical; certainly the most enduring is that an egalitarian society has been created, free from social classes and chronic inequality. Most political institutions in New Zealand are based on the egalitarian principle, yet none of them function in such a way as to achieve this ideal. For example, an educational system freely available to all is compromised by various practices, including a requirement that 50% of all students taking a School Certificate examination must fail to receive that particular Certificate (and the grade necessary to pass may be raised in the event of a more widespread satisfactory performance). As a consequence, essential qualifications may be denied a large proportion of the population whose future educational and occupational choices must become inevitably restricted. Political influence is monopolised, for the most part, by males who are white, middle-class, and middle-aged. Inequality is pervasive, associated with the distribution of: political power; economic rewards; educational attainments; health standards; provision of social services. Inequalities based on sex, age, race and social class have been well established, and in many respects these fissures appear to be widening.

In discussing the position of the Maori in the dominant New Zealand system, the subtle character of inequality has been delicately exposed:

If . . . one considers that political participation means involvement in decision-making affecting one's own affairs at the real level of power, at the bureaucratic level, then [New Zealand has not] allowed power-sharing or fostered political development . . . there is an indigenous desire for equality of opportunity on a strictly bicultural and separatist basis, and in the short term the two may be incompatible in white eyes . . . There is a world of difference between segregation (or assimilation) imposed from 'above' by a dominant society, and voluntary separatism requested from 'below' by the minority concerned. The true, not the emotionally imaginative, nature of 'Black Power' can help us understand this phenomenon: it is the demand that Maoris, Indians, and Aborigines become *legitimate participants* in the decision-making processes and in the social institutions of society, and not simply the *recipients* of what white society determines for them. It is the demand that equal participation is compatible with the retention of cultural forms that *they* see as worthy and valuable, not the 'souvenir' forms that whites perceive as worthy.[30]

For the more recent Pacific Island migrants, from Western Samoa, Tonga, Cook Islands and Niue, the situation may be more desperate, for their claim on resources has yet to progress to the point where they can expect even the patronising sympathy–involving regular, formal obeisance to and invocation of the shared values of a multi-cultural society–so common in the response of successive governments to Maori problems and pressures. At the same time, neither Maoris nor Pacific Islanders have been successful . in efforts to develop separate radio or television stations broadcasting entirely in their indigenous language. Prospects for increased Pacific Island immigration to New Zealand are virtually nil, while the government has increased its efforts to bring to an end the practice of some Pacific Islanders' remaining in New Zealand beyond the expiry date of their permit. Finally, despite the significant movement launched in 1975 by the Te Matakite organisation designed to protest against the loss of Maori lands, and subsequent protests at Parliament and at Bastion Point near Auckland, there appears little likelihood that this exceedingly sensitive and vital issue will be resolved in the near future to the satisfaction of all parties.

Racial prejudice may play a very small role in these issues, and in the disproportionate rewards distributed by the political system to non-white New Zealanders. Thus New Zealanders who claim not to be racist, in terms of their attitudes and behaviour, may at best be obliquely reacting to descriptions of New Zealand as a 'racist' society. An assessment of racism may depend less on the interpersonal dimension than on the more tangible (and measurable) aspects of material attainment: quality of housing; level of income; type of employment; and so on.

New Zealand has established a Race Relations Conciliator, with offices in Auckland and formal powers under the Race Relations Act, 1971. Until recently, the Ombudsman has served as Race Relations Conciliator in conjunction with his other duties. Most complaints originate, not surprisingly, in Auckland, a city with a large non-white population. During the 1974–5 period, 150 formal complaints were received of alleged racial discrimination against persons of the following racial, ethnic or national groups: Maori; Rarotongan; Coloured; Pacific Islanders; New Zealand pakeha; Samoan; Indian; Polynesian; Black American; Australian Aborigine; Chinese; Thai; French; Fijian; English. Accusations were made against five groups of persons: Maori; Chinese; English; New Zealand pakeha; Dutch. Over one-third of all complaints (35.3 percent) were made by Maoris, and another one-third of all complaints (35.3 per cent) were made by Pacific Islanders. In 1977–78 , 44.9% of all complaints were made by Maoris, and 31.3% by Pacific Islanders. However, 95.1% of all complaints were made *against* white New Zealanders (pakehas). The complaints received fell within the following sections of the Race Relations Act, 1971:

TABLE 7:2 *Analysis of Complaints to Race Relations Conciliator, 1974–1978*

		1974–5	1975–6	1976–7	1977–8
Section 3:	Access to public places, vehicles and facilities	0	1	1	1
Section 4:	Provision of goods and services	24	19	28	22
Section 5:	Employment	12	11	24	27
Section 6:	Land, housing and other accommodation	41	22	30	24
Section 7:	Advertisements	14	4	27	3
Section 25:	Inciting racial disharmony	55	44	57	56
Miscellaneous		4	5	10	10

The complaints were classified as following:

TABLE 7:3 *Classification of Complaints, 1974–1975; 1976–1978**

Category	Number		
	1974–75	1976–77	1977–78
Action completed			
Justified and rectified	35	33	19
Rectified, no decision	17	29	38
Not justified	30	47	39
Action discontinued			
Complaint terminated	14	14	7
Complaint withdrawn	11	17	14
Referred to other agency	30	18	23
Under investigation	13	9	3
	150	177	143

* The 1975–76 Figures were reported differently and were not suitable for comparative purposes.

These figures indicate that for the 1974–75 period, barely more than one of five complaints (23.3 per cent) received by the Race Relations Office culminated in a formal decision that the complaint was justified. For 1976–78, the proportion of justified complaints had fallen below 20%. These allegations of discrimination ranged from a complaint about an anti-Irish joke in a newspaper to complaints about the denial of accommodations on grounds of racial background. It is significant, however, that complaints by Pacific Islanders have tended to occupy an increasingly substantial share of the Race Relations Conciliator's workload: 14 (15.2%) complaints in 1973–4, 53 (35.3%) in 1974–5, 34 (30.0%) in 1975–6, 80 (45.2%) in 1976–7, 45 (31.3%) in 1977–8.

While it appears that subtle techniques of investigation and conciliation have a somewhat more widespread influence, nevertheless a purely quantitative analysis of formal complaints to the Race Relations Conciliator would clearly not support contentions that New Zealand was a society with widespread discriminatory racial impacts.

The Race Relations Conciliator concluded, however, that:

> . . . racial discrimination is generally abhorred by New Zealanders. It is regarded as a very serious moral offence and consequently inquiries are often accompanied by a good deal of emotion from either the aggrieved party or the alleged discriminator, or both . . . most people in New Zealand who discriminate upon racial grounds don't recognise their actions as such. For example, it is not uncommon for a defendant to admit to an act of discrimination but then deny that it was racial discrimination on the basis that he had other good reasons for his action and that he had not intended to discriminate on the grounds of race . . . Intent is by no means a necessary ingredient in an act of racial discrimination.[32]

As in the Ombudsman's other duties, two points must be noted in any assessment of the *political* effectiveness of the institution (as against the clearly beneficial activities in terms of individual complainants).

(1) It is likely that other channels are used as well, so that the Race Relations Conciliator becomes a 'last resort'; racial disharmony may therefore be more common than is suggested by the number of annual complaints.

(2) Complaints are made by individuals, and investigation and resolution of 'cases' is on an individual basis. Thus, complaints of racial prejudice are not aggregated into a policy-oriented programme.

Significantly, whites and non-whites appear to hold two different perceptions of 'racism'. To white New Zealanders, racism is uncomfortable in a direct, personal way when associated with interracial crimes of violence, or crimes of property committed by non-whites against white New Zealanders. To non-white New Zealanders, racism is an economic, social and political fact of life, taking its form in tangible and subtle deprivations. Neither form of 'racism' can be affected very much by the effective and diligent labours of the Race Relations Conciliator.

The myth of equality and contentment has been challenged by the demands of the women's movement in New Zealand in the 1970s. New Zealand was the first western country to grant women suffrage, and was also the first Commonwealth nation to have a women Cabinet Minister (Mabel Howard, under Labour). Yet demands for social, political and economic equality have revealed the relative deprivation of women in business and government, and the suffering experienced by women through their exclusion from positions of political power and influence. Women have tended to be politically invisible in the past, incorporated in the New Zealand dream as articulated by men. For example, Mr Muldoon's Maiden Speech concluded with an interesting exchange of cross-floor comments:

Mr Muldoon:	Sir, before I conclude I should say what a privilege it is to stand in this House alongside so many men who have already made or who will make their places in the history of this country.
Hon. Mabel B. Howard: (Labour)	What about the women?
Mr Muldoon:	I use the term 'man' as including 'woman'.[33]

Political science has not been unwilling, however, to make the necessary distinction between the sexes in examining differential political participation and rewards. The criterion of sex alone can be used effectively to describe the formal exercise of influence and power in New Zealand politics. There have been only fifteen women MPs, and only three women Cabinet Ministers: Mabel Howard (Labour), Minister of Health (1947–9) and Minister of Social Security (1957–60); Dame Hilda Ross (National), Minister without Portfolio (1949–57) and Minister of Social Security (1957); Mrs W. Tirikatene-Sullivan (Labour), Minister of Tourism and Associate Minister for Social Welfare (1972–3) and Minister of Tourism and Minister of Environment (1973–5). As women scarcely suffer from an inherent incapacity to contribute to the shaping of public policy, it is necessary to conclude that New Zealand society can ill-afford the casual squandering of its resources suggested by the meagre involvement of women in political decision-making roles. Full political participation by New Zealand women might lead in the short term to new priorities in social programmes, improved child care facilities, and more sensible family planning policies. In the long term, government policies towards emloyment, social welfare, income maintenance and education might be reshaped to enlarge the opportunities for independence and personal achievement amongst women and men.

Political Style

> Power always thinks it has a great soul and vast views beyond the comprehension of the weak . . . [34]

In New Zealand, pragmatism has led to a distrust of universities and 'intellectuals', and a costly aversion to theoretical knowledge. New Zealanders prefer a political style based upon direct experience, communicated in 'ordinary' language, and reflective of involvement in shared experience. In politics, due regard for ceremony is preserved through the Honours List–involving recognition of community, political or military service, awarded by the Crown upon the recommendation of the Government–and other affairs associated with the monarchy.[35] New Zealanders nevertheless appreciate from their politicians an approach which avoids pomposity. By contrast, political rhetoric in the United States tends to be replete with quotations from former Presidents and party leaders, and the summoning of the citizenry to occasions of great purpose. Very few New Zealand politicians will cite the speeches of former Prime Ministers or party leaders. Similarly, while President Carter has indicated that his objective as President was 'to bring justice to a sinful world', Prime Minister Muldoon more modestly declared in 1975 that he would be satisfied merely to leave New Zealand 'no worse off' that he found it–a goal not stressed in the 1978 reelection campaign, however.

There is some evidence, however, that New Zealand politicians may apply an excessively untutored approach to political phenomena;[36] greater evidence of contemplation and reflection, involving an acceptance of the view that 'civility is not a sign of weakness',[37] would be encouraging. However, as Robinson comments, 'The pronounced pragmatic approach to problems which is found in New Zealand . . . appears to be a long-standing tradition in New Zealand politics.[38] Nevertheless, Oliver has identified the durable mould into which aspiring New Zealand politicians must shape their character and political style. Describing Prime Minister Seddon, he observes:

> He did more than any other politician to personalise New Zealand politics. All his successors have attempted to follow his example, to create a friendly and familiar image in the mind of the voter, but few have been able to approach the standard of his wonderful performance. Subsequent politicians, whatever their party, walk in the footsteps of Seddon . . . The solid support of his rule was popularity, and this popularity he institutionalised through an admirable party machine . . . Seddon was much more concerned with power than policy. The crucial test of a proposal was not its abstract rectitude but its electoral magnetism . . . He judged his colleagues' suggestions according to the degree to which he found

they suited the public taste. He would, in all sincerity, have seen himself as an agent for the registration of the popular will, and it was indeed fortunate for his political career that it corresponded so closely to his own prejudices and sentiments.[39]

There is little intrinsically menacing about 'strong' leadership. Politicians who project themselves as insincere or vacillating lack the capacity to persuade people that their conception of the community's needs is compellingly correct. Mr Muldoon's personal style of communicating his political judgements has a demonstrated ability to arouse and intensify public feelings, both approving and disapproving. In itself this may not be a uniformly harmful phenomenon either. Many people objecting to Muldoon's style do so because they object to the goals this style has been mobilised to serve.

Mr Muldoon's confidence in his own grasp of the public mood suggests that he may regard his position in much the same way as orthodox Gaullists have viewed the French Presidency. With De Gaulle, Mr Muldoon seems to view his office as the embodiment of the national will; he emerges above others as the translator and upholder of the nation's 'mandate' to govern. With De Gaulle, Muldoon has an imperious impatience for parliamentary forms which may constrict him, a disdain for the irritating procedures through which the parties manoeuvre towards decision. There is a crucial distinction between the New Zealand Prime Minister and the late French General. De Gaulle took power out of the ruins of a crumbling political system, and governed the nation from outside Parliament through a new constitution providing a diminished role for established institutions. Prime Minister Muldoon has sought to develop a similar style of governing from *within* Parliament. Muldoon emerges therefore as a member of an institution whose role in governing he seeks to diminish to that of one capable of providing as minimum an amount of personal annoyance as possible. Thus, Mr Muldoon's style of government, which has come to overshadow the policies to which they have been wedded, may constitute a *radical* departure from New Zealand political norms, rather than a return to government by *conservative* principles.

However, Muldoon's pre-eminence provides New Zealand politics with its most sustaining interest. Moreover, his style of government, while a challenge to accepted conventions governing some aspects of New Zealand politics, may not be so unique as his more vociferous critics maintain.

Complaints about the dominance of the Prime Minister over his colleagues, and the parliamentary system, are far from unusual. In describing a then-healthy Norman Kirk, Roberts alluded to his commanding presence: '. . . he'll be a leader a long while. He's young, and he so bestrides his narrow world that there's just no possibility of a contestant in my view'.[40]

The Webbs' portrait of Seddon was an exceptionally vivid one:

. . . he struck as a gross, illiterate but forceful man . . . It was obvious that he would be nowhere in the English House of Commons . . . He was noticed only as being incurably rough in manner, and sometimes rather the worse for liquor. But in the New Zealand Parliament he undoubtedly stands out as a giant. His courage is tremendous. He is unabashed by any attack or exposure. He is deterred by no difficulties and few scruples. No sooner does he discover that any considerable section of his electorate have a grievance or desire some particular reform, than he assumes that he must and can produce the necessary bill . . . He is shrewd, quick, genial–but intensely vulgar–tolerant and more devoid of any conception of honour than actually dishonest. Above all, he is intensely responsive to any public opinion that can express itself in a majority of votes . . . The common people throughout the colony feel that he is working for them–that he is their servant, labouring with zeal, intense industry, indomitable pluck, and just the sort of capacity which they can appreciate . . . In order to get over any immediate difficulty he will never hesitate to tell a lie–and a lie that will be inevitably found out after it has served its purpose! Then he bullies his subordinates . . . Seddon is, in fact, a man without traditions and without manners: he acts on impulse. Most of his impulses are vulgar, none of them are distinguished. For all that, I still believe that his dominant desire and most permanent impulse is to conduct the business of government so as to obtain the greatest advantage for the majority of the people, with the expectation that, if he does so, he will be kept in office. That the greatest advantage is, to his mind, always material and immediate, is another way of saying that he is no philosopher and cannot be ranked as a great statesman.[41]

Whether the Muldoon phenomenon fits the Seddon style and image, so entrenched in the New Zealand political culture, is more a matter of partisan sentiment than analytic judgement. An ahistorical obsession with the present can lead to extravagant and unbalanced claims being made, and may have other dangers too. As Mr Muldoon has noted, an obsession with his personality can lead commentators to neglect the more necessary and searching scrutiny of fundamental issues and needs.[42]

The New Zealanders

It has recently been argued that New Zealanders are a 'passionless' people, devoid of any real capacity for spontaneity, intimacy and intense emotional involvement.[43] Such a judgement may only reflect once more McLeod's judgement that in New Zealand 'The small intellectual community, vigorously hostile to its bland, smug environment, continually depleted and replenished, is largely alienated from the wider community whose tastes it ineffectually strives to elevate'.[44]

There seems to have developed a protective xenophobia, a possible reaction against those emigrating from those remaining behind, to justify their continued presence in New Zealand to themselves. New Zealanders may be developing dual standards: one, for themselves, the other, for those perceived as aliens, foreigners, non-New Zealanders. Even 'permanent residents' may find that 'becoming a New Zealander' to New Zealanders requires something more than living and working in the country, something more even than acquiring citizenship, something which cannot be identified or retrieved but without which full acceptance can never be won.

There is a long tradition of intellectual estrangement from dominant cultural patterns, and many New Zealanders embark on their long-awaited 'overseas experience' and never return. Many of those who remain behind enforce conformity, penalise talent and suppress creativity. The stifling of emotional life has been noted as well. These generalisations are true of other contemporary societies as well. As criticisms, they have the accuracy of a glossary of diseases. The symptoms of many of them seem so familiar, and every ache seems to confirm the presence of a multiplicity of ailments. Yet few of them are so severe as to require urgent attention.

> The New Zealander delegates authority, then forgets it. He has shrugged off responsibility and wants to be left alone. There is no one more docile in the face of authority. He pleads rationalisations, 'doesn't want to make a fuss' or 'make a fool of himself', but generally he does what he is told, partly because everyone else is doing it, partly because he wants to be sociable and co-operate in a wishfully untroubled world. Only when things go visibly wrong does he recall his right to question the authority and change it. When he complains half his bitterness is that he has been made to complain because he hates complaint and can't complain with dignity. Anyone who questions too often is a 'moaner', yet in New Zealand the moaner is common. Things never run so smoothly as the New Zealander pretends. So he is suspicious of politics . . . [45]

Pearson's description of morality contributes to an understanding of New Zealand political style. 'In public morality the New Zealander's guiding principle is: Do others do it? I doubt if a New Zealander has any other moral referee than public opinion: crimes he has been in youth educated against he will lose distaste for as soon as the wind changes'.[46]

Interestingly, this assessment, if accurate, fits Kohlberg's 'conventional' level of moral development.

At this level, maintaining the expectations of the individual's family, group, or nation is perceived as valuable in its own right, regardless of immediate and obvious consequences. The attitude is one not only of *conformity* to personal expectations and social order, but of loyalty to it, of actively *maintaining*, supporting, and justifying the order and of identifying with the persons or group involved in it. This level comprises the following two stages:

Stage 3 *interpersonal concordance or 'good boy–nice girl'* orientation. Good behaviour is that which pleases or helps others and is approved by them. There is much conformity to stereotypical images of what is majority or 'natural' behaviour. Behaviour is frequently judged by intention: 'he means well' becomes important for the first time. One earns approval by being 'nice'.

Stage 4 *'law and order'* orientation. There is orientation toward authority, fixed rules, and the maintenance of the social order. Right behaviour consists of doing one's duty, showing respect for authority, and maintaining the given social order for its own sake.[47]

The argument here is that the moral development of New Zealanders, and their politicians, may have failed to progress to a 'principled' level, in which 'there is a clear effort to define moral values and principles that have validity and application apart from the authority of the groups or persons holding these principles, and apart from the individual's own identification with these groups'.[48]

A content analysis of parliamentary debate would reveal the frequency and effects of the form of moral reasoning to which New Zealanders have clung. An explanation in terms of moral development may further illuminate features of the New Zealand political culture, including deference to authority, discouragement of individuality and strong partisan attachment. Moreover, it is insufficiently appreciated that political conflicts are moral conflicts. Thus political judgements must inescapably involve moral implications.[49]

Finally, the egalitarian myth, which prevents inequality from being faced candidly, can have a yet more pernicious influence on the character of New Zealanders and the quality of their social and political intercourse.

Somewhere at the back of the outlook of the New Zealander is a dream, a dream of security in equality. Everybody acts the same, receives the same amount of the world's goods, everyone moves in the same direction. Everyone has simple tastes, explainable desires which can be satisfied with proportionately simple effort. No one has any grievance and accidents don't happen. It is a version of a human dream. The special quality of the New Zealander's version is that the evil is to disagree or be different. The chaos of existence is to be legislated into shape; the varieties of human quality and personality are to be levelled into conformity with the legislation. It is the development of individual talent that destroys the conformity: some men are left resenting their lack of another man's talent, so he must not use it, it is an unfair advantage . . . he fears that if he professes to be, know, feel, or understand more than his neighbour, he is guilty of pretensions to social climbing. He is out to be no better than the next man.[50]

It is particularly vital at this point in New Zealand's history, when the dream of comfort and security for all is jeopardised by challenging and unprecedented economic circumstances, that New Zealanders encourage the pursuit of individual excellence. The expression of diversity, and the development of unique personal talents, in all spheres of life, are legitimate activities which may be reconciled with egalitarian objectives. The danger is that New Zealanders may feel so threatened by the pace of change that, in subtle and yet cumulatively significant ways, they may discourage those qualities of initiative and independence most necessary for New Zealand to prevail, and the entirely admirable egalitarian dream to be realised.

References

1. See C. Wilkes, 'The Great New Zealand Melodrama: Television and the 1975 General Election' in S. Levine (ed.), *Politics in New Zealand: A Reader*, pp. 207–221.
2. Four-year-old girl, Wellington.
3. K.E. Boudling, *The Image*, Ann Arbor: The University of Michigan Press, 1956, p. 4.
4. R.E. Dawson, K.S. Dawson and K. Prewitt, *Political Socialisation* (2nd edition), Boston: Little, Brown and Company, 1977, p. 1.
5. *Ibid.*
6. The major literature on political socialisation would include: D. Easton and J. Dennis, *Children in the Political System: Origins of Political Legitimacy*, New York: McGraw-Hill, 1969; F. Greenstein, *Children and Politics*, New Haven: Yale University Press, 1965; R.D. Hess and J.V. Torney, *The Development of Political Attitudes in Children*, Chicago: Aldine, 1967; K.P. Langton, *Political Socialisation*, London: Oxford University Press, 1969; R. Sigel (ed.), *Learning About Politics: A Reader in Political Socialisation*, New York: Random House, 1970.
7. See Chapter 1.
8. See Chapter 3.
9. R.E. Dawson, K.S. Dawson and K. Prewitt, *op. cit.*, p. 41.
10. See, for example, N. Adler and C. Harrington (eds), *The Learning of Political Behaviour*, Glenview, Illinois: Scott, Foresman and Company, 1970; J. Dennis (ed.), *Socialisation to Politics: A Reader*, New York: John Wiley and Sons, Inc., 1973.

11. See P. Zimbardo and E.B. Ebbesen, *Influencing Attitudes and Changing Behaviour*, London: Addison–Wesley, 1970; M. Rokeach, *Beliefs, Attitudes and Values: A Theory of Organisation and Change*, San Francisco: Jossey–Bass, 1969.

12. This is illustrated particularly well in M. Rokeach, *The Three Christs of Ypsilanti*, New York: A.A. Knopf, 1964, in which three persons in a mental institution cling fiercely to their separate beliefs that each is Jesus Christ despite confrontation with one another.

13. R. Heilbroner claims that attitudes towards authority, by necessity, will have serious effects on man's ability to adapt to social and political change related to various manifestations of ecological catastrophe. See R.L. Heilbroner, *An Inquiry into the Human Prospect*, London: Calder and Boyars, 1975, Chapters 4 and 5.

14. Pericles' enduring Funeral Oration is reprinted in G.W. Botsford and C.A. Robinson Jr., *Hellenic History*, New York: The Macmillan Company, 1956 (fourth edition), pp. 201–3.

15. S. Levine, 'The Fern and the Tiki Revisited: Mapping Political Culture' in S. Levine (ed.), *New Zealand Politics: A Reader*, p. 315.

16. W.A. Rosenbaum, *Political Culture*, London: Thomas Nelson and Sons Ltd., 1975, p. 7.

17. *Ibid.*, pp. 8–21.

18. S. Levine, 'The Fern and the Tiki Revisited: Mapping Political Culture' *op. cit.*, pp. 312–14.

19. For a wry look at New Zealanders, see A.V. Mitchell, *The Half-Gallon, Quarter-Acre, Pavlova Paradise*, Wellington: Whitcombe and Tombs, 1972.

20. See, for example, D.P. Ausubel, *The Fern and the Tiki: An American View of New Zealand National Character, Social Attitudes, and Race Relations*, New York: Holt, Rinehart and Winston, 1965.

21. See the election literature cited in Chapter 5. In addition, see A.V. Mitchell, *Politics and People in New Zealand*, Christchurch: Whitcombe and Tombs, 1969; A.V. Mitchell, 'The People and the System: Some Basic Attitudes', *New Zealand Journal of Public Administration*, vol. 31, September, 1968, p. 22. More recent studies include M. Tower, 'The Political Socialisation of New Zealand School Children' in S. Levine (ed.), *Politics in New Zealand: A Reader*, pp. 343–352; C. Kraus, 'Learning About Politics: Shearing Gangs as a Social Unit' in S. Levine (ed.), *New Zealand Politics: A Reader*, pp. 328–36.

22. W.A. Rosenbaum, *op. cit.*, p. 9.

23. A.D. Robinson, *op. cit.*, p. 17.

24. See B. Kernot, 'Maori Strategies: Ethnic Politics in New Zealand' in S. Levine (ed.), *New Zealand Politics: A Reader*, pp. 228–34.

25. A.D. Robinson, *op. cit.*, p. 25.

26. S. Levine, 'The Fern and the Tiki Revisited: Mapping Political Culture', *op. cit.*, p. 315.

27. W. Gordon, 'Political Socialisation of School Children: A Comparative Study—Urban and Rural', Wellington: Victoria University, 1977.

28. See *New Zealand Yearbook, 1976*, pp. 70–3; 1049; more recent figures on population movement are reported in *The Monthly Abstracts* issued by the Department of Statistics, Wellington.

29. S. Levine, 'New Zealand/United States Relations: A Political Appraisal', in R. Phillips (ed.), *Alternatives to ANZUS*, Auckland: The New Zealand Foundation for Peace Studies, 1977, p. 15.

30. C. Tatz, 'Three Kinds of Dominion', Inaugural Lecture, 1972, pp. 18–20; also see Polynesian Panthers, 'What We Want', in S. Levine (ed.), *New Zealand Politics: A Reader*, pp. 225–227; G.A. Wood, 'Race and Politics' in S. Levine (ed.), *Politics in New Zealand: A Reader*, pp. 333–342; B. Jackson, 'Maori and Pakeha: New Zealand's Race Bomb', *New Society*, vol. 31, no. 1643, pp. 250–2.

31. All figures obtained from *Annual Report of the Race Relations Conciliator* (Wellington: Government Printer) for 1975, 1976, 1977 and 1978.

32. *Ibid.*, p. 9.

33. *NZPD.*, vol. 326, p. 69.

34. John Adams, quoted in H. Morgenthau, *Truth and Power: Essays of a Decade, 1960–1970*, London: Pall Mall Press, 1970.

35. An interesting study of the Honours List, describing its various stratified components and their relationship to each other, as well as providing interesting data on the recipients, is to be found in C.H. Townsend, *Political Patronage in New Zealand: An Exploratory Study*, University of Canterbury, Department of Political Science, 1977, Chapter 2. Townsend also studies New Zealand Justices of the Peace as a 'case' of the exercise of political patronage by MPs.

36. See K. Ovenden, *op. cit.*, p. 191.

37. J.F. Kennedy, 'Inaugural Address' in *Inaugural Addresses of the Presidents of the United States from George Washington to Lyndon Baines Johnson*, Washington: Government Printing Office, 1965.

38. A.D. Robinson, *op. cit.*, p. 24.

39. W.H. Oliver, *The Story of New Zealand*, London: Faber, 1963, pp. 152–4.

40. S. Levine, 'Interview with John L. Roberts: Labour After Nine Months', *op. cit.*, p. 424.

41. See D.A. Hamer (ed.), *The Webbs in New Zealand, 1898: Beatrice Webb's Diary with Entries by Sidney Webb*, Wellington: Price Milburn for Victoria University Press, 1974, pp. 35, 36, 38, 39.

42. Similarly Mr Muldoon has accused the press of being obsessed with his personality, and of insufficient interest in his government's policies and New Zealand's problems. See T. Garnier, 'The Parliamentary Press Gallery' in S. Levine (ed.), *Politics in New Zealand: A Reader*, pp. 149–160.

43. G. McLauchlan, *The Passionless People: New Zealanders in the 1970's*. Auckland: Cassell New Zealand, 1976.

44. A.L. McLeod, 'Introduction' in A.L. McLeod (ed.), *The Pattern of New Zealand Culture*, Melbourne: Oxford University Press, 1968, p. 4.

45. B. Pearson, 'Fretful Sleepers', *Landfall*, vol. 6, September, 1952, pp. 202–3.

46. *Ibid.*, p. 207.

47. L. Kohlberg, 'Stages of Moral Development', p. 87, symposium (no publisher). See N. Porter and N. Taylor, *How to assess the moral reasoning of students; a teacher's guide to the use of Lawrence Kohlberg's stage-developmental method*, Ontario: Ontario Institute for Studies in Education, 1972; R. Druska and M. Whelan, *Moral Development: a guide to Piaget and Kohlberg*, Dublin: Gill and MacMillan, 1977.

48. *Ibid.*

49. *Ibid.*, p. 82.

50. Pearson, *op. cit.*, pp. 217–18.

8 Policy Analysis

The Budgetary Process

'You couldn't have it if you *did* want it', the Queen said. 'The rule is, jam tomorrow and jam *yesterday*–but never jam *today*.'[1]

Alice's experiences in a looking-glass world describe quite well the budgets of successive New Zealand governments, particularly those drawn up in non-election years. Citizens are urged to recall (with nostalgia and regret) past days of prosperity, when New Zealand led the world and social justice ensured a comfortable life for everyone. New Zealanders are admonished to 'tighten their belts' in a budget which will 'hold the line' against inflation; the virtues of sacrifice are stressed, while groups are warned of the dangers of immoderate demands. Excessive selfishness may jeopardise the national interest, for self-interest and sectional claims border on the treasonable. The third National Government, in particular, has urged voters to remember that abundance has vanished through the profligacy of the third Labour Government.[2] Labour's massive overseas borrowing and domestic overspending is deemed responsible for the fact that although 'good times' may be around the corner, that corner is still a considerable distance away. 'Jam tomorrow, jam yesterday–never jam *today*.'

Perhaps the cynicism of voters is responsible for the increasing unreality of the budget message. Thus, the 1977 budget was described in *The Evening Post* as being of little interest to the average citizen.[3] After a brief glance at the headlines to determine whether any harm had befallen them, readers were described as likely to move on to the racing page for a close study of the daily form. Certainly in New Zealand, in contrast with the United States for example, the attention given to the budget concentrates almost exclusively on the *revenue* side. The concern of the citizen, apparently, as reflected in the press, is almost exclusively with the rate of taxation; where will the government be getting its revenue from, compared to the previous year? The very significant *'output'* or *expenditure* side of the budget—how the government will spend its money, the goals it will specify and seek to achieve—receives much less careful scrutiny. It is as though the average citizen has little interest in what the government actually does with the money, with the allocations amongst government departments, so long as minimal damage is done in the way of new revenue-raising measures.

The pattern of consultations amongst officials in government departments, the crucial position of Treasury, the participation of the Cabinet Economic Committee, and the more limited role of the governing party caucus and various parliamentary structures and institutions would need to be thoroughly examined to understand the process by which the budget is developed. Yet the study of the budget remains one of the most critical subjects for political science, for the allocation of resources is inextricably linked to the making of choices, the setting of priorities, and the exercise and implementation of value judgements about the needs and aspirations of the community. As Wildavsky has argued:

> In the most literal sense a budget is a document, containing words and figures, which proposes expenditures for certain items and purposes ... The budget ... becomes a link between financial resources and human behaviour to accomplish policy objectives ... In the most general definition, budgeting is concerned with the translation of financial resources into human purposes. A budget, therefore, may be characterised as a series of goals with price tags attached.[4]

Given unlimited abundance, choices about the deferral of programmes and the setting of priorities would *not* need to be made. The requests of all government departments, interest groups and institutions could be met in their entirety, immediately, by a beneficent government. In fact, politics would cease, for politics involves the competition amongst groups for resources. Were resources unlimited, conflict and competition amongst groups would be precluded; thus politics—and budget-making—assumes *scarcity*, a scramble for the contents of a pie diminished irrevocably by every allocation made from it. Moreover, every decision about budgetary allocation tends to acquire a fixed character; the establishment of a programme creates a vested interest dedicated at least to its defence, and probably to its growth and extension as well.

> Once enacted, a budget becomes a precedent; the fact that something has been done once vastly increases the chances that it will be done again.[5]

For this reason, ministerial discretion may be very limited; the opportunity for creative policy-making within Cabinet is diminished by the fact that a high proportion of a budget merely involves the extension of existing programmes, salaries, costs and commitments into another fiscal year.

If politics is regarded in part as conflict over whose preferences shall prevail in the determination of national policy, then the budget records the outcomes of this struggle.[6]

The budget, 'at the heart of the political process', is usually regarded in New Zealand as a purely economic document. For political science, however, the formulation and evolution of the budget, in a manner not readily accessible to public scrutiny, must remain the central, enduring feature of policy-making. While the Government's Speech from the Throne at the opening of Parliament sets forth the legislative intentions in the coming session, it is the Budget Message which clearly establishes the non-ephemeral policy commitments of the State in relation to social needs and political institutions. With the exception of revenue-raising measures, the Budget rarely raises public passions; yet ultimately an assessment of the democratic character of a political system must involve an evaluation of government programmes as reflected in the allocation of national resources in the Budget.

> . . . the responsive capability is a relationship between inputs and outputs . . . The . . . salient questions are: To whom is the system responsive? In what policy areas is it responsive? How does it manage to sustain a pattern of responsive behaviour?[7]

The answers to these questions, central to an assessment of government 'effectiveness' and the impact of government programmes on individual citizens, are at least partially to be found in patterns of government expenditure.[8] Ultimately, what governments actually *do* is at least as important as how they are selected in determining whether a system satisfies democratic criteria.[9] One of the things which governments *do* is to extract resources from their environment, and allocate or distribute them through the society, through appropriations to institutional channels (such as government departments) or transfer payments to groups and individuals (as in social welfare programmes).[10]

> Governments are responsible to Parliament and the electorate for the use of national resources, and exercise this responsibility primarily through budgetary policy. Although fiscal, monetary, and other policies can be adjusted at any time, the main systems of expenditure control are associated with the annual budget. The Government has to allocate resources, redistribute income and wealth, and stabilise economic activity. These are separate, though interrelated, objectives. Budget policy can be viewed as a function of three interdependent plans, each of which involves different objectives and principles of

of action. These plans are then consolidated into budgets involving a single set of taxation and expenditure measures.[11]

The study of budget messages can trace the evolution of social, political and economic goals and the development of policies designed to secure them. In the United States, the Bureau of the Budget–established by the Congress to process departmental requests–has evolved into an agency of unprecedented authority. In reconciling the various claims of departments to government revenues, this agency plays a critical role in establishing government priorities. In New Zealand, the Treasury Department has come to play a similarly central role in the management of government affairs. Of course it has long been recognised that Treasury is the major branch of *government*; as Roberts observed,

> You can't run government in this country without Treasury unless you are going to restructure it. As it happens, the whole business of government is co-ordinated through Treasury not only because, structurally, that is the place where things have to be finally brought to focus, but also because the able blokes are there. The really capable people who understand the whole system naturally have gone where the power is, and there has been quite a deliberate policy of recruiting ability there and giving them authority . . . you can't do anything about Treasury's primacy of position; it is better to work through them.[12]

Indeed, the party elected to government after a general election is described as 'having captured the Treasury benches'. In New Zealand the economic basis of national politics is well established. As Robinson so acutely notes:

> Each major party is based on sectional interests from which it receives the bulk of its funds and its most solid organisational and voting support. Labour is based on the trade unions, with which it has formal links, while National is based on the business and farming interests . . . *The electoral basis of the parties reflects and contributes to the main issue at stake between them, namely, the distribution of the national income.*[13] (emphasis added)

Nevertheless, it is not well appreciated that the budget is a *political* document; the choices' which are made have implications not merely in economic terms but for the values which citizens may wish to see promoted through government action. As one American President observed:

> A budget is a plan of action. It defines our goals, charts our courses, and outlines our expectations. It reflects hard decisions and difficult choices. This budget is no exception. It is a budget of priorities.

It provides for what we must do, but not for all we would like to do. It is a budget of both opportunity and sacrifice. It begins to grasp the opportunities of the Great Society. It is restrained by the sacrifices we must continue to make in order to keep our defences strong and flexible. This budget provides reasonably for our needs. It is not extravagant. Neither is it miserly.[14]

The 1977 Budget of Prime Minister Muldoon similarly sought to establish goals, priorities, and policy objectives. The budget involved political choices and ethical implications, although decisions were organised in the context of an integrated programme of economic management. As the Prime Minister noted:

After only 20 months in office the Government can claim that substantial results have been achieved in turning around the alarming situation which it inherited. The balance of payments deficit has been substantially reduced and the Government's own deficit has been cut in half. However, our terms of trade are still depressed and the balance of payments deficit is still far too high for comfort. While the rate of inflation has declined, it is still a serious and urgent problem . . . I believe New Zealanders have the resources, the strength, and the courage to win out. The Government can only give a lead and this will not be lacking. The real battle has to be fought by all the men and women in this country and I have every confidence that they will carry the day . . .

Our balance of payments outlook, which is a major determinant of economic policy, will depend on three things: the growth in export production, world demand for our exports, and access to markets. It is our job to expand export production. No one else can do that for us. The other two factors, world demand and market access, are largely beyond our power to influence . . .

Economic growth is not an end in itself. It is, however, a necessary prerequisite to the attainment of our society's individual and collective objectives, whether they be expressed as the spending power of personal incomes, the quality of family life, the quality and quantity of our social services or the economic, social and physical environment in which we and succeeding generations will live.

Traditionally, economic growth in New Zealand has been constrained by external factors. A small country not generously endowed with natural resources, New Zealand is highly dependent on imports of capital equipment and raw materials to sustain the industries in which most of the work force is employed. The extent to which the country can purchase these imports depends on the volume and purchasing power of our exports.[15]

The programme outlined by the Prime Minister was conditioned by his assessment of New Zealand's economic dilemma. In effect, the Budget underscored the disparity between the *demands* for goods and services made upon the system and the *resources* available to the system.[16] Out of the reconciliation of these two 'inputs' into the system emerges policy 'output'. However, the tensions and stresses within a budget reflect the difficulty political institutions have in developing a consensus about the appropriate distribution of resources amongst conflicting political forces.

The extent of state involvement in the New Zealand economy[17] as a proportion of total economic activity is revealed in the following table.

TABLE 8:1 *Government Expenditure in Relation to GNP*[18]

Year	Government current expenditure on goods and services*	Gross National Product	Percentage
	$(million)	$(million)	
1938–39	46.4	464	10.0
1948–49	100.0	978	10.2
1958–59	236.2	2,270	10.4
1963–64	320.2	3,231	10.0
1967–68	442.4	4,128	10.8
1968–69	484.8	4,355	11.3
1969–70	539.3	4,809	11.3
1970–71	657.8	5,539	12.1
1971–72	766.2	6,452	12.8
1972–73	870.7	7,498	11.6
1973–74	999.9	8,636	11.6
1974–75	1,215.9	9,452	12.9
1975–76	1,475.3	10,928	13.5

* This figure' is net of departmental receipts. It also excludes the operating expenses of trading departments, expenditure of a capital nature, and transfer payments to either persons or local authorities such as social security benefits, pensions subsidies, and interest on the public debt paid in New Zealand.

A detailed analysis for the 1976–8 period of the sources of government revenue, and the direction of government expenditure, is provided in the following table. Figure 8:1 examines revenue and expenditure for 1978 only.

The challenge for citizens or groups seeking a share of state resources is to demonstrate that their claim is as substantial as those already being met by the government. For political leaders, the difficult task is to develop room for manoeuvre, to introduce flexibility into

TABLE 8:2 *Financing of Government Expenditure*[19]

	Years ended 31 March			($ million)
	1976	1977	1978	1979 (estimated)
Expenditure				
Administration	475.9	388.3	479.2	517.4
Foreign relations	271.0	288.7	329.0	364.7
Development of industry	573.1	504.9	629.8	775.7
Education	627.0	699.4	807.5	841.4
Social services	997.0	1,158.9	1,569.3	1,784.9
Health	605.7	689.1	808.5	896.7
Transport and communications	275.3	230.6	247.6	278.9
Debt services and miscellaneous investment transactions	311.2	409.5	516.8	562.3
Subtotal	4,136.2	4,369.4	5,387.7	6,022.0
Miscellaneous financing transactions	308.1	208.8	281.0	333.0
Total	4,444.3	4,578.2	5,668.7	6,355.0
Supplementary Estimates	..	..	..	250.0
Total Expenditure	4,444.3	4,578.2	5,668.7	6,605.0
Financed from—				
Taxation—				
Income Tax	2,295.8	2,828.5	3,482.8	3,865.0
Customs, sales tax and beer duty	576.9	652.6	703.0	761.0
Highways tax	101.2	107.4	126.2	151.0
Motor spirits tax	76.3	100.4	102.2	143.0
Other taxation	135.1	156.0	212.1	217.0
Total Taxation	3,185.3	3,844.9	4,626.3	5,137.0
Interest, Profits and Miscellaneous Receipts	257.3	257.3	348.0	418.0
	3,442.6	4,072.1	4,974.3	5,555.0
	1,001.7	506.1	694.4	1,050.0

the budgetary process so that resources can be devoted to urgent, immediate problems without disrupting long-term social and developmental planning. In New Zealand, for the foreseeable future, this effort will be complicated by a precarious economic position which denies to policy-makers the resources necessary for the manifest needs of the community to be fully met.

New Zealand in the International Community

[Macaulay] . . . described the figure of a New Zealander . . . standing on the ruins of London Bridge, while he sketched the time-worn columns and shattered though standing dome of our St. Paul's ... Is the time quickly coming when the New Zealander shall supplant the Englishman in the history of the civilisation of the world? Have the glories of Great Britain reached their climax, culminated, and begun to pale? Is England in her decadence?[21]

New Zealand's orientation in the world has been that of a nation dependent upon others for its security and prosperity. Traditionally, New Zealand has chosen to play the role of a 'good ally', to demonstrate its willingness to make a contribution in return for the continued protection of a strong power.[22] For most of its history, that power has been Great Britain; more recently, the United States has become the guarantor of New Zealand's security. In either case, New Zealand has been willing to adopt a junior role in return for great-power protection.

FIGURE 8:1 *Government Revenue and Expenditure, 1978*[20]

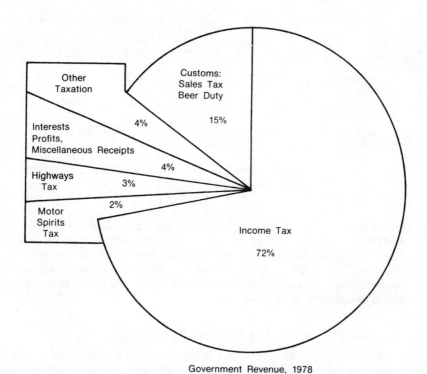

Government Revenue, 1978

The continuity of New Zealand's international preoccupations may be suggested by Dalziel's account of the major tasks undertaken by New Zealand's first overseas representative, the Agent-General in London. Dalziel notes that: 'The government had incurred a very heavy burden of debt repayments; private individuals had been tempted by a buoyant economy to speculate in land and building; and the new immigrants added to the problems of unemployment.'[23]

The Agent-General's activities in arranging for the government's massive overseas borrowing programme to be sustained led to attacks in the colonial press when he failed to secure favourable interest rates. Financial dependence, economic vulnerability and a tendency to indulge in 'scapegoating' as an alternative to more creative problem-solving activities are clearly not phenomena limited to recent times in New Zealand.

Every nation is 'unique' in its circumstances, history, and position; nevertheless New Zealand's involvement in international politics in

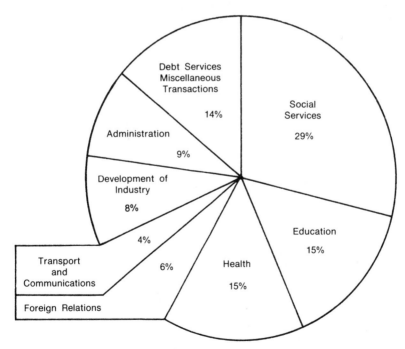

Government Expenditure, 1978

recent years is not too dissimilar from other nations participating in an alliance framework. For example the following passage, written about Brazil, reasonably describes Labour's foreign policy during the 1972–5 period.

... the expansion of ... foreign relations, together with her independent and activist attitude, created domestic enthusiasm and attracted considerable attention from the international community . . .[24]

The breakdown of a rigid bi-polar conflict, between the American-led 'west' and the Russian-led 'east', and the emergence of a world community containing multiple centres of power, has given many nations the opportunity to develop more flexible foreign and defence policies.[25] While the National Government has sought unmistakably to secure New Zealand in a revived American alliance, this effort has not interfered with the enlargement of New Zealand's international relationships. It is only during the post-war period that New Zealand has systematically begun to conduct its own foreign relations. In the past, much of New Zealand's foreign policy was conducted through the British foreign office. Indeed, Prime Minister Savage once observed to his Australian counterpart, Mr Lyons, that an Australian document on the defence of Australian ports was routed through London to reach New Zealand as a British paper, while a paper originated in New Zealand 'has presumably reached Australia as a British paper'.[26]

In larger nations, the establishment of diplomatic representation with virtually every other independent nation may be taken virtually for granted. In a nation-state with limited financial resources and a small diplomatic establishment, however, the decision to establish an embassy or a consulate, or even to cross-accredit one diplomatic representative to represent its affairs in another country, is one which cannot be lightly taken. United Nations membership permits New Zealand to participate widely in international affairs. The need for New Zealand to manage its own diplomatic relations has been relatively recent, however, and made more urgent by British entrance into the European Community and consequential gradual surrender of the British market. New Zealand's Department of Foreign Affairs has had its resources fully stretched. In Europe, New Zealand maintains embassies in Austria, the Federal Republic of Germany, Belgium, France, Greece, Italy, the Netherlands, the USSR and the United Kingdom (represented by a High Commissioner). Several other European countries are represented through the practice of accreditation, which enlarges their responsibilities; thus the New Zealand Ambassador to France has been accredited to Spain as well, while the Ambassador to Austria is accredited to Czechoslovakia, Hungary,

Poland and Romania. In addition, Ambassadors may provide representation to international organisations of which New Zealand is a member. The Ambassador to France, for example, provides permanent representation to the Organisation for Economic Co-operation and Development, while the Ambassador to Belgium has formal responsibilities in relation to the European Community.[27]

Some combinations may be less likely. The Ambassador to Belgium is accredited to Denmark as well as Luxembourg and the European Community in Brussels, while the Ambassador to the Netherlands has responsibility in Norway, Malta and Sweden. The Ambassador to Italy has been accredited to Egypt (as well as Yugoslavia), responsibilities which may flatter Italian aspirations in the Mediterranean but scarcely coincide with the Egyptian perspective of its role in the Arab world. An embassy was established in China in 1973, while direct representation in other Asian countries is maintained in Hong Kong, India, Indonesia, Japan, the Republic of Korea, Malaysia, Singapore and Thailand. In addition, the practice of accreditation has extended New Zealand representation to Bangladesh, Nepal and Sri Lanka (from India), Laos (from Thailand), Pakistan (from Iran), Brunei and Burma (from Malaysia), the Philippines (from Hong Kong), the Maldives (from Singapore), Vietnam (from China) and Mongolia (from the USSR).

The momentum to develop and maintain direct contacts through permanent representation overseas has been powerful. During the period 1970–78, New Zealand either established embassies or accredited ambassadors for the first time to forty-one countries. Representation in South America has commenced with embassies in Chile (1972) and Peru (1971), while access to the Middle East markets may be enhanced through representation in Iran (1975), Iraq (1975) and Bahrein (1977).

A decision by New Zealand to establish diplomatic representation is made with regard to the volume of trade between the two countries concerned, in two distinct ways: (1) setting up an embassy *follows* a sustained pattern of significant trade; (2) the presence of an embassy is presumed to facilitate the *further extension* and growth of a trading partnership. The use of such criteria ensures that the operations of the Ministry of Foreign Affairs are integrated into the overall objectives of New Zealand government policy (i.e. to enlarge the resource base open to policy-makers). At the same time, *purely economic criteria* can be a hazardous basis for conducting foreign relations, and can produce diplomatic embarrassment. Thus, the decision to represent New Zealand in Egypt through an Embassy in Rome, while perhaps economically sound, can scarcely have commended itself to decision-makers in Cairo. Similarly, a 1977 decision to defer the establishment of an embassy in Cairo in order for one to be set up in Bahrein may be economically sound but politically myopic. That an office in Bahrein can 'represent' New Zealand throughout the Arab world is unrealistic, and ignores Egyptian sensibilities about their nation's leadership position in that international sub-system. It may be unduly cautious as well to defer the extension of diplomatic and trade missions elsewhere until sufficient volumes of trade have already been developed. An investment may need to be taken by New Zealand *before* significant markets can be usefully explored.

Even a reliance on purely economic criteria may need to take into account factors *other* than indices of volume of trade. New Zealand's dependence on oil imports from certain Arab countries, for example, makes these relationships peculiarly important, and may already have propelled subtle shifts in New Zealand foreign policy as a consequence of the 1973 Arab–Israeli war and the use by the Arabs of their 'oil weapon'.[28] Certainly it might have been possible for New Zealand to avoid the débâcle surrounding the 1976 All Black Rugby Tour of South Africa had a diplomatic presence been maintained south of the Sahara. Instead, the political consequences of the tour appeared to take the government by surprise. Although warned by anti-apartheid groups such as HART and CARE of the possibilities of reprisals against New Zealand by African nations angered by the tour, the government dismissed the threats as implausible. Mr Muldoon refused to meet with Mr Abraham Ordia, Chairman of the Supreme Council of Sport in Africa, during his fact-finding trip to New Zealand, on the basis that Mr Ordia was not a head of state nor the accredited diplomatic representative of any African government. 'Why should I?', observed the Prime Minister, when questioned by newsmen investigating the likelihood of contacts with Mr Ordia. Mr Ordia's brief visit to New Zealand was eventually followed by the African Nations' attempt to bar New Zealand from the Olympic Games at Montreal, and the subsequent withdrawal of African participation from the Games.

The Ministry of Foreign Affairs has indicated, however, that it would find an expansion of its overseas diplomatic establishment difficult to meet due to a shortage of trained, experienced staff. In addition, New Zealand's total trade with sub-Saharan Africa has amounted annually to around $12 million, less than its exports to Peru. Nevertheless, given the diplomatic ostracism which New Zealand faced during the 1976–7 period prior to the Commonwealth's Gleneagles agreement urging governments to discourage sporting relationships with South Africa, some relaxation of the economic criteria governing the selection of diplomatic postings would be desirable.

New Zealand has been a strong supporter of the United Nations, although Labour more than National has endeavoured more consistently to centre more of New Zealand's foreign policy on that institution. Indeed, during the first Labour Government, New Zealand differed from Great Britain and Australia in seeking to persuade the UN's predecessor, the League of Nations, to implement its collective security policy by imposing sanctions against Italy for its invasion of Abyssinia (Ethiopia).[29] Similarly, Labour and National governments have maintained an active overseas aid programme, with recent efforts being directed towards the South Pacific Island nations. The emphasis has been on programmes whose contribution will involve a significant, measurable impact, rather than becoming a 'drop in the bucket' in proportion to the needs of large populations.

The diversification of New Zealand's trading relationships during the 1970s has become an increasingly urgent necessity. British entry into the European Community (Common Market) has led to a gradual decline in New Zealand-British trade. While the trauma of 'abandonment' by the 'mother country' (despite New Zealand's position as Britain's most loyal Dominion) may have passed, the economic consequences are continuing to ripple through the system. These are likely to increase in severity, as Community guarantees expire and resistance to continued access to the British market for New Zealand intensifies. New Zealand must enlarge its export trade in several respects: (1) develop a wider pattern of enduring trade relationships; (2) broaden the base of its export trade, so as to develop non-pastoral marketable commodities; (3) increase the productive efficiency, size and quality of its pastoral industries.

Trade knows few ideological boundaries; under National, trade with the Soviet Union has exceeded $100 million, making the USSR one of New Zealand's major trading partners. Whether this will lead under National to an alteration of New Zealand's alliance membership is doubtful; however, it is not difficult to envisage pressures on New Zealand to cease attributing hostile intentions to the Russian naval presence in the Indian and Pacific Oceans. Prime Minister Muldoon has already demonstrated a pragmatic, flexible approach to foreign relations where necessary. In China, Mr Muldoon adopted Chinese terminology to describe the Soviet threat. 'We are well aware that there are forces at work in the world that seek to establish hegemony and would subject us to the will of others. We are determined to resist such forces and to maintain for ourselves and our friends the right to decide our own destiny.'[31]

From a vaguely sensed menace, the Chinese had evolved into cordial partners, acceptable to visiting Ministers and MPs. The Vietnam war, and the more recent controversy over Labour's recognition of Peking and the severance of relations with Taiwan, have receded in the memory of the National Party leadership. A similar rapprochement

TABLE 8:3 *Trade Relations, 1860–1976*[30]

Year	Britain	Australia	Japan	United States	Other Countries
			Exports (%)		
1860	70	27	..	—	3
1870	52	46	..	—	2
1880	75	21	..	2	2
1890	75	15	..	6	4
1900	77	14	..	6	3
1910	84	9	..	3	4
1920	74	5	..	16	5
1930	80	3	..	5	12
1940	88	3	..	4	5
1950	66	3	..	10	21
1960	53	4	..	13	30
June Year					
1970	36	8	10	15	30
1971	34	9	9	17	31
1972	31	8	10	15	35
1973	27	7	13	15	38
1974	21	10	14	17	38
1975*	22	11	12	12	43
1976*	20	12	13	11	44
			*Provisional		
			Imports (%)		
1860	56	42	..	1	1
1870	58	36	..	1	5
1880	56	31	..	4	9
1890	67	17	..	6	10
1900	61	17	..	10	12
1910	62	14	..	8	16
1920	48	17	..	18	17
1930	47	8	..	18	27
1940	47	16	..	12	25
1950	60	12	..	7	21
1960	43	18	..	10	29
June Year					
1970	30	21	8	13	28
1971	29	21	10	12	28
1972	28	23	11	10	27
1973	24	25	13	11	27
1974	19	24	13	12	32
1975*	19	20	14	13	34
1976*	17	19	15	15	34
			*Provisional		

with the Soviet Union on a political level, to complement the expanding ties (the Russians have already begun to urge further cultural and scientific co-operation), is no less plausible.

New Zealand defence planning is centred on the ANZUS treaty, a brief though controversial document negotiated by a Labour government and developed from Labour's war-time co-operation with Australia and the United States. The commitment of the United States to antipodean defence to replace the British was foreshadowed as long ago as 1908, on the occasion of President Theodore Roosevelt's dispatch of the U.S. fleet on a round-the-world journey.

> In Sydney and Melbourne, crowds of from 400,000 to 600,000 turned out to greet the American navy. More than a quarter of Australia's population massed the foreshores and streets of the two cities and celebrated the advent of American naval power into the southwest Pacific ... The Americans themselves admitted that nowhere, including the West Coast of America, had they met with such a reception.[32]

Both New Zealand and Australia have sought security–economic, political, military and psychological–to overcome their isolation from Europe, and their limited capabilities and resources. Post-war alliance agreements were foreshadowed as early as 1938 when, following news of President Roosevelt's intention to seek amendments to the United States Neutrality law, the Australian Prime Minister, Mr Lyons, observed (noting the friendly status of Canada in the proposed legislation) in a cable:

> Seems to us that even if chances small it would be well worth while ... to discuss with Roosevelt the possibility of America including Australia and New Zealand in same category as Canada. Such a recognition of common interests and ideals [of] English-speaking countries on Pacific basin would have obvious and tremendous results.[33]

The ANZUS treaty was preceded by the Canberra Pact, signed on 21 January, 1944. This alliance treaty, between Australia and New Zealand, provided for elaborate and permanent machinery for collaboration in defence and foreign policies. Its purpose was to protect 'a regional zone of defence comprising the south-west and South Pacific areas ... based on Australia and New Zealand, stretching through the arc of islands north and north-east of Australia, to Western Samoa and the Cook Islands'.[34] As the cornerstone of Australian and New Zealand defence planning, however, the ANZUS treaty seeks to guarantee the security of each neighbour through a formal alliance with the United States. The pact provides that:

... the parties will consult together whenever in the opinion of any of them the territorial integrity, political independence or security of any of the parties is threatened in the Pacific. Each party recognises that an armed attack in the Pacific area on any of the parties would be dangerous to its own peace and safety and declares that it would act to meet the common danger in accordance with its constitutional process.[35]

ANZUS has been more important to Australia and New Zealand than it has been to the United States. American policy is rarely centred on the South Pacific region, and global concerns give the major alliance partner a quite distinct outlook. For example, while ANZUS initially reflected American concern over Communist expansion, Australia and New Zealand regarded the pact as useful against any renewed Japanese threat as well. One reason for New Zealand's reliance upon ANZUS is the difficulty faced in maintaining a sizeable, modern defence establishment. Defence spending has risen considerably in recent years, but has dwindled in proportion to government expenditure and gross national product (GNP).

TABLE 8:4 *Defence Expenditure, 1968–1979*[36]

Year ended 31 March	Defence expenditure	Percentage of government expenditure*	Percentage of Gross National Product
	$(m)	%	%
1968	87.11	6.8	2.1
1969	85.34	6.3	2.0
1970	89.72	6.1	1.9
1971	109.07	6.3	2.0
1972	121.17	6.0	1.9
1973	129.82	5.1	1.8
1974	140.51	4.7	1.6
1975	166.86	4.5	1.7
1976	193.46	4.1	1.7
1977	214.83	4.2	1.7
1978	252.17	N.A.	N.A.
†1979	280.0	N.A.	N.A.

* Excludes repayment of public debt
† estimate

Moreover, there are few surplus resources to support the kind of modernisation programme required to create a significant defence capability. Yet particularly in naval and air services, the need for such a programme has increased, not merely to overcome deterioration of equipment but to police New Zealand's enlarged territorial seas. The

200-mile economic zone can make a significant contribution to New Zealand's efforts to diversify and stabilise its patterns of trade.[37] Assured markets in exchange for concessions to exploit the zone's resources ought to be complemented by efforts to encourage New Zealanders to enlarge their participation in such developmental programmes. While these opportunities will challenge New Zealand's skills of diplomacy and resource management, the size of the zone may require as well a greater commitment of resources for security purposes.

The detailed pattern of defence expenditure, revealed in Table 8:5, demonstrates that most of the defence budget has covered the cost of personnel, whose wages and conditions of service have been improved in recent years.

TABLE 8:5 *Detailed Analysis of Defence Expenditure, 1972–1978*[38]

Item	1972–3	1973–4	1974–5	1975–6	1976–7	1977–8
	$(m)	$(m)	$(m)	$(m)	$(m)	$(m)
Personnel	79.76	89.72	101.60	114.19	125.03	142.32
Travel, transport and communications	4.94	5.26	6.52	6.70	8.18	10.60
Maintenance, operation, upkeep, and rental	7.85	8.74	10.73	12.48	13.62	18.71
Materials and supplies	19.21	17.71	26.95	32.20	37.69	45.55
Services	2.81	2.99	3.34	3.38	4.51	5.43
Other operating expenditure	0.92	1.25	1.17	1.39	1.47	2.09
Grants, contributions, subsidies	0.08	0.05	0.06	0.16	0.18	0.18
Capital works	1.30	2.00	2.99	5.99	5.54	5.39
Capital equipment	12.95	12.78	13.49	16.98	18.60	21.88
Totals	129.82	140.51	166.85	193.47	214.82	252.15

Nevertheless, the size of New Zealand forces has declined, and during 1977–8 efforts have been made to promote recruitment overseas to augment forces depleted by a declining rate of re-enlistment.

The restraints on defence spending have been challenged by defence spokesmen and, in particular, by the Returned Servicemen's Association (R.S.A.), an organisation of former members of New Zealand forces. The furore during 1976 of a Russian threat to New Zealand–the latest in a succession of 'scares' dating back to the earlier periods of European settlement, involving Russian, French, German and Japanese forces as potential threats–therefore may have been part of an all-too-familiar scenario: public alarms from respected figures

TABLE 8:6 *Strength of Armed Forces*[39]

As at 31 March	Navy	Army	Air Force	Total
1964	3,035	5,559	4,338	12,932
1965	2,976	5,374	4,390	12,740
1966	2,922	5,549	4,381	12,852
1967	2,934	5,620	4,378	12,932
1968	2,912	5,840	4,485	13,237
1969	2,935	5,730	4,498	13,163
1970	2,975	5,782	4,530	13,287
1971	2,941	5,638	4,413	12,992
1972	2,966	5,449	4,222	12,637
1973	2,972	5,498	4,319	12,789
1974	2,845	5,553	4,232	12,630
1975	2,850	5,523	4,297	12,670
1976	2,734	5,432	4,254	12,420
1977	2,726	5,441	4,289	12,456
1978	2,825	5,722	4,217	12,764

over a period of months about a growing danger to national security; publicly expressed dismay from interested parties over the alarming deterioration of the services; demands for more resources to be allocated to the military at the expense of other government expenditures. Americans particularly will be sensitive to and wary of this three-act drama, which the Pentagon has been staging in Washington, in good times and bad, for over thirty years. Given the comparative secrecy with which government departments compete for resources, New Zealanders may be unaccustomed to the staging, and may mistake the theatrical world of Defence Department pressure politics for the real present-day environment in which nation-states interact.[40]

National's Minister of Defence (Mr McCready) has claimed that the armed services face a shortage of 'men, money and materials.' Frequent repetition of this refrain may not make it any more valid. There is no absolute standard against which a nation's commitment of military resources may be measured. These depend on the strategic needs of the country. The level of expenditure and the size of the defence establishment must depend on the resources available to decision-makers and the goals they wish to attain.

Certainly there will be an enlarged role for the naval and air services, for New Zealand's effective and enforceable international boundaries have been expanded in anticipation of a rewritten law of the sea. In this context the reassessment of the material capabilities of the naval and air services by the government in its 1978 'White Paper' on Defence has been useful. Its examination sought to concentrate on the identification of specific needs and the specification of costs associated with available alternatives. What is *not* required in any reappraisal is rhetoric about the dangers of Russian ships, the need for more money for the armed services or the imminent collapse of security guarantees. The latter refrain, in particular, may resemble a self-fulfilling prophecy. The National Government's willingness to permit United States nuclear-powered naval vessels to visit New Zealand ports, for example, was justified as an attempt to save ANZUS from imminent collapse. However, the Australian Prime Minister, Mr Fraser, when asked whether there was any danger of ANZUS's dissolution if New Zealand refused entry to nuclear-powered ships, replied: 'Not for a moment.'[41] As Mr R. Prebble (Labour, Auckland Central) observed:

> I have a copy of the ANZUS treaty. I am a lawyer, and I am prepared to give the Government a free legal opinion. There is no clause in the treaty which obliges New Zealand to allow in nuclear vessels. It is a purely defensive agreement and the operative clauses do not come into effect except in a time of war. Our allies have made it quite clear that they do not regard the ANZUS agreement as conflicting with the concept of a nuclear-free zone. I draw attention to the statement made on TV1 on 2 April by Vice-President Rockefeller, who, when asked whether America would consider withdrawing from ANZUS if New Zealand were to ban nuclear vessels, said: 'No. I don't know where you got that idea from.'

Countering charges that Labour was opposed to ANZUS, Mr Prebble noted:

> The ANZUS treaty is a public document, which came to be signed as a result of the initiative of a Labour Government. It is a purely defensive treaty. The operative clauses are those that come into effect only if one of the signatories' territorial areas is attacked.
> There is no obligation under that treaty for anything to be done in a time of peace except to consult and hold talks. The last Labour Government fulfilled its ANZUS obligations to the letter. Every single one of the ANZUS talks that were requested were held. There is nothing in the treaty to indicate that there should be some sort of joint military manoeuvres. And any such manoeuvres must be regarded as being something extra and outside of the treaty.[42]

The position of the United States government towards ANZUS requirements has been clarified in an official statement released by the highest-ranking official responsible for New Zealand affairs in the United States Department of State.[43] The United States government is not re-evaluating its commitment to ANZUS, and American membership has not become a matter of controversy in the United

States. A refusal to admit nuclear-powered alliance vessels would not be in conflict with treaty obligations. While the United States would prefer National's policy, this policy is clearly *an option* open to the government, rather than one *required* by the obligations of alliance membership or compelled by treaty provisions. It would appear that the New Zealand public is being misled when threats of American withdrawal from ANZUS are mooted, or when ANZUS is described as responsible for a policy which is, in fact, freely chosen by the government from a range of possible alternatives each compatible with alliance obligations.

Certainly the concept of a nuclear-free zone in the South Pacific is not viewed with favour by the United States, and Labour spokesmen ought not to disguise this fact. While the zone would not appear to conflict directly with the American view of ANZUS requirements, certainly the depth of American mistrust for the concept is not inconsiderable. These sentiments have been shared by the Australian government as well.

ANZUS ultimately may fall victim to a policy for which it is not directly responsible. At the very least, an obstinate antipathy towards the American partner may well come to permeate the New Zealand political atmosphere, to become a burden ultimately fatal to an evolving and significant relationship. This process may already have begun. Since the admission of American nuclear ships to New Zealand and National's rejection of the 'nuclear-free' zone concept for the South Pacific as incompatible with alliance obligations, Labour and Social Credit have pledged to reverse National's policies on the admission of nuclear ships, while Values has promised a withdrawal from ANZUS altogether. How the United States government would react to the withdrawal of port facilities for its nuclear-powered, nuclear-armed fleet is hypothetical, but if National's predictions may be accepted, then Labour and Social Credit are in practice pledged to policies leading to the termination of ANZUS. Such a development would surprise Americans for,' to the extent that they are aware of New Zealand's existence, their feelings are friendly, and there is an assumption that such affection and trust is reciprocal. Yet this may be a mistaken assumption, and the depth and range of aversion to America in New Zealand may be surprising.

The support for the ANZUS alliance within New Zealand is . . . superficial . . . The United States appears to be regarded by many New Zealanders as a corrupt and violent society, characterised by moral decline and intellectual vulgarity. Other New Zealanders identify the United States with the promotion and extension of imperialist domination in political, military, cultural and economic dimensions, and pronounce New Zealand as one of its victims.[44]

Withdrawal from ANZUS would disrupt defence arrangements with Australia as well as the United States, however. It is difficult to see how New Zealand could continue its close association with Australia on matters of defence, if New Zealand renounced the alliance while Australia retained membership.

Of course, conflicts of interest amongst allies will always exist, and these should not be disguised from the public.[45] The interests of the United States, for example, are so extensive and the perspective of this superpower so different from that of New Zealand that a uniformity of interest and policy on international issues cannot be expected to arise as a matter of course. Similarly, while Australia's security needs will in large measure be similar to New Zealand's, Australia's proximity to Asia is so much greater, and her resource base so much more extensive, that policy-makers should not assume a common 'Australasian' position on security issues. While New Zealand is a nation increasingly oriented towards the Pacific, two of its most important partners for trade, security and cultural purposes will remain Australia and the United States. While New Zealand and the United States are nations *separated* by a common language due to cultural differences, and Australia is a third communicant, distinct and apart from the other two, there remains an opportunity for them to develop policies responsive to their shared problems and needs. There are critics of ANZUS who regard it as an alliance linking New Zealand with an aggressive, imperialist power. Their sentiments towards the treaty were foreshadowed by Dryden:

> Such subtle covenants shall be made,
> Till peace itself is war in masquerade.[46]

Yet the ANZUS nations do constitute a *security community*, as a group of nations between whom war is unthinkable.

> Integration and security community . . . imply stable expectations of peace among the participating units or groups, whether or not there has been a merger of their political institutions . . . The absence of . . . advance preparations for large-scale violence between any two territories or groups of people prevents any immediate outbreak of effective war between them, and it serves for this reason as the test for the existence or non-existence of a security community among the groups concerned. The attainment of a security community thus can be tested operationally in terms of the absence or presence of significant organised preparations for war or large-scale violence among its members, and integration for us is the creation of those practices and machinery–the habits and institutions–which actually results in the establishment of a security community.[47]

As a 'security community', Australia, New Zealand and the United States faithfully conform to the criteria more closely than the various partners in the North Atlantic Treaty Organisation, for example. Both governments and national populations in Greece and Turkey, for example, or Britain and Iceland are unlikely to form a 'security community' in this sense, while within the European Community, West Germany's partners still seek to bind her to them precisely because this requisite degree of trust is still far from established. Indeed, it has recently been argued that New Zealand should place its armed forces under Australian operational control, establish a full free trade area with Australia far beyond the agreements already negotiated, and envisage a customs and monetary union leading towards considerable political integration.[48] While to the rest of the world Australia and New Zealand appear to be regarded almost as a single entity, Australians and New Zealanders themselves tend either to ignore each other's society and culture, or to emphasise their political and cultural differences. As 'neither country seems to be bound up with the political, commercial, sporting and cultural life of the other', New Zealanders may be unprepared for a more intimate association with their larger neighbour. Yet as Mr Brian Talboys, National's Minister of Foreign Affairs, has noted:

> The time has come for New Zealand to recognise that our relationship with Australia is more important to us than our links with any other country in the world. I believe we do recognise this fact instinctively, at the back of our minds. We have to bring it to the forefront, make it explicit in our thinking and in our actions. It has to be the cornerstone of New Zealand's external policies.[49]

Contrasting images of New Zealand as a placid, relaxed society culturally oriented towards Britain, and a more aggressive Australia, more obviously attracted toward the United States (or, more narrowly, Texas), suggest some of the psychological obstacles impeding full harmony between the two.

The influence of political images is most profound when they become 'natural' features of a person's mental and emotional life. When this occurs, these political images–like the other subconsciously structured sources of behaviour in a personality–will emerge to govern political perceptions and orientations in extraordinary ways. The influence of the United States on both trans-Tasman nations, and the dominance of Australia over New Zealand in many facets of their bilateral relationship, suggest that the preservation of a distinctive national identity is in some danger in New Zealand. Withdrawal from international contacts would have its rewards as well as its costs, but whether sensible policies could be devised to protect a 'little New Zealand' is questionable.

New Zealand cannot depend for its security on its isolation or its inoffensiveness, or on inexhaustible reserves of international goodwill. If ANZUS membership is not misused for partisan purposes, or short-term advantage, it can enhance New Zealand security in conjunction with independent diplomatic and trade relationships conducted with sensitivity and maturity. Moreover, the literature on the development of international communities suggests that 'alliances will either evolve towards communities or else dissolve altogether'.[50]

For ANZUS, that sense of shared danger and freely accepted responsibility which emerged in the context of a certain ideological cohesion has been disintegrating for some time. While a security community amongst the member-nations persists, the ANZUS nations will need to enlarge the scope of their activities within the Pacific community if the alliance is to attract significant and stable popular support. In the long run, the challenge for proponents of ANZUS in New Zealand, Australia and the United States is to transform the United States from the ally New Zealanders may *need* into the ally New Zealanders genuinely *want*. At this stage, there is little evidence of the need for such an effort being grasped at government level, so that ANZUS and indeed the entire spectrum of Australia–New Zealand–United States partnership have at best the grudging approval of the public.

Certainly the need to provide for defence can present policy-makers and citizens with dilemmas. The tension between the aspiration for autonomy and the reality of interdependence, reflected as well in desires for seclusion from *and* a parallel involvement in a potentially hostile world, must present policy-makers with difficulty choices. Those who seek to shelter behind a science-fiction view, in which New Zealand emerges as a land of the survivors, the last refuge following a nuclear holocaust extinguishing all other life, might ponder a more sobering message oriented originally towards Australians but equally valid for New Zealanders.

It may be doubted whether civilised life in Australia could in fact continue in a situation in which social life had broken down in the major advanced societies, or in which they had been ravaged by nuclear war. But even if it could be shown that Australia had a prospect of escaping the consequences of a global ecological or nuclear catastrophe, the idea that we should plan for isolated survival in a world that has been stricken by such catastrophe, rather than bending our efforts towards co-operation with other nations in avoiding such a catastrophe, or coping with it if it occurs, is a repellent one.[51]

References

1. L. Carroll, *Through the Looking Glass*, Boston: International Library, 1955, p. 81.
2. *New Zealand National Party Manifesto: A Guide to What the Next National Government Will do for New Zealand, 1975*, pp. 1–2. Despite its title, this mini-manifesto was subsequently described (in relation to the rugby tour issue) by the Prime Minister as the work of its advertising agency and not binding on the government. However, the substance of the mini-manifesto is consistent with the party's campaign oratory and with its full statement of general election policy.
3. *Evening Post*, p. 1, 22 July, 1977.
4. A. Wildavsky, *The Politics of the Budgetary Process*, Boston: Little, Brown and Company, 1964, pp. 1–2.
5. *Ibid.*, p. 3.
6. *Ibid.*, p. 4.
7. G.A. Almond and G.B. Powell, *Comparative Politics: A Developmental Approach*, Boston: Little, Brown and Company, 1966, p. 201.
8. See, for example, the analysis of programmes and expenditures in T.R. Dye, *Politics, Economics and the Public: Policy Outcomes in the American States*, Chicago: Rand McNally, 1966. See also D.S. Ippolito, *The Budget and National Politics*, San Francisco: W.H. Freeman and Company, 1978, which views the budget of the U.S. federal government as a political document.
9. S. Levine, 'Introduction to Part 8' in S. Levine (ed.), *New Zealand Politics: A Reader*, p. 415.
10. G.A. Almond and G.B. Powell, *op. cit.*, pp. 128–63; 190–212.
11. New Zealand Monetary and Economic Council, *The Public Sector*, p. 53.
12. S. Levine, 'Labour After Nine Months: An Interview with John L. Roberts', pp. 422–3, 425.
    For an analysis of the role of the United States Bureau of the Budget, see A. Wildavsky, *op. cit.*, especially pp. 18–62.
13. A.D. Robinson, *op. cit.*, p. 44.
14. L.B. Johnson, 'The Budget Message of the President' in *The Budget of the United States Government for the Fiscal Year Ending June 30, 1966*, Washington, D.C.: U.S. Government Printing Office, 1965, p. 7.
15. R.D. Muldoon, *Budget*, 1977, pp. 43–4, pp. 2–4.
16. See D. Easton, *The Political System*, New York: A.A. Knopf, 1953; the model of 'the political system' with inputs–'black box'–outputs, analogous to an information processing system (i.e. a computer), is developed in D. Easton, *A Framework for Political Analysis*, Englewood Cliffs, New Jersey: Prentice–Hall, Inc., 1965.
17. See I.A. Webley, 'State Intervention in the Economy: The Use of Public Corporations in New Zealand' in S. Levine (ed.), *Politics in New Zealand: A Reader*, pp. 36–49.
18. *New Zealand Official Yearbook, 1977*, p. 876.
19. R.D. Muldoon, *Budget, 1977*, p. 47; *1978*, p. 53.
20. Calculated from figures provided in R.D. Muldoon, *Budget, 1977*, p. 47.
21. A. Trollope, *The New Zealander*, pp. 3–5.
22. For a more detailed account, see R. Kennaway, *New Zealand Foreign Policy, 1951–1971*, Wellington: Hicks Smith, 1972; W.D. McIntyre, *Neutrality, Non-Alignment and New Zealand*, Wellington: Price Milburn, 1969; J.H. Moore, *The American Alliance: Australia, New Zealand and the United States 1940–1970*, Melbourne: Cassell, 1970;

T.R. Reese, *Australia, New Zealand and the United States: A Survey of International Relations 1941–1968*, Oxford: Oxford University Press, 1969; *New Zealand in World Relations*, vol. 1, Wellington: Price Milburn for New Zealand Institute of International Affairs, 1977.

23. R.M. Dalziel, *The Origins of New Zealand Diplomacy: The Agent-General in London, 1870–1905*, Wellington: Price Milburn for Victoria University Press, 1975.

24. W. Perry, *Contemporary Brazilian Foreign Policy: The International Strategy of an Emerging Power*, London: Sage Publications, 1976, p. 11.

25. *Ibid*; see M. Croan, *East Germany: The Soviet Connection*, London: Sage Publications, 1976.

26. R.G. Neale (ed.), with P.G. Edwards and H. Kenway (asst. eds), *Documents in Australian Foreign Policy, 1937–1949, vol. 1, 1937–1938*, Canberra: Australian Government Publishing Service, 1975, p. 480.

27. See Ministry of Foreign Affairs, *New Zealand Representatives Overseas*, Wellington: April, 1977. The information in that booklet was considerably augmented through the kind assistance of Yvonne Ormond, of the Ministry of Foreign Affairs Library. Certain forms of representation are not discussed, including trade missions, information bureaux, honorary consuls and other personnel who may continue to provide important representational services to New Zealand. In addition, the extent to which services are shared, while suggested by cross-accreditation, is not fully revealed. Officials may serve in different capacities in more than one embassy. Finally, certain diplomatic postings may participate in international organisations. Thus, the Embassy in Rome participates in meetings of a United Nations Specialised Agency, Food and Agricultural Organisation (FAO). A very important role is provided by the Embassy in Switzerland which represents New Zealand at meetings of General Agreement on Trade and Tarriffs (GATT). Of course New Zealand's diplomatic representation is augmented at numerous and important points by direct participation of the Prime Minister and/or the Minister of Foreign Affairs in conferences, trade meetings and other important negotiations.

28. See M.H. McKay, *New Zealand and the Oil Crisis*, University of Canterbury, Department of Political Science, M.A. thesis, 1975, p. 27.

29. *Documents in Australian Foreign Policy 1937–1949, vol. 1, 1937–1938*, pp. 498–504; 513–15.

30. *New Zealand Official Yearbook, 1977*, p. 545.

31. S. Levine, 'New Zealand Politics: Annual Review', *op. cit.*, p. 108.

32. N.S. Meaney, *The Search for Security in the Pacific, 1901–14*, Sydney: Sydney University Press, 1976.

33. *Documents in Australian Foreign Policy, 1937–1949, vol 1, 1937–1938*, p. 521.

34. J.A.S. Grenville, *The Major International Treaties 1914–1973: A History and Guide with Texts*, London: Methuen and Co. Ltd., 1974, pp. 549–50.

35. *Ibid.*, pp. 337–9.

36. Annual Reports of the Department of Defence (Wellington: Government Printer), 1975–1978.

37. C.D. Beeby, *The United Nations Conference on the Law of the Sea: A New Zealand View*, Wellington: Ministry of Foreign Affairs, October 1975, p. 27.

38. Annual Reports of the Department of Defence (Wellington: Government Printer), 1975–1978.

39. *Ibid.* See S. Levine, 'Defence' in R. Goldstein with R. Alley, *op. cit.*, pp. 173–83, for further analysis of New Zealand's armed forces requirements.
40. See S. Levine, 'A Pernicious Three-Act Drama', *The Week*, vol. 1, no. 1, 2 July 1976.
41. See S. Levine, 'ANZUS: The American View', *New Zealand International Review*, vol. 2, no. 3, May–June 1977, p. 15.
42. *Ibid.*, p. 16.
43. *Ibid.*
44. S. Levine, 'New Zealand–United States Relations: A Political Appraisal', pp. 11–12.
45. F.S. Northedge, *The International Political System*, London: Faber and Faber, 1976, pp. 127, 254–5; 264.
46. J. Dryden, 'Absalom and Achitophel' in E.N. Hooker *et al.* (eds), *The Works of John Dryden*, Berkeley: University of California Press, 1961.
47. P.E. Jacob and H. Teune, 'The Integrative Process: Guidelines for Analysis of the Bases of Political Communities' in H.E. Jacob and J.V. Toscano (eds), *The Integration of Political Communities*, New York: J.B. Lippincott Co., 1964, p. 4.
48. See A. and R. Burnett, *The Australia and New Zealand Nexus*, Canberra: Australian and New Zealand Institutes of International Affairs, 1978.
49. B.E. Talboys, *N.Z. Foreign Affairs Review*, vol. 27, July–September, 1977, p. 28.
50. R. Aron, 'The Spread of Nuclear Weapons', *Atlantic Monthly*, vol. 215, no. 1, January 1965, p. 50.
51. H. Bull, 'Australia and the Nuclear Problem: Some Concluding Comments' in R. O'Neill (ed.), *The Strategic Nuclear Balance: An Australian Perspective*, Canberra: Australian National University Press, 1975, p. 140.

9 Politics in New Zealand: Alternatives and Obligations

'Would you tell me, please, which way I ought to walk from here?'
'That depends a good deal on where you want to get to . . . '
'I don't much care where— . . . '
'Then it doesn't matter which way you walk . . . '
'—so long as I get somewhere . . . '
'Oh, you're sure to do that . . . if you only walk long enough.'[1]

Despite years of advance warning, New Zealand's failure to diversify its economy has finally produced a 'permanent economic crisis'. Persistent inflation, low productivity, a declining British market for New Zealand's primary products, repeated balance of payments deficits, and chronic deficits in internal government accounts have meant that the Values Party's goals of a 'no-growth' economy and zero population growth may have been unexpectedly and inadvertently achieved, or even exceeded. For many New Zealanders, economic decline appears to have been a stimulus to external migration.

New Zealand's population appears to have undergone a remarkable transformation in the past decade. Table 9:1 describes the pattern of long-term migration during the 1970–78 period.

TABLE 9:1 *Permanent and Long-term Arrivals and Departures, 1970–1978*[2]

	(as at March) Year	Arrivals	Departures
	1970	26,825	29,822
	1971	39,377	38,165
	1972	45,099	37,546
	1973	54,651	35,483
	1974	69,815	42,338
	1975	65,900	43,461
	1976	48,460	43,160
	1977	37,020	56,092
	1978	36,972	63,680
Apr–Jul	1978	10,564	27,480

What is most astonishing about these figures is the sheer *volume* of migration into and out of New Zealand, in proportion to the total population. During the term of the third Labour Government, for example, there were approximately 310,000 permanent and long-term migrants either entering or leaving the country, a figure equalling 10 per cent of the total population. Examining the *emigration* figures only, it would appear from recent experience that a government can expect that 3 per cent (or 1 per cent per annum) of the population will leave New Zealand during its three-year term. Finally, under the National government during the 1976–1978 period, there has been an excess of departures over arrivals of significant proportions, a loss of skilled and vigorous young New Zealanders which is perhaps more serious than the massive immigration to New Zealand during the 1973–75 period for which the country was ill-prepared. Certainly National's 1975 pledge to reduce immigration has been more than fulfilled, with a vengeance, so that now what needs to be considered is whether the process by which New Zealanders choose to vote 'with their feet' can be halted, or indeed reversed.

One way of categorising the political choices open to citizens is as follows: *exit*, withdrawal from community affairs; *voice*, partisan involvement to secure political change; *loyalty*, support for the status quo; *silence*, a passive orientation towards politics.[3] While most New Zealanders have regularly opted for loyalty or silence, an increasing number of people have regularly chosen *exit*, literally, as the only viable option for themselves and their families. In the 1976–8 period, National's policies of economic austerity have, seemingly, contributed to a net loss of over 57,000 persons from New Zealand. The position of New Zealand, according to the Organisation for Economic Co-operation and Development, seems to be deteriorating.

New Zealand's current deficit, which amounted to $US1,600 million in 1974, remained very large in 1975 at $US 1,450 million. These deficits were equivalent to about 13½ per cent of GNP in both years, the largest recorded among OECD Member countries in each year and comparing with a longer-run deficit equivalent to just over 1 per cent . . . New Zealand's terms of trade have traditionally been subject to significant fluctuation, but movements over the past few years have exceeded past experience . . . New Zealand has typically recorded a trade surplus; indeed since 1950 a deficit had been registered in only one year prior to 1974. During the 1950's, the surplus averaged the equivalent of 3.5 per cent of GNP, but then fell quite noticeably to 2.1 per cent in the 1960's. On the other hand, invisible transactions have yielded a large deficit, primarily on account of substantial interest and dividend payments as well as expenditure on transportation. Thus, the current account of the balance of payments has typically been in deficit–during the 1950's to the tune of 0.6 per cent of GNP, rising in the 1960's to 1.8 per cent . . .

Current developments need to be seen in the context of the adjustment of the economy to an exceptionally steep decline in the terms of trade, amounting to some 40 per cent in two years–the equivalent of 12 per cent of gross national income. Until well into 1975, the strategy adopted–based on the assumption that the world recession would be short-lived–envisaged a relatively gradual adjustment . . . But the balance of payments deteriorated more than expected, partly on account of the unexpected severity of the recession abroad and the particularly sharp terms-of-trade deterioration: New Zealand's current deficit was the biggest, in relative terms, of all OECD countries in both 1974 and 1975, and foreign indebtedness was built up rapidly . . .

The New Zealand authorities are . . . faced with two sets of problems–achievement of a higher level and greater stabilisation of export receipts, and better insulation of the domestic economy from external impulses. As regards the first, one approach which might seem promising would be a greater degree of commodity price stabilisation; *but there does not appear to be a great deal that New Zealand can do on its own in this area.* Another approach would be diversification of the export base. *The scope for significantly broadening the product base, in anything but the very long term, is probably relatively limited.* (emphasis added)[4]

As Mr Muldoon observed in his 1977 Budget message:

The extent to which the deterioration in our terms of trade will be reversed is impossible to determine. What is clear is that there have been far-reaching structural changes in the world economy which have adversely affected our country. We cannot expect, and would be foolish to depend upon, an upturn in the near future of sufficient size and permanence to restore New Zealand's economic fortunes. If we are to complete an economic recovery and achieve sustained growth once again, we shall have to rely on our own efforts.[5]

It is no longer a matter of 'holding the line', or imposing 'restraints' described as temporary until conditions improve. New Zealanders' Candidean optimism–the belief that 'things always work out for the best', the 'she'll be right' mentality–while admirable in certain circumstances, is a far from effective response to a worsening social, economic and political crisis. Political leadership involves more than a loud voice, an aggressive manner, or special skill at savage repartee. It involves, primarily, an understanding of the present, and a vision of the future, so as to shape social and economic programmes for humane and compassionate purposes.

I can't help thinking of the Venetian Republic in their last half-century. Like us, they had once been fabulously lucky. They had become rich, as we did . . . A good many of them were tough-minded, realistic, patriotic men. They knew, just as clearly as we know, that the current of history had begun to flow against them. Many of them gave their minds to working out ways to keep going. It would have meant breaking the pattern into which they had crystallised. They were fond of the pattern, just as we are fond of ours. They never found the will to break it.[6]

Certainly we can expect that politicians who fail to plan for New Zealand's future, in an obsession with short-term advantage and partisan manoeuvring, will pass out of memory, and no one will ask

Who or what they have been
More than he asks what waves
Of the midmost ocean have swelled,
Foamed for a moment and gone.[7]

Any point in the life of a community, subjectively experienced, can be regarded as a 'turning point'; nevertheless, the Report of the Government's Task Force on Economic and Social Planning argues the accuracy of its title–New Zealand At the Turning Point–by declaiming that 'time is not on our side . . . '

. . . while we agree that 'economic' objectives must be given very high priority in the foreseeable future, it is not enough, as some submissions suggested, to concentrate planning on 'economic' issues. Planning for social justice, for a positive reduction of social problems, for a greater sense of community, for a pleasant environment, and for cultural and recreational activities which both refresh us and develop our national identity, is not only important in its own right, but also an essential element in any scheme to overcome our economic difficulties, while keeping New Zealand a place where both young and old will wish to live.[8]

For New Zealand to 'go boldly forward to what could well be a distinguished future'[9] will require a creative renewal permeating all features of the political system–the institutions, parties, groups, political culture, public policies. More than a sense of community, New Zealand's predicament demands the reality of shared participation in common struggle, to provide a rational basis for the belief that New Zealand may overcome its economic, political and cultural flaws.

There is certainly cause for alarm, but not for despair. As Camilleri reminds us, 'Hope is . . . an integral part of man's present commitment . . . Hope is not prediction but openness to the movement of history . . . annunciation of what is not yet, anticipation of a new order . . . [10]

In this spirit, we may be cautiously hopeful that the New Zealand people themselves will be able to accept and share their common responsibility for shaping the collective future of their communities. Viewed broadly, New Zealand's goals–equality, freedom, and social justice–derive from majestic concepts, and the hope of their realisation may be utopian. On the other hand, perhaps the country's objectives may be little more than to ensure that a future visitor may echo the sentiments of an earlier one.

> The harbours of New Zealand are romantic, and the countryside wild without being desolate. And it is delightful to be in a country where there are no millionaires and hardly any slums, among a people characterised by homely refinement, and by a large measure of vigorous public spirit . . . We met no distinguished persons . . . but any number of pleasant cultivated men and women. Judged by English standards, the New Zealanders are an easy-going race, moral but gay, lacking in puritan pugnacity . . . taken all in all if I had to bring up a family outside of Great Britain I would choose New Zealand as its home.[11]

To create a comfortable life for its people, in a placid social setting, may seem an uninspiring goal to some, yet it is one fittingly New Zealand in scale and tone. More importantly, it may be one within reach of a creative politics, whose realisation in so small a society may be an example to larger, more generously endowed nations. To fulfil the New Zealand promise, however, will require compassion, understanding and sustained effort. The temptation to condemn the unfamiliar, or to revile those in need of support (whether these be solo parents, the elderly, the unemployed or the overtaxed), will need to be resisted, for this kind of judgmental approach to social problems and individual needs is one fundamentally incompatible with a commitment to democratic values. From politicians, voters and political commentators alike, there will need to be a fresh approach to politics, involving a candid willingness to admit the possibility of error, and a recognition of the potential virtues in the criticisms of an adversary. In the long run, humility and intellectual honesty may prove to be the orientation to politics most likely to provide New Zealand with a future both materially comfortable and politically distinctive.

References

1. L. Carroll, *Alice's Adventures in Wonderland*, New York: Doubleday, 1961, pp. 93–4.

2. *New Zealand Official Yearbook, 1976*, pp: 71; 1049; Department of Statistics, *Monthly Abstract of Statistics*, Wellington: Government Printer, June 1977, p. 10; October 1978, p. 13.

3. This typology has been developed by A. Hirschman, *Exit, Loyalty and Voice*, Cambridge: Harvard University Press, 1970. For an application to New Zealand politics, see G.M. Fougere, 'Undoing the Welfare State: The Case of Hospital Care' in S. Levine (ed.), *Politics in New Zealand: A Reader*, pp. 407–417.

4. Organisation for Economic Co-operation and Development, *New Zealand: OECD Economic Survey, Annual Review*, Paris: OECD, August 1976, pp. 5, 6, 12, 33–5.

5. Rt. Hon. R.D. Muldoon (Minister of Finance), *Budget, 1977 (Financial Statement, House of Representatives, 21 July, 1977)*, Wellington: Government Printer, 1977, pp. 43–4. In this context, a relatively generous 1978 election-year budget involving taxation concessions and assistance to various groups must be viewed as a temporary measure. It follows a general pattern of election-year budgets, which tend to emphasise the allocation of resources rather than the more stringent economic management practised in non-election years.

6. C.P. Snow, *The Two Cultures and the Scientific Revolution*, Cambridge: Cambridge University Press, 1960.

7. See F. Farmer (ed.), *The Wilson Reader*, New York: Oceana Publications, 1956, p. 63.

8. Report of the Task Force on Economic and Social Planning, *New Zealand at the Turning Point*, Wellington: Government Printer, December 1976, p. 45.

9. L. Lipson, *op. cit.*, p. 503.

10. See J.A. Camilleri, *Civilisation in Crisis: Human Prospects in a Changing World*, Cambridge: Cambridge University Press, 1976, p. 261.

11. B. Webb, in D.A. Hamer (ed.), *op. cit.*, pp. 54–5.

Appendix

Date of General Election	Political Party	Total Votes	Percentage of Votes	Number of Seats in House of Representatives	Percentage of Seats Won	Turn-out	Size of Electorate	Number of Persons Voting
1890 (5 December)	Liberal	76,548	56.1	38	54.3	40.0	183,171	73,332
	Conservative	39,338	28.9	25	35.7			
	Miscellaneous	20,451	15.0	7	10.0			
1893 (28 November)	Liberal	175,814	57.8	51	72.9	72.6	302,997	220,082
	Conservative	74,482	24.5	13	18.6			
	Miscellaneous	53,880	17.7	6	8.6			
1896 (4 December)	Liberal	165,259	46.0	39	55.7	71.9	339,230	258,254
	Conservative	134,397	37.4	25	35.7			
	Miscellaneous	59,748	16.6	6	8.6			

1. Prior to 1890, general elections were held on the following dates:

1853 14.7; 1.10	1866 12.2; 6.4	1879 28.8; 15.9
1855 26.10; 28.12	1871 14.1; 23.2	1881 9.12
1860 12.12	1875 20.12	1884 22.7
1861 28.3	1876 29.1	1887 26.9

However, the absence of firm political party affiliations does not facilitate a brief descriptive summary of the results. For the period 1890–1943, the four Maori seats are excluded. Until 1951 (from 1881) European and Maori constituencies voted on different days. The dates in the tables refer to the European polling day. In 1908 and 1911 the two dates given are for the first and second ballots. Vote totals for 1908 and 1911 are calculated from the first round figures where this was decisive, and upon the second ballot when it was not.

Date of General Election	Political Party	Total Votes	Percentage of Votes	Number of Seats in House of Representatives	Percentage of Seats Won	Turn-out	Size of Electorate	Number of Persons Voting
1899 (6 December)	Liberal	204,331	52.7	49	70.0	72.1	373,744	279,330
	Conservative	141,758	36.6	19	27.1			
	Miscellaneous	41,540	10.7	2	2.9			
1902 (25 November)	Liberal	215,845	51.8	47	61.8	76.5	415,789	318,859
	Opposition	85,769	20.6	19	25.0			
	Labour and Socialist	10,501	2.5	—	—			
	Miscellaneous	104,847	25.1	10	13.2			
1905 (6 December)	Liberal	209,731	53.6	55	72.4	83.2	476,473	396,657
	Opposition	117,118	29.9	15	19.7			
	Labour and Socialist	3,623	0.9	—	0.0			
	Miscellaneous	60,717	15.5	6	7.9			
1908 (17 November) (24 November)	Liberal	242,261	59.0	47	61.8	79.8	537,003	428,648
	Opposition	114,245	27.8	25	32.9			
	Labour and Socialist	17,492	4.3	1	1.3			
	Miscellaneous	36,508	8.9	3	3.9			
1911 (7 December) (14 December)	Liberal	191,323	41.1	30	39.5	83.5	590,042	492,912
	Reform	164,627	35.4	36	47.4			
	Labour and Socialist	40,759	8.8	4	5.3			
	Miscellaneous	68,859	14.8	6	7.9			
1914 (10 December)	Liberal	222,299	43.1	31	40.8	84.7	616,043	521,525
	Reform	243,122	47.1	39	51.3			
	Labour and Social Democrat	49,482	9.6	6	7.9			
	Miscellaneous	1,004	0.2	0	0.0			
1919 (17 December)	Liberal/United	155,708	28.7	17	22.4	80.5	683,420	550,327
	Reform	193,676	35.7	43	56.6			
	Labour	131,402	24.2	8	10.5			
	Miscellaneous	61,954	11.4	8	10.5			

Date of General Election	Political Party	Total Votes	Percentage of Votes	Number of Seats in House of Representatives	Percentage of Seats Won	Turn-out	Size of Electorate	Number of Persons Voting
1922 (7 December)	Liberal/United	162,149	26.4	21	27.6	88.7	700,111	620,650
	Reform	245,281	39.9	35	46.1			
	Labour	150,448	24.5	17	22.4			
	Miscellaneous	56,192	9.2	3	3.9			
1925 (4 November)	National (Liberal)	135,419	20.2	9	11.8	90.0	754,113	678,877
	Reform	312,932	46.6	51	67.1			
	Labour	184,616	27.5	12	15.8			
	Miscellaneous	39,004	5.8	4	5.3			
1928 (14 November)	Liberal/United	219,648	29.9	25	32.9	88.0	844,633	743,691
	Reform	256,014	34.8	25	32.9			
	Labour	197,759	26.9	19	25.0			
	Miscellaneous	61,970	8.4	7	9.2			
1931 (2 December)	Labour	242,301	35.0	24	31.6	83.3	838,344	698,027
	National[2]	304,750	44.0	42	55.3			
	Miscellaneous	146,021	21.1	10	13.2			
1935 (27 November)	Labour	392,321	47.4	53	69.7	90.7	919,798	834,682
	National[2]	258,270	31.2	17	22.4			
	Democrat	65,217	7.9	—	0.0			
	Miscellaneous	111,987	13.5	6	7.9			
1938 (15 October)	Labour	513,397	55.9	50	65.8	92.9	995,173	924,057
	National	368,809	40.2	24	31.6			
	Miscellaneous	35,478	3.9	2	2.6			
1943 (23 September)	Labour	439,207	48.2	41	53.9	92.1	1,000,197	921,327
	National	390,343	42.8	34	44.7			
	Democratic Soldier Labour	40,423	4.4	—	0.0			
	Miscellaneous	41,397	4.5	1	1.3			
1946 (27 November)	Labour	536,994	51.3	42	52.5	97.5	1,081,898	1,055,204
	National	507,139	48.4	38	47.5			
	Communist	1,181	0.1	—	0.0			
	Miscellaneous	1,891	0.2	—	0.0			

2. An electoral alliance of the United and Reform parties.

Date of General Election	Political Party	Total Votes	Percentage of Votes	Number of Seats in House of Representatives	Percentage of Seats Won	Turn-out	Size of Electorate	Number of Persons Voting
1949 (30 November)	Labour	506,100	47.2	34	42.5	94.0	1,148,748	1,079,905
	National	556,805	51.9	46	57.5			
	Communist	3,499	0.3	—	0.0			
	Miscellaneous	6,777	0.6	—	0.0			
1951 (1 September)	Labour	490,143	45.8	30	37.5	89.0	1,205,772	1,073,423
	National	577,630	54.0	50	62.5			
	Communist	528	0.0	—	0.0			
	Miscellaneous	1,490	0.1	—	0.0			
1954 (13 November)	Labour	484,082	44.1	35	43.8	91.4	1,209,670	1,105,609
	National	485,630	44.3	45	56.3			
	Communist	1,134	0.1	0	0.0			
	Social Credit	122,068	11.1	0	0.0			
	Miscellaneous	3,979	0.4	0	0.0			
1957 (30 November)	Labour	559,096	48.3	41	51.2	93.4	1,244,748	1,163,061
	National	511,699	44.2	39	48.7			
	Communist	706	0.1	0	0.0			
	Social Credit	83,498	7.2	0	0.0			
	Miscellaneous	2,366	0.2	0	0.0			
1960 (26 November)	Labour	508,179	43.4	34	42.5	90.3	1,303,955	1,176,963
	National	557,046	47.6	46	57.5			
	Communist	2,423	0.2	0	0.0			
	Social Credit	100,905	8.6	0	0.0			
	Miscellaneous	1,950	0.2	0	0.0			
1963 (30 November)	Labour	524,066	43.7	35	43.8	90.5	1,332,371	1,205,322
	National	563,875	47.1	45	56.3			
	Communist	3,167	0.3	0	0.0			
	Social Credit	95,176	7.9	0	0.0			
	Miscellaneous	11,761	1.0	0	0.0			
1966 (26 November)	Labour	499,392	41.4	35	43.8	86.6	1,399,720	1,212,127
	National	525,945	43.6	44	55.0			
	Communist	1,060	0.1	0	0.0			
	Social Credit	174,515	14.5	1	1.2			
	Miscellaneous	4,183	0.3	0	0.0			

Date of General Election	Political Party	Total Votes	Percentage of Votes	Number of Seats in House of Representatives	Percentage of Seats Won	Turn-out	Size of Electorate	Number of Persons Voting
1969	Labour	592,055	44.2	39	46.4	88.9	1,519,889	1,351,813
(29 November)	National	605,960	45.2	45	53.6			
	Communist	368	0.0	0	0.0			
	Social Credit	121,576	9.1	0	0.0			
	Miscellaneous	20,209	1.5	0	0.0			
1972	Labour	677,475	48.4	55	63.2	89.9	1,569,937	1,411,301
(25 November)	National	581,422	41.5	32	36.8			
	Social Credit	93,231	6.6	0	0.0			
	Values	27,467	2.0	0	0.0			
	Miscellaneous	21,364	1.5	0	0.0			
1975	Labour	634,453	39.6	32	36.8	83.1	1,938,108	1,611,104
(29 November)	National	763,136	47.6	55	63.2			
	Social Credit	119,123	7.4	0	0.0			
	Values	83,211	5.2	0	0.0			
	Miscellaneous	3,755	0.2	0	0.0			
1978	Labour	691,756	40.4	41	44.7	83.8	2,057,840[3]	1,724,666
(25 November)	National	683,857	39.9	50	54.3			
	Social Credit	274,876	16.0	1	1.0			
	Values	41,226	2.4	0	0.0			
	Miscellaneous	22,131	1.3	0	0.0			

3. For size of electorate, the figure given refers to the number of people aged 18 and over in New Zealand as of 31 December 1977, rather than to the total number of names on the electoral rolls (2,487,594, an excess of 429,754). A new system for compiling the rolls was introduced for the 1978 general election, and the scale of errors and duplications seems to have been significantly more substantial than for previous general elections. The results obtained from the Chief Electoral Office are provisional and subject to recount.

Sources: T.T. Mackie & R. Rose (eds), *The International Almanac of Electoral History,* London: Macmillan, 1974; L. Lipson, *The Politics of Equality,* Chicago: Chicago University Press, 1948; S. Levine and A.D. Robinson, *The New Zealand Voter,* Wellington: Price Milburn, 1976; Chief Electoral Officer (Department of Justice, New Zealand).

New Zealand Governments

1854–1890 (pre-party era)

1. James E. Fitzgerald Ministry, 14 June 1854–2 August 1854.
2. Thomas S. Forsaith Ministry, 31 August 1854–2 September 1854.
3. Francis D. Bell/Henry Sewell Ministry, 18 April 1856–20 May 1856.
4. William Fox Ministry, 20 May 1856–2 June 1856.
5. Edward W. Stafford Ministry, 2 June 1856–12 July 1861.
6. William Fox Ministry, 12 July 1861–6 August 1862.
7. Alfred Domett Ministry, 6 August 1862–30 October 1863.
8. Frederick Whitaker Ministry, 30 October 1863–24 November 1864.
9. Frederick A. Weld Ministry, 24 November 1864–16 October 1865.
10. Edward W. Stafford Ministry, 16 October 1865–28 June 1869.
11. William Fox Ministry, 28 June 1869–10 September 1872.
12. Edward W. Stafford Ministry, 10 September 1872–11 October 1872.
13. George M. Waterhouse Ministry, 11 October 1872–3 March 1873.
14. William Fox Ministry, 3 March 1873–8 April 1873.
15. Julius Vogel Ministry, 8 April 1873–6 July 1875.
16. Daniel Pollen Ministry, 6 July 1875–15 February 1876.
17. Sir Julius Vogel Ministry, 15 February 1876–1 September 1876.
18. Harry A. Atkinson Ministry, 1 September 1876–13 September 1876.
19. Harry A. Atkinson Ministry, 13 September 1876–13 October 1877.
20. Sir George Grey Ministry, 15 October 1877–8 October 1879.
21. John Hall Ministry, 8 October 1879–21 April 1882.
22. Frederick Whitaker Ministry, 21 April 1882–25 September 1883.
23. Harry A. Atkinson Ministry, 25 September 1883–16 August 1884.
24. Robert Stout/Sir Julius Vogel Ministry, 16 August 1884–28 August 1884.
25. Harry A. Atkinson Ministry, 28 August 1884–3 September 1884.
26. Sir Robert Stout/Sir Julius Vogel Ministry, 3 September 1884–8 October 1887.
27. Sir Harry A. Atkinson Ministry, 8 October 1887–24 January 1891.

1891–1935 (initial alignment of parties)

28. John Ballance Ministry (Liberal), 24 January 1891–27 April 1893.
29. Richard J. Seddon Ministry (Liberal), 1 May 1893–10 June 1906.
30. William Hall–Jones Ministry (Liberal), 21 June 1906–6 August 1906.
31. Sir Joseph G. Ward Ministry (Liberal), 6 August 1906–28 March 1912.
32. Thomas MacKenzie Ministry (Liberal), 28 March 1912–10 July 1912.
33. William F. Massey Ministry (Reform), 10 July 1912–12 August 1915.
34. William F. Massey Ministry (Liberal and Reform coalition), 12 August 1915–25 August 1919.
35. William F. Massey Ministry (Reform), 25 August 1919–10 May 1925.
36. Sir Francis H.D. Bell Ministry (Reform), 14 May 1925–30 May 1925.
37. Joseph G. Coates Ministry (Reform), 30 May 1925–10 December 1928.
38. Sir Joseph G. Ward Ministry (Liberal), 10 December 1928–28 May 1930.
39. George W. Forbes Ministry (Liberal), 28 May 1930–22 September 1931.
40. George W. Forbes Ministry (Reform & United coalition), 22 September 1931–6 December 1935.

1935–1978 (realignment of parties)

41. Michael J. Savage Ministry (Labour), 6 December 1935–27 March 1940.
42. Peter Fraser Ministry (Labour), 1 April 1940–13 December 1949.
43. Sidney G. Holland Ministry (National), 13 December 1949–20 September 1957.
44. Keith J. Holyoake Ministry (National), 20 September 1957–12 December 1957.

45. Walter Nash Ministry (Labour), 12 December 1957–12 December 1960.
46. Keith J. Holyoake Ministry (National), 12 December 1960–7 February 1972.
47. John R. Marshall Ministry (National), 7 February 1972–8 December 1972.
48. Norman E. Kirk Ministry (Labour), 8 December 1972–31 August 1974.
49. Wallace E. Rowling Ministry (Labour), 6 September 1974–12 December 1975.
50. Robert D. Muldoon Ministry (National), 12 December 1975–

Leaders of the Opposition[1]

1891–1935

John Bryce (Conservative), 23 June, 1891–31 August, 1891.
William Rolleston (Conservative), 31 August, 1891–8 November, 1893.
Captain William Russell (Conservative), June, 1894–3 July, 1901.
William F. Massey (Opposition; Reform), 11 September, 1903–10 July, 1912.
Sir Joseph G. Ward (Liberal), 10 July, 1912–12 August, 1915; 21 August, 1919–27 November, 1919.
William D.S. MacDonald (Liberal/United), 21 January, 1920–31 August, 1920.
Thomas M. Wilford (Liberal/United), 8 September, 1920–13 August, 1925.
George W. Forbes (Liberal/United), 13 August, 1925–14 October, 1925.
Henry E. Holland (Labour), 16 June, 1926–18 October, 1928.
Sir Joseph G. Ward (Liberal/United), 4 December, 1928–10 December, 1928.
Joseph G. Coates (Liberal/United), 10 December, 1928–22 September, 1931.
Henry E. Holland (Labour), 22 September, 1931–8 October, 1933.
Michael J. Savage (Labour), 12 October, 1933–6 December, 1935.

1935–1978

George W. Forbes (Liberal/United), 6 December, 1935–2 November, 1936.
Adam Hamilton (National), 2 November, 1936–26 November, 1940.
Sidney G. Holland (National), 26 November, 1940–13 December, 1949.
Peter Fraser (Labour), 13 December, 1949–12 December, 1950.
Walter Nash (Labour), 17 January, 1951–12 December, 1957.
Keith J. Holyoake (National), 12 December, 1957–12 December, 1960.
Walter Nash (Labour), 12 December, 1960–31 March, 1963.
Arnold H. Nordmeyer (Labour), 1 April, 1963–16 December, 1965.
Norman E. Kirk (Labour), 16 December, 1965–8 December, 1972.
John R. Marshall (National), 8 December, 1972–4 July, 1974.
Robert D. Muldoon (National), 4 July, 1974–12 December, 1975.
Wallace E. Rowling (Labour), 12 December, 1975–

Leaders of the Major Third Parties, 1954–1978

Social Credit

W.B. Owen, 1954–60.
P.H. Mathews, 1960–63.
V.F. Cracknell, 1963–70.
J.B. O'Brien, 1970–72.
B.C. Beetham, 1972–

---

1. The dates are for date of election when the party concerned was recognised as the Chief Opposition Party; otherwise the date of the opening of the Session is given. Between 1915–1919, there was no Leader of the Opposition since there was a Coalition Government.

Values

A.J. Brunt, 1972–3.
R.C. Clough, 1974–6.
A.H. Kunowski, 1976–

Sources: G.H. Scholefield (ed.), *New Zealand Parliamentary Record, 1840–1949*, Wellington: Government Printer, 1950; J.O. Wilson (ed.), *New Zealand Parliamentary Record: Supplement, 1950–1969*, Wellington: Government Printer, 1969; *New Zealand Parliamentary Debates (Hansard), 1969–1977*.

Select Bibliography

The first group of references provide a useful starting point for further reading in New Zealand politics. The brief list of general references to political science literature can serve as an introductory guide to the comparative study of political behaviour.

New Zealand politics

M. Bassett, *The Third Labour Government*, Palmerston North: The Dunmore Press, 1976.

R.M. Chapman, W.K. Jackson and A.V. Mitchell, *New Zealand Politics in Action: The 1960 General Election*, London: Oxford University Press, 1962.

S.H. Franklin, *Trade, Growth and Anxiety: New Zealand Beyond The Welfare State*, Wellington: Methuen, 1978.

R. Goldstein and R. Alley (eds), *Labour in Power: Promise and Performance*, Wellington: Price Milburn for New Zealand University Press, 1975.

W.K. Jackson, *New Zealand: Politics of Change*, Wellington: A.H. and A.W. Reed, 1973.

S. Levine (ed.), *New Zealand Politics: A Reader*, Melbourne: Cheshire Publishing Pty Ltd, 1975.

S. Levine (ed.), *Politics in New Zealand: A Reader*, Sydney: George Allen & Unwin Ltd., 1978.

S. Levine and J. Lodge, *The New Zealand General Election of 1975*, Wellington: Price Milburn for New Zealand University Press, 1976.

S. Levine and A.D. Robinson, *The New Zealand Voter: A Survey of Public Opinion and Electoral Behaviour*, Wellington: Price Milburn for New Zealand University Press, 1976.

L. Lipson, *The Politics of Equality*, Chicago: Chicago University Press, 1948.

Sir John Marshall (ed.), *The Reform of Parliament: Papers Presented in Memory of Dr Alan D. Robinson*, Wellington: New Zealand Institute of Public Administration, 1978.

A. McRobie and N.S. Roberts, *Election '78: The 1977 Electoral Redistribution and the 1978 General Election in New Zealand,* Dunedin: John McIndoe, 1978.

R.S. Milne, *Political Parties in New Zealand,* Oxford: The Clarendon Press, 1966.

A.V. Mitchell, *Government by Party,* Christchurch: Whitcombe and Tombs, 1966.

A.V. Mitchell, *Politics and People in New Zealand,* Christchurch: Whitcombe and Tombs, 1969.

A.V. Mitchell, *The Half-Gallon, Quarter-Acre Pavlova Paradise,* Wellington: Whitcombe and Tombs, 1972.

G. Palmer (ed.), *The Welfare State Today: Social Welfare Policy in New Zealand in The Seventies,* Wellington: Fourth Estate Books, 1977.

D. Pitt (ed.), *Social Class in New Zealand,* Auckland: Longman Paul, 1977.

K.J. Scott, *The New Zealand Constitution,* Oxford: The Clarendon Press, 1962.

K. Sinclair, *Walter Nash,* Auckland: Auckland and Oxford University Presses, 1976.

A.D. Trlin (ed.), *Social Welfare and New Zealand Society,* Wellington: Methuen, 1977.

I. Wards (ed.), *Thirteen Facets,* Wellington: Government Printer, 1978.

G.A. Wood, *Why National Won,* Dunedin: John McIndoe, 1975.

Comparative Political Behaviour

D. Aitkin, *Stability and Change in Australian Politics,* Canberra: Australian National University Press, 1977.

G. Almond and G.B. Powell, *Comparative Politics: A Developmental Approach* (second edition), Boston: Little, Brown, 1978.

D.E. Apter, *Introduction to Political Analysis,* Cambridge, Massachusetts: Winthrop Publishers, 1977.

A. Campbell, P.E. Converse, W.E. Miller and D. Stokes, *The American Voter,* New York: John Wiley, 1960.

I.H. Carmen, *Power and Balance: An Introduction to American Constitutional Government,* New York: Harcourt Brace Jovanovich, 1978.

D. Easton, *A Systems Analysis of Political Life,* New York: John Wiley, 1966.

H. Elcock, *Political Behaviour,* London: Methuen, 1976.

L.D. Epstein, *Political Parties in Western Democracies,* New York: Praeger, 1967.

R. Forward (ed.), *Public Policy in Australia,* Melbourne: Cheshire Publishing Pty Ltd, 1974.

D.A. Kemp, *Society and Electoral Behaviour in Australia*, St Lucia: University of Queensland Press, 1978.

P. King (ed.), *The Study of Politics: A Collection of Inaugural Lectures*, London: Frank Cass, 1977.

R.D. Lumb, *The Constitutions of the Australian States* (fourth edition), St Lucia: University of Queensland Press, 1977.

W.J.M. Mackenzie, *Free Elections*, London: George Allen and Unwin, 1958.

M. Mackerras, *Elections 1975*, Sydney: Angus and Robertson, 1975.

H.R. Penniman (ed.), *Australia at the Polls, The National Elections of 1975*, Washington: American Enterprise Institute for Public Policy Research, 1977.

H.R. Penniman (ed.), *Britain at the Polls: The Parliamentary Elections of 1974*, Washington: The American Enterprise Institute for Public Policy Research, 1975.

R.M. Punnett, *British Government and Politics*, London: Heinemann, 1976.

J. Rasmussen, *The Process of Politics: A Comparative Approach*, New York: Aldine–Atherton, 1969.

R. Rose (ed.), *Electoral Behaviour*, New York: The Free Press, 1974.

D.F. Roth and F.L. Wilson, *The Comparative Study of Politics*, Boston: Houghton Mifflin, 1976.

L.T. Sargent, *Contemporary Political Ideologies: A Comparative Analysis*, (fourth edition), Homewood, Illinois: The Dorsey Press, 1978.

B. Stacey, *Political Socialization in Western Society*, London: Edward Arnold, 1978.

D.S. Strong, *Issue Voting and Party Realignment*, University, Alabama: The University of Alabama Press, 1977.

Index

202